The flashligh
the tunne

"Stay on the pathway, lads," one of the men said as we began our approximately twenty-foot descent into the depths of the tunnel. Stay on the pathway, lads? That sounded very much like a certain quote from *An American Werewolf in London*. Someone was having a laugh at our expense. Thankfully, the concrete steps were easy to negotiate. Having reached the floor, we looked up and I half expected to see the two RAF men wearing malicious grins as they replaced the lid and encased us forever in this icy cold tomb. Instead they waved genially and suggested that we head left. We decided to go right.

PRAISE FOR NICK REDFERN'S BESTSELLING CHRONICLES OF THE UNEXPLAINED

"This is a trove of entertaining stories for *X-files* fans and government skeptics."

—*Publishers Weekly* for *Strange Secrets*

"Anyone with a remote interest will be held spellbound. . . . His book gives much food for thought."

—*Daily Express*, for *A Covert Agenda*

THREE MEN SEEKING MONSTERS

Six Weeks in Pursuit of Werewolves, Lake Monsters, Giant Cats, Ghostly Devil Dogs, and Ape-Men

NICK REDFERN

PARAVIEW POCKET BOOKS

NEW YORK LONDON TORONTO SYDNEY

PARAVIEW
191 Seventh Avenue, New York, NY 10011

POCKET BOOKS, a division of Simon & Schuster, Inc.
1230 Avenue of the Americas, New York, NY 10020

ISBN: 978-0-7434-8254-7   0-7434-8254-9

First Paraview Pocket Books trade paperback edition April 2004

10 9 8 7 6 5 4 3 2 1

*For Jon and Rich—two better and madder friends
a man could never find.*

CONTENTS

INTRODUCTION

Hey Ho, Let's Go!

"BLITZKRIEG BOP," THE RAMONES

As I sit typing these words, it is a relatively warm and pleasant day in the southeast Texan town on the outskirts of the city of Beaumont where my wife, Dana, and I reside. Midway through the first year of the new millennium, however, I was living on the other side of the world in the somewhat colder climes of rural England and, with two good friends, I was having a bizarre adventure chasing monsters around the British countryside. Writing the story that you are about to read was a very strange experience for me, because in many ways the inevitable passage of time, the fact that England seems so far away now, and the distinct unreality of the whole adventure have all ensured that to those of us involved in these events, our nature and perception of reality, imagination, and day-to-day living have all radically changed.

While we once thought that we lived in an orderly world, we now realize that orderly is the last thing that this world is. It is one filled with chaos, hidden realms, shadowy manipulators, dreams that may be real, a reality that may be all a dream, secret histories that some would have—and indeed, may have—killed to keep secret, bizarre characters and freaks of nature hidden, or hiding, from prying eyes, a catalog of monsters, myths, and mysteries that penetrate the heart of the British establishment and English folklore, and much, much, more, as you are now about to learn.

1

1

THE MONSTER BUSTERS

We're a happy family, we're a happy family . . .

"WE'RE A HAPPY FAMILY," THE RAMONES

My story begins on a hot summer weekend in 1997. Everything was good in the world. My first book was about to be released by a major British publisher and we had secured serialization for the title in a leading Sunday newspaper. I had just eaten an artery-blocking English breakfast after a beery night with Matthew Williams, then editor of the conspiracy-based journal *Truthseeker's Review,* and the man who would find fame in the latter part of 2000 as the first person to be arrested, charged, and convicted for making a crop circle. And in roughly two hours time I was due to deliver a lecture on the history of UFOs and the British government to the assembled throng of the curious, the mad, the paranoid, and the allegedly normal that had congregated at Sheffield University, England, for the yearly conference of the British UFO Research Association.

I turned off my Walkman from which the mighty and punk-dominated sounds of the Neurotic Outsiders echoed, entered the main auditorium of the university, and looked to see who was there. Right away, among the crowd of several hundred, an assortment of stalls, booths, and a group of spotty youths in Trust No One T-shirts, I was accosted by a greasy-haired old geezer who asked me in an accusing tone: "You're one of the lecturers, aren't you?" I nodded. "You can't do a lecture in a black T-shirt, jeans, and a motorbike jacket!" he yelled. "Didn't you bring a shirt and tie?"

"No, I did not. I don't wear shirts and ties," I answered quickly and firmly. I continued on my way and left the man complaining about my lack of commitment to the seriousness of the event as he accused me of being "with the government."

Suddenly, I was stopped in my tracks by a veritable behemoth of a character in a badly ironed brown suit (that was covered with a number of suspiciously positioned stains) striding purposefully toward me.

"Graham, come on!" the man bellowed mightily at a painfully thin, bearded fellow in a sweater and jeans behind him who, carrying an assortment of boxes crammed with books and magazines, was struggling to keep up. "Out of my way, peasants!" screamed the Hulk-like figure at all and sundry while waving a half-consumed bottle menacingly in front of them. "I have brandy and harlots to devour!"

As the assorted and astonished crowd made way in a fashion that reminded me of the parting of the Red Sea, the man stopped in front of me. Towering over me at around six feet six inches in height, surely four hundred pounds in weight, and sporting a wild beard and even wilder hair, he boomed, "Who the hell are you?"

"I'm Nick Redfern; who the hell are you?"

The man's tone suddenly changed; his voice took on an outrageously affected style and a beaming smile came over his face. "My dear, dear boy. I'm Jon Downes. I've been looking for you; I want to interview you for *Sightings* magazine."

"Oh, yeah, I know who you are. You do those lake monster and big cat investigations, don't you? Don't you run a group or something?"

"My boy, my boy, I do. Let's go and sit down at my stall and we can talk. Graham, come!" barked Jon. The thin man muttered something under his breath and followed. I scanned Jon's table closely. It was full of all manner of magazines and books on lake monsters, Bigfoot, the Yeti, the Loch Ness Monster, and more.

"God almighty, I need a drink," said Jon wearily, as he fell back into his chair. It buckled and strained alarmingly under his mighty girth. "Anyway, dear fellow, it's good to meet you," Jon said to me in cheerful tones. He gestured toward the thin man. "Sit, Graham!" The thin man scowled but did as he was told. "This is Graham Inglis, my manservant and special friend. *Very special friend.*"

"Okay." I laughed. "Hi, Graham; how's it going?" The thin man smiled back in a slightly sinister fashion, nodded, and said nothing. He crossed his legs, flipped open a can of Carlsberg Special Brew lager, and turned his attention to a magazine on computer games. I watched him take a CD out of his bag and insert it into his own Walkman. It was those 1970s progressive rock atrocities, Gong. I cringed to myself. Jon proceeded to open a shopping bag and I expected to see him take out a pile of books. Instead, out came a small, lovingly crafted, wooden box with ornate brass handles. I leaned forward to see what was inside. Noticing this, Jon took an inordinate amount of time to open it and did so in a way-over-the-top camp fashion. When he finally lifted the lid, however, I was amused to see that it contained two small glasses and a bottle.

"Would you care to indulge in a small, dry sherry, dear Nicholas?" inquired Jon, with a twinkle in his bloodshot and sleep-deprived eyes. Jon was not your average UFO investigator I was relieved and pleased to find out. He was my kind of guy—but not in the biblical sense, you understand.

Over the next hour or so, we talked about wine, women, and song, and just about everything *but* UFOs. It transpired that we had probably already met without realizing the fact—at one of the many record and CD fairs that we regularly attended, bought and sold at in the 1980s and early-to-mid 1990s—and we struck up an enjoyable rapport. Jon went on to tell me how, as a boy growing up in Hong Kong, he had been fascinated with unknown animals and monsters; and he now ran the Center for Fortean Zoology and could boast of being Britain's only full-time monster hunter. He had written numerous books on *zooforms*, those "nonanimate things that appear to be animals," he explained, edited two magazines—*The Goblin Universe* and *Animals & Men*—and regularly launched expeditions to the darkest corners of the globe in search of lake monsters, sea serpents, still-living dinosaurs, and ape-men.

Jon told me how he loathed the world of nine-to-five and wanted to earn a living his way while having an uproariously good time in the process. Yes, indeed, we were going to get along just fine. Over the course of the next six months or so Jon and I would keep in touch by telephone and met regularly at conferences around the U.K. But it wasn't until the early part of 1998 that I finally visited him at home in Exeter.

As I sat on the train to Exeter on a snowy Tuesday morning in January, my mind began to wander. I knew that Jon had grown up in Hong Kong; was widely traveled; went to school with Princess Diana's lover, James Hewitt; had a father who was high up in the British government's Colonial Service; a brother who was a vicar; and he seemed to live the life of a veritable English dandy and nineteenth-century explorer. Knowing that Jon resided in the wilds of Devonshire (in a Court, no less), and that his brother and father had both been decorated by the queen, I tried to imagine the scene that would greet me.

Doubtless, I thought, Jon's little Devon hamlet was unchanged since the eighteenth or nineteenth century and he lived in a large manor house constructed out of ancient stone that looked like it came straight out of *The Hound of the Baskervilles* or the pages of a Brontë or a Hardy novel. It would be a resplendent Gothic affair, complete with a large attic and a well-stocked wine cellar. Every day would be an adventure and every meal would be a banquet. Was Jon akin to being the local squire, held in high esteem by the village folk? I would soon find out.

On arriving at Exeter St. David's railway station, I trudged through the ever-deepening snow, got myself a taxi, and asked the driver to take me to Holne Court, Exwick. After first being mistakenly taken to Home Court on the other side of Exeter, I finally arrived. But this wasn't Brontë or Hardy country, and where was the windswept moorland? The taxi pulled up outside a row of houses; I got out and asked the driver to hit the horn.

"Nicky!" I heard a familiar voice boom. "Get up here," shouted Jon, leaning head-and-shoulders out of a small window of a modestly sized house. I headed up the steps and the front door of the house swung open. Immediately an old and gnarly dog pounced on me and bared its teeth in a menacing fashion. "Toby!" Jon exclaimed. "That is *not* the way to greet Britain's baldest ufologist," he said, in reference to my daily-shaved head. He gently and fondly castigated the dog. It turned on its tail and glared at me. "Well, come on in to my Bohemian squalor and I'll get us a sherry," said Jon as I struggled with my bags.

I sat down on the couch and scanned the room. It wasn't what I had imagined but it was a perfect little bachelor pad and had a pleasantly chaotic, warm, and homely feel to it. But Jon was not the local squire. Like my rooms at home, books, shelves, CDs, and magazines filled every last inch of space; and around the lounge large glass tanks housed every conceivable type of insect, lizard, and reptile that you could possibly imagine. A large poster of The Golden Girls was pinned to the wall—that, like Jon's brown suit, was also covered in suspiciously positioned stains—and a human skull sat atop an old piano.

"You don't want to know where I got that from," Jon said, leaning forward, in conspiratorial tones.

"Er, Jon," I motioned to the corner of the room.

"For goodness' sake!" he exclaimed.

His two cats, Carruthers and Isabella, were tugging on a copy of Tim Matthews's book, *UFO Revelation,* and Toby was busying himself playfully tearing up a copy of *When Girls Fight* magazine. "Drop," shouted Jon, and all three animals headed with precision for the kitchen and shot up the stairs. At that moment, something truly bizarre happened. The late comedian John Belushi walked into the room. Not only that, he appeared to be dressed as an eighteenth-century pirate.

Actually, it wasn't John Belushi, nor was it an eighteenth-century pirate. It turned out, in reality, to be Jon's roommate and partner-in-crime at the Center for Fortean Zoology, Richard Freeman. At that time, Richard was in his late twenties and had for three years worked as Head of Reptiles at Twycross Zoo. Like Jon, Richard had had a lifelong fascination with monsters and unknown beasts; and as with many of us who spend our lives investigating the mysteries of this planet and beyond, he had taken that make-or-break step from the world of nine-to-five to, as he put it, "chasing monsters and lasses and having a laugh." Richard was also a Goth—for the uninitiated, a devotee of rather depressing and doom-laden rock music played in a slightly inept fashion by groups for whom (like Henry Ford) any color will do just as long as it's black. Richard had also undergone an intriguing initiation to the world of monsters.

As a boy in the 1970s Richard holidayed with his grandparents in Devon, England. One summer, when Richard was about nine, his grandfather got talking to a retired trawler man in Goodrington harbor. The old man recounted his life as a fisherman and one particular incident that was firmly and forever stuck in his mind. Some years previously he and his crew were trawling off Berry Head, where the seas of Britain are almost at their deepest. Indeed, such are the depths of this part of the English Channel that the area is commonly used as a graveyard for old ships and the drowned wrecks of these vessels have made an artificial reef that has attracted vast amounts of fish. Good catches are therefore almost guaranteed and the area has become a popular place for fishermen to drop their nets.

On one particular night, the crew had trouble lifting the nets and began to worry that they had got them entwined about a rotting mast. Soon, though, they felt some slack and duly began to haul the nets up. The men thought that their catch was a particularly good one, so heavy were their nets. As their nets drew closer to the trawler's lights, however, a frightening sight took shape. The crew had not caught hundreds of normal-sized fish but one gigantic one.

"It was an eel, a giant eel. Its mouth was huge, wide enough to have swallowed a man; the teeth were as long as my hand," said the fisherman. Even now Richard still remembers the words of the ancient mariner and is convinced that this was not a tall story designed to entertain gullible tourists. "While it was still in the water," said the frightened fisherman, "it was buoyed up, but as soon as we tried to pull it onboard the nets snapped like cotton and it vanished back down. I was glad it went; I've been at sea all my life but I've never been as scared as I was that night. I can still see its eyes, huge, glassy." And from that moment onward, Richard's life was forever changed.

He was an immediately unforgettable figure as he strode purposefully into the room in tails, with hands on hips and wearing an Adam Ant–style pirate shirt and pointed, thigh-length leather boots. He sat down next to me on the couch.

"Are you Nick?" he asked.

"Yeah, I am."

"I'm Rich. Jon told me you were coming down for a while. Has he got you a drink?"

"Yeah, he did, thanks."

"You're from up north, aren't you?" he quizzed me suspiciously.

"Well, the Midlands, yeah."

"Thank God," he shouted loudly and clapped his hands. A beaming smile came over his face. "You don't know what it's like living down here in the south. It's all red wine and pasta and Perrier-drinking southerners. Decent folk, proper beer, and home-cooked grub like you get up north just don't exist here. And—" He stopped in midsentence and stared at the floor.

"That bloody dog!" screamed Richard. "Is that my new *When Girls Fight* ripped up?"

"Sorry, Richard," said Jon meekly, while simultaneously and steadfastly staring at his feet. "He doesn't do it on purpose; he's just old." Richard scrambled to the floor and frantically began trying to salvage what was left of his precious magazine.

"Look at her," he said to me, pointing lovingly to a crumpled photograph of a girl nicknamed The Fight Madam who, dressed in black leather, and with a mean look on her face and a boxing glove on her right hand, adorned one of the few pages that remained relatively untouched by Toby's fearsome jaws. Jon guffawed from across the room. "Dear Richard, I love you like a brother but you are very strange." We all laughed and got down to some serious drinking.

Richard punched the Play button on the CD system and the monolithic drone of Bauhaus echoed around the room. "Bela Lugosi's dead," repeated the band's lead singer, Peter Murphy, endlessly.

"I'm not surprised he's dead if he had to listen to this tripe," quipped Jon. Richard waved his arms maniacally like some rabid orchestral conductor. Jon and I leaned back in our respective chairs and let the booze take effect. Meanwhile, from behind the kitchen door Toby the dog rested his head on his paws, stared intently at me, and quietly planned his next assault. And that was my initiation to the world of Jon Downes and the Center for Fortean Zoology. In the three years that followed we had some unforgettable moments—most of them alcohol-fueled and bizarre in the extreme.

There was the occasion, for example, that Jon invited me to enter, for the first time, his bedroom, where we sat and watched a masterfully bad, but hugely entertaining, film that Jon had acquired titled *Chainsaw Attack of the Radioactive Lesbian Zombies.* Prior to this invitation, I had been afforded only the barest of glimpses of this most mysterious and darkest of places; and, over dinner on that evening, Richard regaled me with endless tales of how Jon kept a hydrocephalic, twelve-fingered great-grandmother locked in a part of the attic above his bedroom; she was clinically insane. Indeed, I *had* heard a low moaning in the early hours of one particular morning that sounded like it *was* coming from the attic and that always made me wonder if there was any truth to this rumor. But then I realized I was just being an idiot. It had to have been the unnamed and toothless hag who frequented the house from time to time; Jon had picked her up at the local asylum that he visited for psychotherapy once a week. Or was it?

The mystery of who was, or indeed was *not,* imprisoned in Jon's attic aside, there were a number of other impressively memorable incidents that I will always remember with both fondness and hilarity—including the time that we made a riotous film based on Jon's award-winning book *The Owlman and Others.* Telling the story of a huge and fearsome "birdman" that supposedly haunts a Cornwall churchyard and the surrounding woodland, the film gathered rave reviews on its release in 2000, but was essentially an excuse for us to film a couple of naked women cavorting together in a wood. And who can argue with the merits of that? Certainly not I![1]

In the summer of 2000, things turned very, very dark. Toby the dog and the two cats, Isabella and Carruthers, all died within weeks of each other. Despite the fact that they were elderly and had been in failing health for some time, it was a sad time and Jon was inconsolable. Then a close friend of his, Tracey, committed suicide; Jon's car was written off by a drunk driver; the house nearly burned down after Richard cooked a mammoth feast for us; snakes escaped from their tanks (with one even finding its way into my sleeping bag in the middle of the night); the refrigerator became weirdly electrified and fried my fingers; and all manner of calamities piled on top of one another. When Jon told me that this was very possibly all due to a form of "psychic backlash" that was a direct result of his investigation of the Owlman, I believed him. But Jon soldiered on and we collaborated on some writing projects, including *Weird War Tales*, which chronicles the many and varied mysteries of the Second World War.

Shortly after its publication, in September 2000, I was booked to speak at the annual UFO Congress at Laughlin, Nevada. Little did I know it at the time, but it was to be a conference that would change my life. I flew out to the conference on March 1, 2001, and while there I met a beautiful lady named Dana who would, eight months later, become my wife. Before long the pleasant English countryside would be replaced by the sunny and blisteringly hot climes of southeast Texas. But I'm getting ahead of myself here. Two months after I returned from Laughlin, Dana came to live with me in England for a month and while over, she and I attended yet another UFO conference and met Jon, Richard, and the rest of the gang.

A fine time was had by all, as we sat around at the Edenfield Hotel drinking wine and beer and playing Sex Pistols songs on Geordie Dave's guitar. By now there was a growing and serious realization on my part that I might soon be leaving the country for a totally new life. And as is the case at all conferences where new friendships are formed and old relationships are rekindled, thoughts of the United

States filled my mind and I sensed somehow that an era had come to an end.

On Sunday night, the four of us sat in the bar until the early hours planning the future and discussing old times. Jon, Richard, and I had come to a decision. We elected to pass approximately six weeks leading up to my departure for the United States having a wild adventure in pursuit of the mysterious and devilish, beginning with an entity that all three of us, at some point, had crossed paths with: the macabre Man Monkey of Ranton.

2

HEY, HEY,
WE'RE THE MONKEYS

He's the devil's apprentice; he's a prehistoric man.

"APE-MAN HOP," THE RAMONES

On the cold and moonlit night of January 21, 1879, a man was riding home with his horse-and-cart in tow from Woodcote in the county of Shropshire to Ranton, Staffordshire, England. Enveloped in darkness, he pulled his jacket tightly around him to keep out the biting wind. The day had been a relatively uneventful and tiring one spent moving furniture from one residence to another and he was not only fatigued, he was already more than an hour late in getting home to his wife. All was normal until around 10.00 P.M., when approximately a mile from the village of Woodseaves and while crossing a bridge over the Birmingham and Liverpool Canal, the man got the shock of his life. Out of the trees leapt a horrific-looking creature. Jet black in color and with a pair of huge, glowing eyes, it was described by the petrified witness as being half-man and half-monkey.

Naturally, all hell broke loose. The creature jumped onto the back of the man's horse, which proceeded to bolt out of sheer fright, and a fierce battle for life and limb began atop the cart. Incredibly, according to the man, when he attempted to hit the beast with his whip, it simply passed straight through its body. Suddenly and without warning the spectral man-beast vanished into thin air, leaving one exhausted horse and its shell-shocked owner in a state of near collapse.

Rushing to a nearby tavern at Woodseaves for a much-needed drink, the man recounted his story to a concerned and frightened crowd. He then headed home and retired to his bed, where he apparently spent several days in a state of nervous exhaustion. But that is not the end of the tale. A somewhat exaggerated account from the villagers of Ranton reached the ears of the local constabulary and a policeman was dispatched to the home of the man's employer to ascertain the truth. When the man's employer relayed the facts, however, the policeman asserted that this was not the first time such a creature had been seen in the vicinity. Indeed, the policeman advised him, he knew precisely what lay behind the bizarre event: "That was the Man Monkey, sir, as does come again at that bridge ever since a man was drowned in the cut."[1]

And so it was with these few, scant facts in hand that I, Jon, and Richard began our quest to ascertain the truth behind the mystery of the Man Monkey. Little did we know, but that quest would take us from the depths of a Staffordshire forest to the shores of Loch Ness, from the man who worked for Royal Air Force Intelligence to an underground government facility, and from an old Victorian hospital to the wilds of Dartmoor. And along the way, our lives would be changed forever.

You might ask: What would prompt us to look into a one-hundred-and-twenty-plus-year-old case about which almost nothing was known, except for these few, meager, and admittedly hard-to-believe "facts"? That's a damned good question. But actually it's one for which the answer is (or the answers are) very simple. All of us had heard of and read accounts of the Man Monkey's exploits but no one, it seemed, had ever tried to resolve the mystery once and for all. It was time for that situation to change. As someone who had spent years investigating mysterious animals, Jon relished the chance to get his teeth into a case of this caliber and for me it was a way of passing the time with some good friends before I left the U.K. for pastures new. For Richard, it was, as he so eloquently put it, "a chance to get the hell out of the bloody south for a while." In early summer 2001 I traveled to Jon's home and from there we coordinated our hunt to seek out the truth about the Man Monkey.

⁙ ⁙ ⁙

It was 7:00 P.M. when I arrived.

"That you, Nick?" I heard Jon scream as I knocked on the door.

"Don't open the door whatever you do. The snapping turtle's escaped; the bastard will have your hand off!"

I dropped my cases and scrambled on top of a huge pile of black trash-liner bags that seemed to be permanently positioned outside of Jon's home, and I peered through the window into the candlelit room. There, sure enough, was the fearsome-looking creature circling the floor and snapping its even more fearsome jaws. Richard and Jon were perched on the sofa, gripping the cats and the dog that, incredibly, were struggling to engage the turtle in mortal combat.

"It's alright, Arnie will be around in a minute," shouted Jon, waving to me with a concerned look on his face. I knew Arnie, a very untrustworthy but friendly used-car salesman, and the guy from whom Jon had bought the wretched beast in the first place. Sure enough, Arnie was quickly on the scene, but it seemed like an eternity before Dee Dee the Snapping Turtle was well and truly locked inside one of Arnie's glass tanks.

"How the hell did he escape?" I asked.

According to Richard, he was in the middle of reciting an ancient, black-magical ritual designed to invoke the presence of "the great horned one" when Dee Dee's tank had exploded, showering both Arnie and glass all over the carpet. Jon's version of events was slightly different, however, and he suggested that having got "bevvied up" during the day, a drunken Richard had stumbled into the sideboard and had simply knocked the tank onto the living-room carpet.

"I don't know how much more of this insanity I can take," said Jon wearily while mopping his ever-fevered brow. "Now, what about this bloody Man Monkey business, then?"

And so it was that our investigation truly began in earnest. Over a splendid chicken dinner cooked by Richard and several bottles of Chianti, Jon regaled us with tales of ape-men, Bigfoot, the Yeti, and a host of other creatures that seemed to bear an uncanny resemblance to the Man Monkey.

"My boys, if we're to conduct a detailed and exhaustive study of the Man Monkey legend, it's vital that all three of us are acquainted with the facts concerning these elusive creatures," Jon told us.

With the curtains drawn and the room lit by only the dimmest of flickering candles, Jon's face took on a strange appearance and the howling wind and driving rain outside only added to the weird atmosphere. At that point, Jon seemed to go off into a mystical world all of his own as he sat back in his chair, pulled out his notes, and regaled us with the facts.

"In the late 1950s the Belgian zoologist Bernard Heuvelmans defined the science of what today we call cryptozoology—the study of mysterious, or hidden animals. Bernie the Belgian, as I like to fondly remember him, proposed a scientific name for the Yeti, and called it *Dinanthropoides nivalis*—the giant ape of the snows."

"So what do you think the Yeti is, then?" I asked.

Jon thought for a moment and continued. "Well, several quite convincing theories exist that have been promulgated to explain its identity."

"Jon, no one says promulgated, mate," I interjected.

"*I* do," he replied matter-of-factly, as Richard rolled his eyes at me with a grin on his face. "One very plausible theory is that the Yeti is an evolved descendant of an extinct giant primate called Gigantopithecus, that was first described after giant teeth were discovered in an apothecary's shop in Hong Kong by a Dutch zoologist named Ralph Von Koenigswald shortly before the Second World War."

After an examination of other fossil remains found alongside those of Gigantopithecus, Von Koenigswald established that the giant ape had lived some five hundred thousand years ago in caves in the Chinese province of Kwangsi, and could have lived as recently as one hundred thousand years ago—something that was, as Jon correctly put it, "in purely paleogeological terms, a mere bagatelle."

As the Chianti began to take effect, Jon was in full flow. "Now, of course, Yeti-like creatures have been seen in North America for centuries. The Native Americans were familiar with the creature, which some of them called Sasquatch. It's been suggested that these animals are close relatives of the Yeti, which crossed to North America from mainland Asia through the long-submerged land bridge across the Bering Strait.

"But did you know that there also seems to be a second unknown primate in North America? In the southern states of the United States they get recurrent reports of chimpanzee-like creatures, known as Skunk-Apes. These, I have to say, sound very much like the Man Monkey. A colleague of mine, Loren Coleman, has suggested that they're evolved descendants of an extinct ape called Dryopithecus. And I must say that there are many reputable zoologists who are prepared to at least consider his hypothesis."

"So could this be what the Man Monkey is, or was?" I asked.

"Well . . ." Jon mused for a moment. "The problem is that there is no evidence to suggest that Dryopithecus or Oak Ape—so called because the fossils were all found in areas that had been covered in deciduous forests—ever existed in North America, never mind in England."

"Really?" said Richard in mock astonishment.

Jon cast a weary eye and a pointed finger in Richard's direction. "Oh yes. And the original inhabitants of what's now Queensland in northwest Australia believe in a man-beast, too, that they called the Yowie. Their folklore refers to Yowies as being as real as the kangaroos, wombats, and thylacines that prehistoric artists painted on the walls of caves and secret, holy places.

"But that ain't all, mate," he said, smiling, as he leaned forward and clasped his fingers together. "There are also cave paintings of shambling, gorilla-like creatures, which the native Australians identify as the Yowies. Although these creatures are still seen occasionally in the wilder parts of the Queensland bush, the so-called scientific community is divided on the veracity of the reports.

"The main problem, of course, is that if it does exist as a living creature, how the hell did it get to Australia in the first place? Although Australia *was* once connected to mainland Asia, the land bridge ceased to exist about at least sixty million years ago, and this was years before even the most primitive primates evolved.

"Now, the eyewitness reports suggest that even if Yowies are some form of human, it seems unlikely that they could have had the ability to build boats to have got them to Australia. It has, however, been suggested that the Yowie is a de-evolved human. This theory would mean that the Yowie shared the same ancestors as the native Australians of today, but that for sociological and/or physiological reasons, they abandoned the complex social structures of tribal existence, and now live as wild men.

"But there's a problem. If the Yowie *is* an ape, the same question arises. How did it get there? The nearest anthropoid apes, geographically speaking, are the orangutans of Java and Sumatra. And what are the chances that these apes could swim such a distance across shark-infested waters? It's almost equally unlikely that the earliest human settlers in Australia, or indeed any subsequent visitors, should have taken anthropoid apes along with them as traveling companions.

"And now we come to what I think we are going to find is behind the Man Monkey story. Fill the glass up, Richard, dear boy. There is another group of so-called man-beasts, and these are ones that have, as far as I'm concerned at least, been unjustly ignored by most cryptozoologists. Whereas logical scientific explanations have been offered for the Yeti, Bigfoot, and the Yowie, there are some that are not so easily explained.

"Nicky," Jon continued, as he drained his glass, lit an enormous Havana cigar, and proceeded to open a bottle of absinthe, "I'm the first to admit that the Himalayan mountains, the Australian outback, and the vast forests of the northwestern United States are—even today—relatively unexplored. And mapped and visited many times they may be, but there are still numerous places in these countries where large apelike animals could live, relatively free from fear of detection. But in England? Forget it. Of course, the big problem is that people *do* see man-beasts in the U.K. even though the existence of such things just can't be. So I think that whatever we learn about the Man Monkey, of one thing we can be very certain: the thing is *not* flesh and blood, whatever it is. It's paranormal. Now, wait right there."[2]

Jon stood up and went to a four-draw filing cabinet that stood in the corner of the room. He rummaged around for a few seconds and pulled out a large and well-worn folder that was about three inches thick.

"This," he whispered in a low voice, "is the Holy Grail."

"It's not an original *Dr. Who* script, is it?" asked Richard.

"Shut up, Richard," said Jon curtly. "This is where we must begin if we are going to get anywhere with the investigation. In here you will find what is—even if I say so myself—probably the finest collection of man-beast accounts from within the U.K. These are my personal investigative files that few, if indeed anyone else, have ever seen. Privileged, you are, indeed."

"He can't half tell a story, can't he?" I said laughingly to Richard.

"Huh," he replied, "I have to put up with his southern nonsense every day."

Jon ignored our comments, opened the folder, scanned the pages, and began to read his notes. "One particularly intriguing series of records comes from the area around Torphins, near Aberdeen, Scotland, and took place in 1994. Three young men were walking along a wide track through a forestry plantation when they encountered what, if this sighting had occurred in the United States, I would have no compunction in identifying as a Bigfoot.

"One of the youths saw what he described as a dark, human-shaped figure run across the track, from the left-hand side to the right two hundred yards in front of them. He felt an immediate sense of terror and foreboding, but his friends saw nothing. Well, they were teasing him and accusing him of having made up the whole incident, when all three saw a face, that they afterward described as being human but not human, peering out at them from between the branches of the fir trees. One of them threw a stone in the direction of this apparition, and the creature disappeared.

"The three young men had a second encounter with the same, or a very similar creature, a few weeks later. They were driving into the town of Torphins, about two miles away from the site of their first experience, when a large, dark, and hairy figure appeared at the side of the road. It began to run up the road behind them and was soon running level with the car. What was surprising was that although the figure was running at a speed that sometimes approached forty-five miles an hour, it did not seem to be fatigued. At one point the creature stared into the car at the three youths, with an inquisitive expression, but after about five minutes it stopped abruptly in the middle of the road, leaving the three friends to carry on, feeling somewhat flustered, with their journey. One of the three claimed later that a female friend of his, living in a secluded cottage, has twice seen a dark, hairy figure standing in the forest watching her cottage, before slinking away into the undergrowth.[3] Now, coincidence or not, but there is another well-attested, and very similar phenomenon known as Jack the Runner, a phantom seen regularly in the drive of Glamis Castle."

Situated just west of Forfar, Glamis Castle is referred to by Shakespeare in *Macbeth,* Macbeth having killed Duncan there in 1040, and it is also at the castle where assassins murdered King Malcolm II in 1034. Glamis Castle was also the childhood home of Queen Elizabeth, the Queen Mother and the birthplace of Princess Margaret. Jon continued. "And the castle is, of course, the site of yet another, well-known and semilegendary beast known as the Monster of Glamis. It's said that the creature was supposed to have been the hideously deformed heir to the Bowes-Lyon family and who was, according to popular rumor, born in about 1800, and died as recently as 1921.

"Legend has it that the monster was supposed to look like an enormous flabby egg, having no neck and only minute arms and legs but possessed incredible strength and had an air of evil about it. Certainly, there *is* a family secret concerning the monster, which is only told to the male heir of the Bowes-Lyon family when they attain majority. But according to the author Peter Underwood, who has looked into this case, the present Lord Strathmore knows nothing about the monster, presumably because the creature has long been dead, but he always felt that there was a corpse or coffin bricked up behind the walls."

I had looked into this story myself and had learned that, according to legend, the existence of the creature was allegedly known to only four men at any given time, namely the earl of Strathmore, his direct heir, the family's lawyer, and the broker of the estate. At the age of twenty-one each succeeding heir was told the secret and shown the rightful—and horrendously deformed—earl, and succeeding family lawyers and brokers were also informed of the family's shocking secret.

As no countess of Strathmore was ever told the story, one Lady Strathmore, having heard of such rumors, approached the then broker, a Mr. Ralston, who flatly refused to reveal the secret and who would only say, "It is fortunate you do not know the truth, for if you did you would never be happy."[4]

Jon continued. "But perhaps the best-known apparition of a Scottish man-beast is the Big Gray Man of Ben Mcdhui. This Yeti-like creature has been reported on many occasions over the past hundred years or so, and a similar entity has been reported from Dundonald Hill and Dundonald Castle in Ayrshire. Take a look at these."[5]

Jon passed to Richard and myself a hefty pile of reports. The first concerned an Englishwoman who, in 1994, was on holiday in Scotland and who had decided to visit Dundonald Castle. As she walked her dogs on the hill, a large, hairy creature appeared some distance away. Immediately the dogs were spooked and began pacing around in circles, growling and snapping.

The thing was not dissimilar to a gorilla in shape, although it stood well over ten feet tall and was covered in longish, charcoal-colored hair. What struck the woman the most was the creature's face. It had two long slits for eyes, which glowed red, two holes where the nose should have been, and very thick lips. After a few moments the creature moved off out of sight and the lady quickly left. She never returned.

"Remember the glowing eyes, boys; that is a clue that we are dealing with something distinctly and diabolically paranormal," said Jon quietly.

The Beckermet area of Cumbria was apparently the location of a similar incident in January 1998 that had caught Jon's attention. He carefully unfolded a copy of a newspaper clipping from the *Whitehaven News* of March of that year and proceeded to read to us the text of a letter from a man who had seen yet another mystery man-beast.

"It was about 5:00 P.M. and starting to get dark so my visibility was not that good, but as I walked past the woods I heard the snapping of branches. Thinking it was an animal, I stopped to try and see it. Looking through the trees I noticed a large creature covered in a sort of ginger brown hair that seemed to be drinking from a pond about 150 meters into the woods. As the lighting was getting bad I was straining to make out what it was, but as I stopped and stared, it appeared to notice me. At this point it reared up onto its hind legs and made off slowly further into the woods. I would estimate its height when upright, to be around 6 feet 6 inches."[6] And the reports kept on coming.

"One of the most credible reports brought to my attention," Jon said, "came from a family that had a daylight encounter with a similar beast in the Peak District in the summer of 1991. This all occurred as they were driving near Ladybower Reservoir on the Manchester-to-Sheffield road. On a hillside, one of the family members had spotted a large figure walking down toward the road. But this was no man.

"Well, they brought the car to a screeching halt and came face-to-face with an enormous creature about eight feet tall that was covered in long brown hair with eyes just like a man's. Its walk was different, too, almost crouching. But just as the man-beast reached the road, another car pulled up behind the family and blasted their horn—apparently wondering why they had stopped in the middle of the road. Suddenly the creature—which I presume was startled by the noise— ran across the road, jumped over a wall that had a ten-foot drop on the other side, and ran off, disappearing into the woods. Now, I know that the family has returned to the area but has seen nothing since."[7]

"Snowdonia in Wales is a typical location for sightings, too," explained Jon, pulling out another report and sipping on his absinthe. "The locals know it as the Brenin Llwyd, or the Gray King, and even the mountain guides are said to be wary of it. It's been seen in recent years including once by a forester, who, with some friends, had mounted an expedition to search for the beast. His account was typical of many others. Here's his report."

Jon passed me a copy of two emails that he had received describing the encounter in question. It read:

I am a forester in North Wales, living for much of my time in a remote mountain bothy in Snowdonia. A bothy is a small mountain hut, and there's nothing I like more than to spend some quality time on my own, amongst the hills and nature. Over the years, I have received many reports of sightings of an extremely unusual creature, a "monstrous beast," as one visitor called it. This has puzzled me for a long time, and I became determined to seek out this beast for myself. It was while searching on the internet that I came across the British Beast on your website, and the thought occurred to me that maybe there is a population of these beasts spread across Britain.

I have spent the last month or two preparing for an expedition base from my mountain bothy. The authorities refuse to give us any support, thinking that we are all crackpots. However, me and a group of colleagues managed to pull together enough resources to mount the expedition, which has just finished. I am afraid our success was limited and there is much still to do, but we did see the creature for ourselves. It attacked our camp one night, and much of our equipment was damaged. It was at least ten feet high, and stood on two legs. It seemed to be more bearlike than apelike; it seemed to be investigating our camp when a dog we had with us tried to attack it. There followed a few minutes of absolute terror, as the beast was clearly quite distressed by our invasion, and sought an escape from what must have been a confusing situation.

It was fortunate that no one was injured, and we are fairly sure that the beast is not inherently dangerous to people. . . .

The second email read:

We have returned to the campsite twice since the incident, to try and salvage what we could. One important point is that the beast could definitely not have been a bear, from a behavioral point of view; the only time a bear stands on two legs is to sniff the air, but this animal was rampaging about on two legs. We feel it is also vital to point out that the beast was in no way aggressive, but merely felt threatened by our presence. All of our camera equipment had been damaged beyond repair, and the terrain there is mostly rock, scree and heather, so there were no tracks etc. We have spent many hours trying to piece together what we would consider to be a fairly accurate description of the beast's appearance, bearing in mind we have been unable to rely on photographic evidence. The beast was roughly ten feet tall when standing on two legs and gave off a strong, musky type of smell. It had dark brown hair, probably fur, and massive hands. Its eyes appeared to be red in color, and we could really sense the fear which the poor beast was enduring. For most of the time we were ducked down behind some rocks, and the campfire smoke was making it keep a fair distance away. It did attack our tent though, tearing through the sides. It was a dull and gloomy day, so when we began to take photos, the flash naturally went off. This really frightened it, and it began to head for us. So we ran off and were forced to leave the camera on its tripod. Alas, the beast picked it up and threw it against the rocks. We feel that this bizarre animal is indeed very intelligent, and eagerly await some finer weather before embarking on another expedition. This disaster has not deterred us, and preparations are being made for next time. People are calling it the "Brecon Beacon Beast," despite it being nowhere near there. The local press seem to go for any excuse for a good alliteration!

Jon also had in his files a copy of a report from September 1998 that originated from within the depths of Cannock Chase, Staffordshire— a huge area of forest land only seven or eight miles from my old home in the West Midlands and a short distance from Ranton, the home of the Man Monkey. It was just after midnight on the night in question when a group of four was driving along the A34 road from Stafford to Cannock.

"Listen to this," said Jon. "These are the exact words of one of the witnesses. 'It was a star-filled night, clear but dark, and we were all in the car driving home, happily chatting and joking. Suddenly we all fell dead serious, the people in the back sat forward and we all pointed to the same shape. It was a tall manlike figure, sort of crouching forward. As we passed, it turned and looked straight at us. In my own words I would describe it as around six feet eight inches tall, legs thicker than two of mine, very strong-looking and with a darkish, blacky[sic]-brown coat. I just could not explain it and I still get goose bumps thinking of it.'

"Now, if you think that's impressive," said Jon, suddenly interrupted by an almighty crashing sound that coincided with what was unmistakably glass breaking. "Mother of God! What the hell was that?" he cried as all three of us jumped to our feet and while chairs, glasses, bottles, and our solitary source of light—the candle—fell to the floor. Whatever it was, it came from the kitchen. Fumbling in the blackness, I finally reached the light switch, only to find that the house's electrical system had been blown out. I cursed loudly. I do not know if it was my imagination or not, but the wind seemed to howl even louder and the rain had turned into a veritable deluge. As my eyes adjusted to the darkness, I could see the outline of Jon's unmistakable bulky form lumbering around frantically in the lounge.

"Got it," he muttered, as he turned on a powerful flashlight that he kept on the shelf near his computer. Jon reached the door to the kitchen and flung it open. All three of us entered warily.

"Bloody hell!" I exclaimed. There, lying dead on the floor amid a pile of blood and feathers was a huge crow that had evidently flown headlong into—and right through—the kitchen window. Fragments of shattered glass lay everywhere and the broken remains of several plates and dishes were scattered all around the unfortunate bird.

"I can't believe this," said Richard. "I cannot bloody well believe this. First the turtle, now this *and* the lights, and all in one bloody night! Do you get the feeling that we've opened the door to something that should have stayed closed with all this Man Monkey stuff?"

Jon shone the torch on us. He had a deadly serious and frightened look on his face the likes of which I had never seen before. "This is precisely the psychic backlash I was telling you about and that I fear," he said. "You mess with this stuff and it will come right back at you. You think it's a coincidence that the lights went out at the same time that . . . *this* happened and right when we're delving into this Man Monkey thing?" he asked, gesturing toward the remains of the bird. "No. This is a warning."

It took us an hour and a half to restore the kitchen to normality. We managed to patch the window with a piece of plywood until it could be properly repaired the next day and what was left of the bird was relegated to the dustbin. Richard and Jon cleaned up the lounge and I got the electricity flowing again. No less than three fuses had blown. I opened the kitchen door and noticed that the rain had stopped. On the horizon, however, another huge storm cloud was brewing. And it was heading our way.

3

THE COSMIC ZOO

I don't have a monkey's brain; I am not an animal.

"ANIMAL BOY," THE RAMONES

By this time it was around 12:30 A.M., but the adrenaline surge of the last few hours had ensured that none of us were ready for sleep. We returned to the table and Jon opened one of his prized bottles of claret.

"Nicky, Richard, listen to me," Jon began. "I don't pretend to have all of the answers to what we're getting into, but I've been down this path before and I don't like it. I don't like it one bit. But we've started and we're sucked in, so we might as well carry on. We're dealing with forces, occult forces, paranormal forces, call them what you will. I've had this same type of psychic backlash before while investigating not just ape-men, but UFOs, big cats, lake monsters, and sea serpents. Somehow, these phenomena are all linked and behind them is a force—or an entity—that screws with the human mind when we try to unravel it all."

Jon explained that while he still held the opinion that *some* of the mysterious creatures that he had investigated *were* indeed flesh-and-blood animals, others were nothing of the sort. There were countless reports and legends pertaining to lake monsters, big cats, ghostly black dogs, man-beasts, and sea serpents on record where the creatures were reported to have literally appeared and then vanished in the blink of an eye. Cameras would jam as people tried to photograph the elusive beasts. No one could ever catch one of the creatures. Movie film was inconclusive. Investigators of these phenomena would begin to experience weird coincidences—or synchronicities—as they delved ever further into the heart of the mystery. Those same people would become obsessed with finding the answers, and marriages and lives would be wrecked and torn apart in the process as an ever-spiraling descent into unreality and madness took an unrelenting hold of them. Jon was unsure of the cause of all this mayhem and mystery, but speculated that some form of ethereal, superior intelligence coexisted with us—and had done so for millennia—and that, for reasons of its own, was constantly manipulating and molding the human mind with images of bizarre and unexplained phenomena.

"Whatever this intelligence is, and it may even be a part of us," said Jon, "we are its plaything and have been for centuries, if not longer even. Indeed, we may be responsible for its existence in the first place." And as Jon also noted, the phenomenon seemed to change and progress as our society did likewise.

The fairies that would kidnap children in the Middle Ages and take them to their twilight world have been replaced by today's bug-eyed aliens abducting people for their DNA. The dragons of yesteryear are our lake monsters. The Wild-Men-of-the-Woods so prevalent in the legends of Europe centuries ago have given way to the gargantuan ape-men of America's great forests. In place of the ghostlike black dogs that can be found in the mythology of numerous towns and villages around the U.K., there now exists phantom felids, such as the so-called Beast of Bodmin and the Beast of Exmoor. And tales of mermaids captured centuries ago and kept in secret locations by sailors have been replaced by accounts of alien bodies hidden in secure government installations such as the infamous Area 51.

"Now, I am not—repeat *not*—saying that there is absolutely no physical reality to any or all of these phenomena; there may well be," Jon elaborated. "But for the most part we are dealing with a form of intelligence that is playing with the human mind and conjuring up these semi- or fleetingly real things and mystifying us in the same way that the imagery on a TV screen would have paralyzed with fear someone from the time of Julius Caesar."

"So," I inquired, "what exactly is this phenomenon and why does it keep throwing up these same images—the big cats, the ghost dogs, UFOs, lake monsters, and ape-men like the Man Monkey?"

"Well," Jon replied, "that's the $64,000 question. Perhaps we're going to finally find out. But let's get back to the reports, shall we? Richard, time for another bottle, I think." As we sat drinking claret, Richard opened up a box of delicious Belgian chocolates and Jon returned to his notes.

"Hangley Cleave, in Somerset, has been the scene of two very similar sightings," Jon continued. "One occurred in a local quarry and another on the nearby barrows where what was described as a large, crouching manlike form, covered in dark, matted hair and with pale, flat eyes, was seen.

"And the area around Smitham Hill in Somerset has also been the site of a number of such encounters. For example, many years ago the area around what is now an abandoned mine was linked to tales of strange beasts seen watching the miners. Sometimes on returning to work in the morning, the men would find that carts and equipment had been pushed over and thrown around during the night.

"But these things, whatever they were, are still seen in that area today—or at least as late as November 1993. This is an exact quote taken from a witness whose case is in my files," added Jon. He picked up a loose sheet of paper and began reading.

"I was on a walk through the woods, when I heard a twig snap. I thought nothing of it and continued on. Suddenly the dogs became very agitated and ran off home. At this point I became aware of a foul smell like a wet dog, and a soft breathing sound. I started to run, but after only a few feet, I tripped and fell. I decided to turn and meet my pursuer only to see a large, about seven feet tall, dark brown, hairy, apelike man. It just stood, about ten feet away, staring at me. It had intelligent-looking eyes and occasionally tilted its head as if to find out what I was. After about twenty seconds it moved off into the forest."

And still the accounts continued. "I have many similar reports of such creatures being seen in Devonshire woodland," said Jon. "And this one is a real cracker because it has so much separate and credible corroboration to it."

The location, Jon revealed, was Churston Woods, close to the holiday resort of Torbay. "Over a six-week period, in the summer of 1996," Jon grandly told us, "fifteen separate witnesses reported seeing what they could only describe as a green-faced monkey running through the woods. Granted, some of the descriptions were quite vague, but most of the witnesses told of seeing a tailless animal, around four to five feet tall, with a flat, olive-green face that would run through the woods and occasionally would be seen swinging through the trees.

"Now, to me at least, this sounds like some form of primitive human, but again, of course, such things simply cannot exist in this country—and yet they seem to. And this area—Devon, Somerset, and Cornwall—is rich with such tales, you know."

In many ways the 1996 encounters at Churston Woods were echoed by a similar tale concerning the infamous Beast of Brassknocker Hill. It had all begun in September 1979, amid rumors that a terrifying monster was haunting the woods of Brassknocker Hill, near the British city of Bath. Described as resembling a chimpanzee, baboon, spider monkey, gibbon, or lemur, the creature was of more concern to some than others. Eighty-one-year-old Brassknocker Hill resident Frank Green took up a shotgun vigil and said, "I am very fond of some animals, but I reckon this creature could be dangerous and I am taking no chances." By the following summer the mystery seemed to have been solved when a policeman caught sight of a chimpanzee in the woods. "We were sure this mystery creature would turn out to be a monkey of some sort," said Inspector Mike Price. "After all, men from Mars aren't hairy, are they?" But rumors of strange activities at Brassknocker Hill persisted.

Two years later, the stories returned, only this time the rumors concerned a four-legged creature—a stag, polecat, or even a Japanese deer. Then one day in the summer of 1984, reports started coming in to the news desk of the *Bath Chronicle* of a strange-looking creature holding up traffic on Brassknocker Hill. "I grabbed my notebook," said reporter Roger Green, now editor of the *Littlehampton Gazette*. "Colin [Shepherd] the photographer grabbed his camera, and we rushed out to the hill. The reports were pretty credible, so we were convinced that there was something there," Green recalled. "It was with slight trepidation that we entered the woods. After several minutes of stalking, we came across the 'beast,' by then calmly grazing in a field. It was an alpaca, a type of llama, and had escaped from a paddock. It was later reunited with its owner by the police." But this did not explain the earlier sightings of a monkeylike animal, of course. Needless to say, the mystery was never resolved to everyone's satisfaction.[1] Jon then passed to me his notes that detailed further aspects of his research into Devonshire beasts and I read them carefully:

From the Cannibals of Clovelly to the Brew Crew of Treworgey, the whole area has attracted people who wish to live outside of our recognized society; and these people have often degenerated into a wild and lawless existence, sometimes even reverting to a surprisingly primitive lifestyle. As well as these people who though undoubtedly wild men were not *wild men*, there are a number of reports of entities whose nature seems far more analogous to some of the stranger "big hairy men" reports from around the world.

The Devon folklorist Theo Brown collected a number of such stories, including one chilling recollection by a friend of hers who had been walking alone at dusk near the Neolithic earthworks at the top of Lustleigh Cleave on the extreme east side of Dartmoor. Lustleigh Cleave is an extraordinarily strange place, and it appears to be one of those "window areas" where an inordinate number of unexplained incidents and anomalous phenomena seem to take place on an almost monotonous basis. I have got reports of sightings of a ghostly Tudor hunting party, mysterious lights in the sky, and even the apparitions of a pair of Roman centurions, but Theo Brown's friend saw, clearly, a family of "cavemen," either naked and covered in hair or wrapped in the shaggy pelts of some wild animal, shambling around the stone circle at the top of the cleave.

As I finished reading his notes, Jon continued: "And there's something else that I've discovered about many of these historical British accounts. Whereas people in the United States and Tibet are content to accept that Bigfoot and the Yeti are real, living creatures, here in the U.K. things are a little different." For a moment Jon sat staring at me in silence with a smug look on his face.

"Okay, Jon, you've got me hooked. What is it?" I asked.

He smiled. "Well, unlike the phenomena in other parts of the world, each of the historic British cases have a convenient little folk story, or ghost story, attached to them to explain the presence of these apparitional creatures in the relevant region. The Ghost Ape of Marwood, for example, was, when alive, a pet of a local landowner who one day grabbed the landowner's young son and climbed a tree with him, refusing to come down. And after being killed, the monkey's ghost supposedly haunted the surrounding area.

"Whereas the well-known specter of Martyn's Ape at Athelhampton House in Dorset is supposed to have been the pet of a member of the Martyn family that was either accidentally bricked up alive during building work, or was entombed when the daughter either committed suicide in a locked, secret room, or was walled up by an unforgiving parent—depending on which account you read and accept.

"The Martyn family built the earliest part of this house in the fifteenth century; and, interestingly enough, their family crest was of an ape sitting on a tree stump and the family motto was: He who looks at Martyn's ape, Martyn's ape will look at him. Now, my theory is that *none* of these assertions are correct. I earnestly believe that these stories—which are all *very* similar to that of the Man Monkey—were invented by village folk in centuries past to try to explain the sightings of monkey-shaped apparitions that would fleetingly appear from time to time and then would vanish as if into thin air. And now, Nicky, dear boy, we come to your area of expertise: UFOs."

I knew that there was a wealth of reports on record where man-beasts, lake monsters, and out-of-place big cats had been seen in the exact same vicinity as UFOs, but the area of research that suggested a common link between all of these issues was one that I had never really delved into before to any great extent. Jon, fortunately, had.

"The idea that some people hold—that Bigfoot, the Yeti and some of these other creatures are seen in the vicinity of UFO sightings because the animals are the property, or even the 'pets' of the UFO intelligences or that they are some form of alien genetic experiment—is, in my view, ridiculously and pathetically simplistic and would be far more at home in a 1950s sci-fi B-movie," said Jon.

"A far more plausible theory is, as I have said, that these things tend to be seen together precisely because they both have a common source of origin and are very much a part of the same phenomenon—which is largely apparitional in nature. Let me give you a few examples." Again, he stood up and went to the filing cabinet and pulled out an even bigger folder titled Men in Black. "You think it's only UFO investigators who have files on Men in Black, Nicky? Take a look at *this*."

Jon handed me a twelve-page, stapled report that told a remarkable tale. It consisted of a transcript of a telephone conversation that Jon had had with a man named Alistair Baxter. In 1968 Baxter—who had a lifelong interest in lake monsters—traveled to Loch Ness and spent nine weeks armed with a camera and binoculars quietly and carefully monitoring the loch for any unusual activity.

Baxter had informed Jon that he never did see the elusive beast of Loch Ness, but he did speak with numerous people who *had* seen it. However, after being at the loch side almost constantly for five weeks, an unusual event occurred. He was awoken in the middle of the night by a curious humming sound that was emanating from a bright, small ball of light about the size of a football that—at a height of around fifteen feet from the ground—was slowly and carefully making its way through the surrounding trees that enveloped Baxter's modestly sized tent.

Suddenly and without warning the ball of light shot into the sky to a height of several hundred feet and hovered in deathly silence over the still waters of Loch Ness. For reasons that Baxter was at a loss to explain, he felt an overwhelming urge to go back to sleep and the next thing he knew it was daybreak. But the strangeness had barely begun.

Shortly after breakfast three men in black suits appeared outside of Baxter's tent seemingly out of nowhere and proceeded to ask him if he had seen anything unusual during the night. He replied that he hadn't and one of the three men turned to his two colleagues and made what Baxter said was "a strange smile." He turned to face Baxter. "We might return," said one of the mysterious men in black and all three departed by simply walking off into the woods. They never returned.

Most interesting of all was the fact that for the following three nights, Baxter had a recurring and frightening dream of a large and lumbering ape-man that would pace outside of his tent and that would then head down to the shores of the loch, whereupon, under a starlit sky, it would tilt its head back, wail loudly, and stand staring at the ink-black water. The dream would always end the same way, with an image of a huge and ominous atomic mushroom cloud exploding in the distance and the beginning of the Third World War and the end of civilization.

"Now, I have no way to explain this," said Jon, "except to say that Baxter was credible—he's dead now so I can name him—and he held a position of responsibility with a mining company for his whole working life before retiring in the mid-sixties and was very scared by this whole experience. But here you have the key ingredients of what I'm talking about all intertwined: the ape-man, the lake monster, and a strange ball of light that was, by the literal definition, a UFO. Then there were the Men in Black. Baxter told me that for a reason he could never quite explain, he failed at the time to even wonder why three men dressed entirely in black would be down at the loch side asking questions about weird goings-on in the middle of the night. And the image of Armageddon and the apocalypse is one that appears regularly in alien abduction accounts."

Jon wasn't wrong. I had numerous accounts in my own files from people who believed that they had undergone some form of "alien abduction" and who, they said, had been shown images by the aliens of a desolate and irradiated Earth in the near future that had been ravaged by a worldwide nuclear war.

"This is a warning of what will happen if we don't change our ways," one of the abductees had said to me. Interestingly, she, too, told of a frightening and futuristic scene that she believed showed a ruined and permanently cloud-covered London where the starving survivors were forced to do battle for food with strange, hairy ape-men that would surface at night out of the remains of the London Underground rail tunnels. What the hell was going on? I wondered.

"Now we come to the real icing on the cake," said Jon, grinning proudly. "What time is it, Richard?"

"Quarter to three."

"Be a good boy and fetch the whisky, will you?" Richard trotted off dutifully to the drinks cabinet; I made us a big plate of toast and Jon settled down to relate the next piece in the puzzle.

"Now, Richard, this is for you as Nick is well acquainted with this story. During the last few days of December 1980 there were a series of UFO reports in and around Rendlesham Forest in Suffolk that occurred on the doorsteps of the Air Force bases Bentwaters and Woodbridge and—"

"I know about that," said Richard quickly. "It was all a lighthouse and a big mistake, wasn't it?" Richard was not a devotee of UFOs.

"Well, that's not exactly true," replied Jon. "On the third night, which was probably—although no one seems too sure—the twenty-eighth of December, something happened which, according to U.S. Air Force eyewitnesses, involved the landing of an apparently alien spacecraft and sightings of what appeared to be its diminutive occupants.

"While *that* was for Richard, *this* is for you, Nicky-boy. The area around Rendlesham Forest is a very strange place—and not just because of the UFO incident. As well as being one of the most eastern points in the British Isles, it's also been the focus of a massive range of truly bizarre paranormal activity. In the thirteenth century, Ralph of Coggershall described a wild man that was caught in fishing nets off Orford Castle and very near to Rendlesham Forest. This creature—whatever it was—apparently lived at the castle for several months.

"And on top of that, the lanes that surround the forest are reputedly haunted by giant, spectral black dogs—such as the one seen by Lady Rendlesham in Leiston Churchyard at the end of the nineteenth century—and mysterious black panthers. But the clincher is this: There is an even more disturbing specter that has been seen deep within Rendlesham Forest called the Shug Monkey, which is described by witnesses as an unholy combination of mastiff and great ape.

"And to add mystery upon mystery, researcher Maxine Pearson is in possession of some videotape taken in Rendlesham Forest that shows the paw print of a huge animal—like that of a cat or a dog, but far bigger and with strange flattened fingernails rather than claws. She thought that it was a print from a big cat of some description, but when Richard and I saw the film, our immediate thought was of the Shug Monkey. So, here again, at the exact site of arguably Britain's most significant UFO landing case, you have an untold number of other inexplicable phenomena including phantom big cats and spectral, apelike creatures."

By now, as the ever-plentiful supply of alcohol began to take effect and even the huge candle was beginning to get perilously close to burning out, the three of us were beginning to wane. Jon closed his file and stood up. "And that, gentlemen, is that for tonight, I think. I'm ready for a decent night's sleep—or whatever is left of it—and I'm sure you are, too." I was, but after hearing Jon's stories, I was also itching to begin our search for the truth about Britain's monsters.

"After all that bloody stuff with the turtle and that bird, you can say that again," said Richard.

"Yeah, that *was* weird," I added. "How could the lights have gone out like that and at the exact same time?"

"I told you. There really *are* dark forces at work. Very dark forces," said Jon as he moved toward the staircase with the candlestick in his hand. "But I hope that what I had to say this evening was useful."

"It was. And *I* have a few things to tell *you,* Jon," I said with a smile.

"Oh?" he replied in a way that I knew I had caught his attention but that he was trying to play down.

"But I think it can wait until the morning."

"You're sure? I can manage a bit longer," he said, totally giving away the fact that he was itching to know what I had to say.

"No, tomorrow will be fine," I responded casually as I unpacked my sleeping bag.

"Until the morning then," Jon said. "My boys, I bid you good night."

4

THE GAME'S AFOOT—
WELL, NEARLY

The kids are all hopped up and ready to go . . .
"SHEENA IS A PUNK ROCKER," THE RAMONES

After what seemed like only half an hour of sleep I was awoken from my slumber by the sound of what—to the uninitiated— could have been misinterpreted as the charge of a herd of marauding elephants. But, having traveled to this merry abode on numerous oc- casions across the course of the previous three years, I knew better. It was simply Jon descending the staircase in the way that only Jon can.

"God almighty," I muttered under my breath as Jon's pounding on the staircase seemed to make the whole room rattle to its very core and rattle me to my bones. After the thirteenth step Jon thrust open the lounge door and bounded into the room. And if any of you have ever met Jon or seen photographs of him, you will know that to see him bounding is an extraordinary and distinctly rare sight indeed. It is also very rare to see Jon surfacing from his lair at such an early hour due to the fact that he much prefers to keep vampirelike hours.

I stuck my thumping and hungover head out of the sleeping bag just as Jon flung open the curtains. A cascade of blinding light en- tered the room. The storm of the previous night had well and truly vanished and it was a bright summer's day of the sort that only merry

England can muster. Wiping my eyes, I focused on Jon, who was looming over me, dressed in a gold, sequined dressing gown that had a large image of Liberace emblazoned on the back. He bent down and bellowed in my ear in true Sherlock Holmes style, "Come on, Nicky, time to get up. The game's afoot!"

I crawled out of the sleeping bag, made us a pot of tea and toast and then headed for the bathroom and a much-needed shower. By the time I came down, it was just turning 8:30 A.M. Richard was just getting up and Jon was perched on the edge of the sofa.

"So what's this news that you had to tell me, then?" he asked, trying his hardest to sound only vaguely interested.

"Sorry, what?" I answered, pretending not to have heard him.

"The news, man, the news!" Jon boomed in reply as he fidgeted with his fingers. "What do you have to tell me?" He looked at me almost pleadingly. "You know how I abhor secrets."

"Oh, *that*. Well, maybe we should wait until Richard is here," I suggested.

Jon jumped to his feet and hurried purposefully to the bottom of the stairs and shouted upward at the top of his voice: "Richard! Come on, boy, blast you!" Five minutes later, Richard strolled into the room and I announced my "news."

"Well," I began, looking at them both with arms folded, "you thought I had come down by train again, didn't you? And you thought we were gonna have to travel around the country in your less-than-reliable old Jag, didn't you, Jon? And you thought we were going to have to pay out on expensive motels and hotels over the next six weeks. Correct?"

"Guilty as charged, my lord, on every count." Jon laughed as he slapped his hand to his heart. "Guilty as charged."

"Here, here," Richard chimed in.

"Ah," I replied, with a knowing grin. "Well, you're wrong on every count. Look out the window." Jon and Richard squabbled like little kids to get to the window first until I suggested it would be easier to simply open the front door. We all three spilled out onto the pavement in a tangled heap as a startled little old lady came walking past.

"My deepest apologies, madam," said Jon, struggling to his feet and bowing his head as the lady hurried on, wondering who on earth these three strange fellows were—one built like the proverbial outhouse and dressed in a sequined, gold dressing gown, one attired like an eighteenth-century highwayman, and one with a shaved head and adorned all in black.

"Er, so what are we supposed to be looking at?" asked Richard, munching on a blackened slice of toast and raspberry jam. I pointed to the other side of the car park that dominated Holne Court.

"That's ours?" asked Richard, with a distinct look of surprise on his face.

"Yep," I replied.

"What—for the whole six weeks?" said Jon, with a mounting tinge of excitement in his voice.

"Yep," I repeated. "It's ours and for the whole six weeks."

"Nicky-boy, that is fabulous, truly fabulous!" Jon gushed.

You may be wondering about the source of all this excitement. I have a friend in the East Midlands named Dave who owns a large camper that sleeps four and that has all of the amenities of home. And when I told him of the plans that Jon, Richard, and I had made, Dave offered to loan us his trusty camper for the period of our adventure. It was an offer that came quite out of the blue and one that will always indebt me to Dave. He had made me promise that when he comes to visit Dana and me, that I fix him up for the week with the finest of Texan belles. It's a promise I'll keep.

Suddenly, Jon's face took on a worried expression. "You *can* drive this, can't you, Nicky?"

"Of course I can," I exclaimed. Before my writing career took off, I had worked for a couple of years as a driver for a paint and wallpaper retail company and had spent weeks (if not months) driving vehicles of this size and bigger up and down and around the U.K.

"No problems at all, mate. I got here safely, didn't I?" I added cheerfully. "And there's more." For several months I had been writing a column on the mysteries of Staffordshire for a local newspaper in the area, *The Chase Post*. While most of the columns focused on issues such as UFOs, big cat sightings, and ghosts, shortly before I came down to Jon's, I wrote a feature on the Man Monkey and asked if anyone knew anything about it could they get in touch with me via the newspaper.

Well, it turned out that, much to my surprise, I received seven letters from people in the region. Two of the letter-writers had had first-hand encounters with very similar creatures on the Cannock Chase in the 1990s; one had seen such a beast in the area in the1980s; three had friend-of-a-friend-style accounts to relate of a similar nature and one—and perhaps the most crucial of all—came from an elderly woman who asserted that members of her family had passed down through the generations a tale of a relative who had seen the Man Monkey itself.

"And I've lined up interviews with them all," I told Jon and Richard. I also told them about a retired Royal Air Force man who had written to me while I was researching my book, *Cosmic Crashes*. He lived in Devizes, Wiltshire, and claimed that British RAF Intelligence had conducted research into some of the more bizarre crypto-zoological accounts that originated from within the U.K. and that this research was somehow linked with clandestine UFO studies. Although I had been able to determine that the man's credentials were utterly sound, I had largely dismissed his claims since I thought—perhaps too rashly—that they seemed just too way out. Based on what Jon had to say on the previous night, however, I began to re-evaluate my dismissal of his account.

"Why don't I give him a call, too?" I said. "I never really did look into what he wanted to tell me. Let's face it: We've got six weeks, a camper to drive around and live in that's like a home away from home and plenty of time on our hands."

Richard could not hold back his excitement. "This is gonna be like a Scooby-Doo adventure!" he exclaimed with glee as he slapped his thigh and we all erupted into fits of laughter. The game really *was* afoot.

The next two days were spent loading the camper with the items that we had on hand, and buying those things that we were going to need and that, altogether, included a state-of-the-art night-vision scope that a friend of ours—who, sadly, *must* remain anonymous—had obtained on the black market from a former member of the East German military; binoculars; cameras; camcorders; tape recorders; blankets, sheets and pillows; a plentiful supply of compact discs for Jon's new CD player; notepads; food; drinks; Jon's trusty laptop computer; and just about anything and everything else that the modern man requires if he is going to run around the U.K. in an absurd pursuit of monsters.

Jon also telephoned his many and varied contacts throughout the country who could conceivably shed light on the puzzle and we had, collectively, almost twenty interviews lined up that extended from one end of the country to the other—never mind what else might turn up when our hunt began in earnest. And we had made another decision, too. Since it was now abundantly clear to all three of us that the Man Monkey legend was, in reality, only a small part of a much bigger picture, we decided that we would not limit our investigation to that single case. Instead, in the one and a half months that we had at our disposal, we would attempt to solve the mystery of Britain's many and varied monsters once and for all and in its entirety. We were nothing if not ambitious.

As Jon explained: "The people I've arranged for us to see will, I think, supply us with our answers. There are a lot of dedicated researchers of mystery animals around the country, but most of them make the same monumental mistake. Like UFO investigators, they faithfully record every sighting of a lake monster or a big cat that comes their way and then try to analyze the data as if the animals were flesh and blood—which, mostly, they're not. That's their downfall and why they never catch one of the accursed things.

"So, I've got us interviews lined up with a bunch of people who can shed light on monster sightings, but also, whose experiences or research should give us more of the clues we need for resolving the paranormal angle of these mysteries. As you know, my published research on mystery animals already points in the direction of the paranormal, and I suspect that we are all going to learn something new about this aspect of monster hunting in the next few weeks."

"You really think we are going to find the truth about these things?" I asked Jon.

"Nicky, we are going to give it a bloody good try," he said.

By late afternoon we were packed and ready to go. Jon had arranged for Graham—his trusty manservant and special friend, *very special friend*, remember—to look after the house for him while we were away and to feed the new pets: Tessie the dog and the cats Tommy, Helios 7, and Chastikos the Deceiver. And yes, those *are* the real names of the animals.

"I expect to return to the house precisely as I left it, Graham," said Jon, holding a battered brown suitcase under his arm and with a stern tone in his voice. "I'll have your balls served up cold on a platter, otherwise."

"Mmmm," said Graham—who was deeply engrossed in a game of Doom on Jon's computer and who was either *pretending* not to listen or was *genuinely* not listening.

"And don't invite any of your women around, either," Jon barked. "I don't want the police knocking on the door."

"Mmmm."

"Is that all you have to say, Graham?"

"Eh?" replied a disinterested Graham.

"Forget it!" cried Jon, who turned and marched out the door with his head held high and huffing and puffing in disgust.

I turned to Graham, who had a big grin on his face. "Have a good time, Graham," I said.

"Oh, I will. I will, indeed," he said in an eerie tone, adding: "The attic awaits."

"Lord!" groaned Richard and we all trundled off to the camper. We loaded the final few items into the back of the vehicle, made sure that everything was secure, and jumped into the cab. I turned the ignition on and the Mystery Machine—as Richard had fondly dubbed it—rumbled into life. It was now 6:00 P.M. and we were off to the Devonshire village of Widecombe-in-the-Moor where we were due to meet a man who, Jon said, could supply some of the answers that we were seeking.

For a moment we discussed the idea of paying homage to the god-like Ramones and considered that for the length of our adventure we should all wear black leather motorcycle jackets. Both Richard and I habitually wore them and the idea amused us immensely. Jon, however, said that he was of such high breeding that to be reduced to wearing a biker's jacket, "and running around the countryside like some street gang," would undermine his family's history and its reputation in the community. And so we concentrated on the events ahead of us.

"Which way, Jon?" I asked as we pulled out of Holne Court.

"Yonder!" he shouted and thrust a finger in the general direction of the main road. Richard hit the Play button on the CD player and the opening chords of the Sex Pistols's classic song "Anarchy in the U.K." blasted out of the speakers. We were on our way.

5

THE CAVEMAN

**The moon is full, the air is still,
all of a sudden, I feel a chill.**

"PET SEMATARY," THE RAMONES

In what seemed like only a few minutes, we had left the hustle
and bustle of the city of Exeter behind us. We were out into the
Devonshire countryside and driving along a pleasant but—for the
vehicle that *we* were in, at least—perilously narrow lane that was
bordered by ten foot high, thick bushes that brushed alarmingly
along the side of the Mystery Machine as we rumbled on toward the
centuries-old village of Widecombe-in-the-Moor.

"So who are we going to see, Jon?" I asked, as I carefully maneu-
vered the vehicle along the lane.

"Now, this is a veritable story and a half," he replied, while trying
less-than-successfully to pour himself a glass of Baileys from the bottle that he had brought along for the journey.

As Richard and I listened, Jon told a remarkable story. As I
already knew, from 1982 to 1985, Jon had worked as a nurse for
the mentally handicapped at the Royal Western Counties Hospital
in Starcross, ten miles from Exeter. However, what I *didn't* know—
and neither did Richard—was that more than a decade before he
established the Center for Fortean Zoology, Jon had been told a
bizarre tale of truly epic cryptozoological proportions by one of the

doctors at the hospital and who, in 1982, was then fast approaching retirement.

According to the doctor, he had been on duty in the early hours one morning in the winter of 1948 when he received several strange telephone calls: one from a senior source within the Devonshire Police Force, one from the Lord Lieutenant of the County, and one from an individual associated with the then earl of Devon—all informing him in a distinctly cryptic manner that a highly dangerous patient would be brought to the hospital within the hour who would require specialist care and an isolated room. It was made clear to the doctor that he should prepare himself for a shock.

While it was certainly unusual and unprecedented to get telephone calls of this manner, the doctor and two of his assistants made preparations for the arrival. Within forty-five minutes a police van arrived at the hospital, reversed with a screech up to a side door, and seven police constables tumbled out of the back of the vehicle while simultaneously trying to hang on to what the doctor said resembled a dirt-encrusted and hair-covered caveman!

Not quite believing what he was seeing, the startled and dumb-struck doctor quickly motioned the police into the hospital and a violent struggle ensued as they fought to keep control of the patient, prisoner, or prize—depending on your perspective. For what seemed like a lifetime, the doctor recalled, the policemen dragged the wild man along the hospital's corridors and into what was known as a Side Room—an isolation room that was "similar to a rubber room but without the rubber," Jon helpfully explained. The doctor ran ahead, flung open the heavy door and the police forcefully propelled the kicking and punching creature headlong into the room. The door was quickly slammed shut behind it.

"What on earth is *that?*" the trembling and ashen-faced doctor asked a senior officer who came rushing along the corridor in a breathless fashion. So the story went, said Jon, a "strange man" had been seen "throwing large rocks around the place" at Ashburton, Dartmoor, and in the vicinity of the old Hexworthy Mine earlier that same evening and the authorities had been called. Needless to say, the police got the shock of their lives when they finally confronted their quarry and saw the creature leaping and bounding across the windswept moorland as if it had the Devil himself on its tail. After a pursuit that lasted for well over three hours, the creature was finally captured and transferred to a local police station before being brought to the hospital.

For a near eternity the creature kicked the walls and punched the door of its room with its powerful fists and screamed and growled in what sounded like the most primitive forms of rage and frustration. After a day, it seemed to settle down but continued to pace the length and breadth of the room, stopping only occasionally to eat the food and water that was carefully and quietly placed into the room while it lay curled and asleep in the farthest corner.

And it was while the creature was sleeping, Jon was told, that the doctor had a chance—albeit from a distance and from behind the safety of a locked door—to look at it in some detail. By now the doctor had concluded that whatever this being was, it was definitely some form of man; it stood slightly over six feet in height, was completely naked, had a heavy brow, wide nose, and very muscular arms and legs. He was covered in an excessive amount of body hair that enveloped his whole body apart from the palms of his hands, the soles of his feet, and his face, and he had a head of long, matted hair. The man never spoke a word. It was quite clear that this was not some unfortunate soul who had spent a few months hiding out on the moors, Jon was told. This was something else. This was something that looked *prehistoric*.

Over the course of the next three days, telephone calls bombarded the hospital from the police, the Lord Lieutenant of the County, and the Home Office in London. Then came the news that the man-beast was being transferred to a secure location in London for examination.

Again late at night, the same group of police constables removed the creature from the hospital. This time, however, they succeeded in holding the thing down long enough for it to be heavily sedated by the doctor, whereupon it was tied with powerful straps to a stretcher and loaded again into a police wagon with an unidentified doctor in attendance for the journey that lay ahead. Less than twenty minutes after they had arrived, the police departed into the frosty night and the creature was gone forever.

The doctor told Jon that he had no idea where in London the wild man was taken. He'd heard no more about him after receiving a call from someone the doctor refused to identify to Jon, but who was a senior source from Scotland Yard informing the doctor that the matter was being taken care of and that he should discuss the bizarre events of the previous few days with no one.

For several years the doctor *did* remain silent—as did his two colleagues who were the only other people at the hospital directly aware of what had occurred. In 1983, however, Jon was told a similar account by a woman who worked as a night nurse at Diggby Hospital. She had had an affair with the same doctor and related essentially the same story and told Jon that it had severely disturbed the doctor for years.

"There was more to this story, though, she implied, but would never tell me," Jon explained as we listened intently and closed in on Widecombe-in-the-Moor. The nurse had apparently died in 1993 and took whatever secrets she knew to the grave with her. But perhaps now, twenty years after he had related the basics of the story to Jon, more than half a century after the events in question, and as he was fast-approaching his mid-to-late eighties, the doctor would finally reveal all.

Shortly after Jon had finished his epic tale we arrived at Widecombe-in-the-Moor, parked the Mystery Machine near the village churchyard and, since it was such a warm and pleasant evening, strolled on foot to our location: a delightful little cottage owned by the sister of the doctor we were due to meet.

It must be said that our attire received some rather unusual looks from the locals as we headed purposefully through the village toward our destination. I had chosen black jeans, black T-shirt, black leather jacket, and Doc Martens; Richard had insisted on dressing in full Goth gear, which consisted of black leather trousers, ornate boots, white pirate shirt, and a floral waistcoat; and Jon's gear included his deerstalker hat, monocle, pocket watch—which he insisted on checking every couple of minutes—and a walking cane.

Like so many other villages in Devonshire, Widecombe-in-the-Moor appeared unchanged by the passing of the centuries and we embraced the chance to breathe in some unpolluted country air of the caliber that is sadly and distinctly lacking in central Exeter—and, indeed, in much of the rest of the country, too.

And also like so many other villages in Devon, Widecombe-in-the-Moor had a curious history attached to it. On October 21, 1638, the village church, St. Pancras, was badly damaged by a lightning strike that killed four people and injured sixty-two. It transpires that there is far more than initially meets the eye with respect to this lightning strike. At the time of its occurrence, the clergyman was one George Lyde, who was born at Berry Pomeroy in 1601, and who was standing in the pulpit when the lightning struck and narrowly avoided serious injury—if not death, even.

Interestingly, Mark Norman, a Fortean researcher as well as a film cameraman (and the producer of Jon's *The Owlman and Others*) investigated the case at length. He offers the possibility that the lightning strike, which some had suggested at the time was the work of the Devil, had, in fact, been caused by that rarest of aerial phenomena known as ball lightning.

Strangely enough, this event had eerie parallels with a very similar incident at St. Mary's Church, Bungay, Suffolk, England, on Sunday, August 4, 1577, when an immense and veritable spectral hound from hell materialized within the church during a powerful thunderstorm and mercilessly tore into the terrified congregation with its huge fangs and claws. So powerful was the storm that it reportedly killed two men in the belfry as the church tower received an immense lightning bolt that shook the building to its very foundations.

According to an old local verse: "All down the church in midst of fire, the hellish monster flew. And, passing onward to the quire, he many people slew." Then, as suddenly as it had appeared, the beast bounded out of St. Mary's and was reported shortly thereafter at Blythburgh Church, about twelve miles away, where it killed and

mauled even more people with its immense, bone-crushing jaws—
and where, it is said, the scratch marks of the beast's claws can still be
seen imprinted on the ancient door of the church.

Even more intriguing is the fact that Bungay's legend of a satanic
black hound parallels that of yet another local legend: that of Black
Shuck, a giant, spectral dog that haunts the Norfolk and Suffolk
coasts and also has links with the aforementioned Shug Monkey of
Rendlesham Forest. Indeed, such is the popularity of the Bungay
legend, that it has resulted in an image of the beast being incorporated into the town's coat of arms—and the Black Dogs is the name
of Bungay Town Football Club.[1]

So here we were: on our way to meet a doctor to talk about wild
men, in a village that had suffered a centuries-old calamity that was
tied in with spectral black dog legends and that, in turn, led indirectly back to the Shug Monkey of Rendlesham Forest—the site
of Britain's most well-known UFO incident. What goes around
comes around, I thought. Within a few minutes we arrived at the
cottage and headed up a small path that was surrounded by all manner of roses and flowers. Jon lifted the ornate door knocker and
tapped lightly.

"Jon, you've got Baileys in your beard, mate," I pointed out
quickly, noticing a large smear of the drink on the bottom of Jon's
hairy growth.

"Eh?" he replied blankly.

"Your beard, mate—there's Baileys in it."

"God," he muttered, hastily wiping the offending stain onto his
arm. At that moment there appeared a white-haired lady with a
pleasant smile, who must have been ninety-five years old and about
four feet ten inches in height.

"Anna, my dear, how are you?" bellowed Jon as he gave the
woman a bear hug of the type that would have nearly killed a man of
my age. "It's so wonderful to see you again. These are my boys,
Nicholas and Richard," he added, introducing us.

"Jon, do you have to keep referring to us as your boys?" I asked
him quietly as we entered.

"Of course I do," he replied, looking slightly hurt.

Having exchanged greetings we were ushered into a splendid little home filled with all manner of antique furniture, thick and rich carpeting, oak beams that looked like they had been put into place millennia ago, and a huge stone fireplace that dominated the living room.

"Please have a seat," said Anna, who then proceeded to bring us a plentiful supply of tea, biscuits, and cake. "Alfred'll be with y'all directly."

I should interject here and point out that Alfred is not the doctor's real name. Unfortunately, Richard made the mistake of bringing up almost immediately the fact that Jon had told us about the doctor's affair with the nurse from Diggby Hospital and this led to some anger on his part, to the extent that I am forced—to my regret—to create a false identity for the doctor. The nurse may now be deceased, but her husband most certainly is not.

Five minutes later, the man we had come to see—our first interviewee of many as we sought to solve the mystery of Britain's monsters—entered the room. A striking figure, he was over six feet in height and had a thick shock of white hair, and even though he was in his mid-eighties, the doctor looked fit, tanned, and in the finest of health. Again, pleasantries were exchanged, and after we got past the air of hostility that briefly threatened to end the interview when the details of the doctor's love affair surfaced, we got down to business. Jon gave an account of the story that he had related to Richard and me and asked if there was anything that he had forgotten or had omitted.

"Only a few minor points," Alfred replied. "I do recall that I was told—by whom I can't remember now—that I should refrain from drawing up any paperwork in connection with the man being brought to the hospital. But that would have come in one of the telephone calls. I just can't remember which. I also recall that when I first began working there shortly after the end of the war, there was a legend or story, which may very well have been true, about *another* wild man being brought into the hospital in 1944 under similar circumstances.

If I remember correctly, the staff had been told to prepare for a special patient and the first thought was that perhaps a Nazi spy had crashed his aircraft. I didn't pay it much attention until I saw one of these things with my own eyes."

"What do you think it was?" I asked.

"That's a damned good question," he chuckled. "All I can say for certain is that for a brief few days in the winter of 1948 I saw what I would class as a semihuman or protohuman being. I don't believe that what we had was simply a man who had lived wild on the moor for a few months. And I say that because of the man's facial features more than anything else. This was *not* an evolved man. I can only sit here and tell you that I saw it. But I *do* have a theory that I'll discuss with you later."

For a moment, Alfred sat back and looked at all three of us. "There is one other thing I can tell you," he added. "I knew one of the policemen involved in later years—named Heath—and he told me that word had got back to them that the creature had been kept in a room that had been constructed out of one of the old London Underground train tunnels used during the war for storing government files and the like. From there, it was supposedly taken into care by the medical authorities."

"Would you know where?" I asked.

"Well, I would imagine to somewhere where it could be examined and hopefully provide some answers," he replied with a smile.

"And do you know where that might be?" I pressed.

"If I did know, or didn't know, I've forgotten," Alfred replied, somewhat enigmatically. Having established that we had all of the facts in hand (as far as could be determined, at least), we told Alfred of our plans for the next six weeks. This seemed to intrigue him greatly and he made us an offer that we could not, under any circumstances, turn down.

He explained that the reason why he had asked for the meeting to be held at his sister's cottage was because her husband had recently passed away and he was helping her to get her affairs in order. However, if we wanted to take him up on the offer he would open up his home to us for two days and nights and let us stay there. He had, he said, a huge library and a rare-document collection that we were sure to find interesting—that included references to wild men and similar creatures seen on Dartmoor as far back as the Middle Ages. He also employed a small staff—including a cook and a cleaner—who would be happy to look after us. We got the impression that Alfred welcomed our somewhat unusual intrusion into his life and we immediately—and unanimously—said yes. And so it was that at approximately 10:00 P.M. we returned to the Mystery Machine and, following our kindly host along the winding roads of a moon-lit Devon, headed in the direction of his abode. By 10:25 P.M. we had arrived.

Having been informed that Alfred employed a small staff, we expected him to have an impressively sized home; however, none of us were quite prepared for what greeted us.

6

BORN TO BE WILD

**I don't wanna go down to the basement;
there's something down there.**

"I DON'T WANNA GO DOWN TO THE BASEMENT," THE RAMONES

We turned onto a side road from the main route and approached a graveled driveway surrounded by large bushes that prevented us seeing what lay beyond. In but a few short moments we had our answer. We continued up the long driveway and there, lit up by an array of powerful spotlights that extended from the ground upward, was a huge, old manor house, three stories high, that must have contained thirty or more rooms.

"Mother of God!" exclaimed Jon as the cathedral-like structure began to take shape as we closed in.

"This looks like one of those places where an Agatha Christie murder would be set, doesn't it?" I added with a laugh.

"Jon, I take back everything I said about the south," said Richard.

Thankfully, the house had ample grounds to park the Mystery Machine and we climbed out of the cab, collected a few items that we would need for the night and followed Alfred into his fine home.

Alfred was amused by our wonderment as we entered. Suits of armor stood by the doorway; huge paintings that must have been two or three hundred years old adorned the walls; a large winding staircase extended from the floor at a distance of about one hundred feet from us; all along the hallway there were rooms full of expensive antiques and lovingly cared-for furniture from a bygone era; and the ceilings were covered with delicate artwork lit up by an array of chandeliers.

"Leave your bags by the door and come this way." Alred motioned and we followed him into his library. Never before have I seen such a collection of books. There were, quite literally, thousands of titles, many of which appeared to be aged in the extreme.

"Please, take a seat," he said to us. In a moment a well-dressed man in his fifties named Robert brought in a tray on which sat four glasses of sherry.

"And so, gentlemen, here we are," said Alfred, stretching his arms wide and still amused by the looks of surprise and wonderment on our faces. It transpired that his family had been landed gentry and had lived in Devonshire for centuries; the house had been built by the family two hundred and fifty years previously. When Alfred's father had passed away the estate had gone to Alfred and his sister, Anna, neither of whom had any children. Anna and her husband had declined to move into the house from their cottage; and, as a result, Alfred had bought her share of the house and property and Anna could now live out the rest of her life in financial comfort in the little village of Widecombe-in-the-Moor, as was always her dream.

After we had indulged in the sherry and taken a light supper, Alfred showed us to our rooms. We climbed the huge staircase, bags in hand, turned left as we reached the next floor, and headed down a long corridor that, again, was filled with paintings, sculptures, and a wide array of the finest furniture.

"I have two guest rooms that have a connecting doorway that you are welcome to use," said Alfred, opening a door. We entered into a room that contained two double beds, a private bathroom, wardrobe, dressing table, and a Regency-style fireplace. Alfred headed to a connecting door that opened into a similarly furnished room but that contained one large four-poster bed.

"Jon," said Alfred with a chuckle in his voice, "you are still the man that I remember twenty years ago and I would therefore suggest that you make use of the four-poster and leave the lads to have the smaller ones."

"Suits me," said Richard as Jon nodded and offered his sincere thanks.

"Would you like to see something interesting?" asked Alfred innocently.

We all looked at each other for a moment in silence. "What's that?" I asked, breaking the ice. Alfred walked over to the large, paneled wall next to the fireplace and pressed gently on one of the panels. The wall swung around and revealed a hidden passageway. I laughed aloud. "Ha! You have got to be kidding."

"I had many a merry time in there as a child and had mapped it all out by the age of eleven," said Alfred, who told us how an extensive system of corridors had been constructed behind and between the framework of the rooms of the house that afforded the person using them the ability to stealthily enter and leave the various rooms at will. Three small staircases existed within the corridors, too, at various points around the house and that allowed a person to travel from the attic down to the cellar.

"You're welcome to have a look at them," Alfred added. "When you get into the corridors you'll see that I've pinned small white flags to the various entry points to the rooms. I would ask that you don't open any of the panels to the left of this room, as they are my rooms. And I would also ask that you don't open the two doors immediately to the right. My cook and Robert both live here and those are their rooms.

"But, as I say, you are welcome to explore. To this day, we don't really know why they were built, but it's a fascinating piece of history. Well, I'll leave you to sleep and tomorrow I'll show you my library. I actually took a big interest in stories of wild men after what happened and have a lot of titles that I think you'll want to see."

Alfred moved to the door. "Oh, one final thing. Don't use the staircase on the south side of the house if you go into the corridors. That's the one that leads to the cellar. It's not safe. Breakfast is at eight. Good night." Alfred closed the door behind him.

"Well, this is brilliant," I said to Richard, as we unpacked our cases. "I thought we were going to be driving all night or sleeping in the camper." Not that the camper wasn't comfortable, but who could turn down an opportunity like this? At that point, Jon came from his room clutching a hip flask and three glasses.

"My dear boys," he said, having changed into a pair of pink pajamas and matching slippers, "this is the life. This is what I aspire to. One day the Center for Fortean Zoology will have a home like this. Aren't you glad I introduced you to Alfred?" We could only agree. We talked for a few minutes about the day's events and drank a toast to what was to come. It was now getting close to the witching hour, however, and we decided to get some sleep; but not for long. At around 2:00 A.M., I was awoken by the whispered tones of Richard from across the room.

"Nick . . . Nick . . . *Nick!*"

I quickly woke from my sleep and sat bolt upright. Surely it wasn't morning already?

"What's wrong?" I asked, wiping my eyes.

Richard clambered out of bed and came over. "I've been thinking," he began. "You know how Alfred reacted funny when you asked him if he knew where the wild man was taken after it left the Underground?"

"Yeah."

"You know what I think?"

"Yeah, I think I do, but go on," I replied with a grin.

"I think Alfred *was* the guy all along who looked after it. And all that stuff about keeping away from the cellar; I think he's got it locked up down there."

I burst out laughing. "That's exactly what I thought you were going to say. Now, that *would* be a cracker of a story." We then did the only thing that we could do. We went to wake up Jon.

"Don't give him a heart attack, whatever you do," said Richard as we tiptoed in the darkness toward the four-poster and from where Jon was snoring loudly. As I got close and could see his face as the moonlight entered the room, I initially thought that his eyes were wide open; however, it turned out that he had a slice of cucumber on each eye that Richard said he used regularly to keep wrinkles at bay. Only Jon, I thought. Only Jon.

"Jon, wake up, mate," I whispered.

In a moment he was awake but, as he flung the cucumber from his eyes, was somewhat disoriented by the fact that the room was pitch-black and there were two darkened forms looming over him from either side of the four-poster. The fact that we were half masked by the bed's drapes didn't exactly help calm the situation, either.

"Who's there?" he shouted. "What the bloody hell's going on?"

"Ssshhhh!" said Richard, clasping a hand over Jon's face and threatening to cut off his air supply.

"What is it? What's going on? I thought you were a bloody incubus!" Jon blurted out. We sat down and told him of Richard's theory.

"For heaven's sake, Richard!" said Jon, throwing his hands into the air. "First you tell dear Nicky that I have an insane grandmother locked in my attic and—"

"*Great*-grandmother," Richard corrected.

"*Great*-grandmother, then," replied Jon, exasperated. "And now you think that Alfred, a kindly old gentleman in his eighties who has been good enough to open his home to us, is some sort of Dr. Frankenstein keeping a monster locked in his cellar? Please!"

"Well, it wouldn't hurt to look," I added.

Jon threw his head back onto the pillow. "How do I get myself mixed up in things like this? And why do I *allow* myself to get mixed up in things like this? We are supposed to be undertaking a serious quest to determine the truth behind Britain's monsters and you two want us to go poking around a grimy old cellar in the middle of the night?"

"Yeah," Richard and I both said in unison, grinning.

"I warn you: This expedition is going to turn into a pure farce," grumbled Jon. Despite his reluctance to seize the day, within five minutes Jon entered our bedroom with a Liberace dressing gown over his pink pajamas. To my everlasting regret, I had left my camera in the Mystery Machine. I pulled on a pair of jeans and a T-shirt and Richard did likewise. We walked quietly over to the wall.

"Okay," I said, "let's give it a try."

I pushed on the panel as Alfred had done and sure enough it opened. Fortunately, Jon had had the presence of mind to pack his flashlight in his suitcase so we had light. I entered first, followed by Richard and then Jon, who wedged the panel open with my Doc Martens.

First, we shone the flashlight up and down the corridor and began to stealthily make our way along its narrow wooden floor. As we rounded the first corner and then a second and a third, it became clear to us how intricate the corridors were and how well crafted the layout was. Indeed, it seemed to snake throughout the entire house, as we had deduced by the fact that at times on our left there appeared to be exterior walls and then at other times it was quite clear that the walls were internal ones—something that suggested we were moving within the body of the huge house itself. And there was something else that had become readily apparent to all three of us. After nearly an hour within this maze-like construction, we were hopelessly disoriented and lost.

"Alright, this is getting ridiculous," seethed Jon. "Here I am, lost in a secret passageway with an insane Goth and a paranoid ufologist trying to find a cellar. God, give me the strength to live another day— so I can kill the two of you."

"Stop panicking, mate," I said, trying to reassure him. "All we have to do is go back the way we came and we should be fine."

"Oh, you think?" said Jon incredulously. "That's alright, then. If Nicky says it's going to be alright, then who am I to worry? We're only lost in someone else's house in the middle of the night and in a god-awful tunnel that we can't get out of. And what about my eyes? They need that cucumber, you know." The panic in Jon's voice was rising. We shuffled along—hands on each other's shoulders—for another five minutes and finally came to a small wooden staircase rather like an attic ladder.

"This must have been what Alfred was talking about," said Richard.

Jon stared at the tiny staircase with a look of horror and disbelief on his face. "And you expect *me* to traverse *that*, do you?" he asked incredulously.

Nevertheless, we successfully descended the staircase and as we reached the bottom, to the left of it was a white flag, clearly indicating the entry point to a room. To the right of it was another small staircase that descended to a lower level: the cellar, presumably. Since we were totally unsure of our location, we had little choice but to get off at the first level and find out where we were. Fortunately it turned out to be the breakfast room and the panel that we pushed revealed on its other side a white, four-paneled door. We walked through the room and found ourselves in the hallway that we had entered when we had first arrived at the house.

"Okay," I said, "we're on the first floor. Let's get back to the staircase."

"What?" cried Jon in a loud voice, and forgetting that this was the middle of the night. "You can forget *that!*"

"Look," I replied, "you saw that the staircase went down to another floor. Correct?"

"Correct," said Jon, arms folded.

"This is the first floor, so that must lead to the cellar. Correct?"

"And your point is, Nicholas?" he responded in hostile tones.

"Well, if there's nothing to see, then we climb back up the steps, get off here and just walk along the hall, up the main staircase and back to the bedrooms that way."

Jon thought for a moment. "Very well," he seethed, repeatedly stamping his pink slippers in frustration like a little boy who has just been told that Christmas has been canceled. And so we returned to the corridor and began to descend the second staircase. When we reached terra firma, it became obvious from the musky and damp smell that we were underground and there in front of us was a solitary white flag.

"This is it! This is it!" said Richard, jumping up and down.

"For goodness' sake, Richard," said Jon, laughing, as he finally began to relax and the fear that we would remain forever doomed to walk the house's secret corridors by night subsided from his ever-tortured mind. We pushed the panel and we were in what was unmistakably a large cellar. We had arrived. Either we had spent what was certainly the most bizarre hour of my life on a fruitless search borne out of the certifiably deranged imagination of Richard, or we were about to come face-to-face with a creature from the dawn of history. Which was it to be? We would soon find out. Jon shone the flashlight around the cellar and it became clear that not only was it huge, but it appeared to have on its far side seven or eight smaller rooms with heavy wooden doors that had a solitary glass window in each.

"He's in one of those! I know it! I know it!" screamed Richard, who was, by now, verging upon hyperventilation.

"Keep your voice down, boy!" Jon whispered in vexed tones as he slapped Richard around the back of his head. We headed for door number one.

"Turn the key, then, turn the key!" a feverishly impatient Richard kept repeating like a manic parrot.

"I am! Hang on; it's stiff," I replied. Nevertheless, in a few seconds the rusted lock turned. I pushed and the door creaked open in a style that would have been perfectly at home in one of those old horror films of the 1960s. Jon shone the flashlight around the room but it contained nothing except for the broken remains of an old machine for drying clothes. We exited the room and headed for door number two. That, too, opened with relative ease, despite the fact that its lock was also rust-coated in the extreme.

"What's there?" asked a jumpy Richard, peering over my shoulder.

"Just cardboard boxes, mate. That's it."

"Damn," he replied, thumping his right fist into his left hand.

Doors number three and four led to rooms that were even more unimpressive and contained precisely nothing. However, as we entered room number five, we were faced with a sight that *did* genuinely spook us. I wish I could tell you, dear reader, that we found ourselves in the company of a genuine Neanderthal man but, sadly, that was not the case. What we *were* faced with, however, was a pair of chains that extended from the rear of the wall at a height of around four feet.

Could the chains have been used to restrain someone—or *something?* They certainly could have. Like the locks on each of the doors, however, the chains were coated with rust and the stench of stale air that dominated each of the rooms indicated to us that the cellar had probably been unused for any purpose for decades.

"Now what do you think *they* were for?" I asked Richard, pointing at the chains.

"The wild man!" he screamed in a voice that echoed and trembled at the same time.

"Richard, I won't tell you again. Keep the noise down," Jon groused. We checked the chains to see if there was any evidence of hair or fibers attached to them that might have conceivably confirmed such a theory. There were none.

"You know, those chains could have been used for anything, really," said Jon.

"Yes, they could," replied Richard, looking at him. "But how many people do you know who have a cellar with a locked room in it that has chains coming out of the wall?"

It was a fair question and one that neither Jon nor I had an answer for. After having checked the remaining rooms, we scoured the rest of the cellar for anything incriminating; but finding nothing, we finally headed out and negotiated the steps back up to the first floor of the house. What had we got ourselves into? Were we staying in a residence that had once harbored a creature from an age long gone—or was the whole affair borne out of the minds of a trio that had overdosed on too much Conan Doyle, Lovecraft, and Stoker? For now we had far more questions than answers and so we dutifully headed back to our rooms to try to salvage some sleep from what was left of the rapidly diminishing night.

"And don't wake me again," said Jon as he entered the room. "If you tell me you suspect that the bodies from the Roswell crash are locked in the refrigerator, I don't want to know—at least not tonight. Until tomorrow, my boys."

I stopped him. "Jon, before you go. Alfred told us not to go down to the cellar because the steps weren't safe. Remember? Did *you* see anything wrong with them? I didn't."

He looked at me for a second with a puzzled expression on his face and quietly closed his door; and Richard and I retired to our beds with thoughts of the secrets that Alfred's cellar might once have held firmly imprinted on our minds.

:: ::: ::

There is something unique about waking up to a sunrise on a summer's morning in England's green pastures that, no matter what the circumstances and no matter how dire the situation may be, seems to make everything well with the world. And this was one of those days. Despite only managing a couple of hours of sleep, I was awake by 6:30 A.M. and was showered and dressed by seven. By seven-thirty, Richard and I were ready for breakfast and we knocked on Jon's door. No answer. We entered Jon's room but he was nowhere to be seen.

"Maybe he's gone for breakfast already?" said Richard.

"Yeah, maybe he has."

We headed downstairs and toward the breakfast room. By the light of day the huge house had a distinctly different atmosphere and the dark and angular shadows that had filled its presence on the previous night—and that gave every impression that we had entered Castle Frankenstein—had been replaced by cascading beams of sunlight that flooded the long hallway.

"Good morning," said Alfred with a smile as we entered the room. Jon was sitting across the table from him holding an absurdly small cup and saucer of Earl Grey tea in one hand and waving at us in the other what we later found out was a signed first edition of *Swallows and Amazons* that Alfred had loaned him.

"Take a seat," added Alfred, pointing to the two vacant breakfast chairs.

"Did you sleep well?" he asked.

"Yes, great, thanks. I was out like a light," I responded in a voice and with a look on my face that I suspect were not entirely convincing. Out of the corner of my eye I could see that Jon was wearing a worried expression.

"Indeed?" replied Alfred. For a moment there was silence.

"Er, yes, indeed," I said.

"Well, I'm glad to hear it," Alfred said affably. "No desire to go marauding about the passageways?" Jon not only had a worried look on his face; he had now gone deathly white, too.

"No, but we wouldn't mind having a look, would we?" I responded, nodding at Jon and Richard and trying to sound innocent.

"No, we wouldn't mind having a look," they both chimed almost in unison—something that only added to the unease.

Alfred eyed all three of us closely and then returned to his breakfast plate. "Please, help yourself," he said, changing the subject and pointing to a large table atop which sat cereal, milk, toast, preserves, and a hot plate containing scrambled eggs, bacon, sausages, and fried bread. Richard and I needed no coaxing and heartily tucked into the food.

Over breakfast and during the course of the morning as we sat and talked with Alfred, it became apparent to all three of us that he was not only interested in the issue of his bizarre experience in 1948, he was downright obsessed by it and would talk of nothing else. Alfred had, he said, pondered on the incident for decades and rarely a day went by when it did not cross his mind. But not only that, in the late 1960s he had begun a project to catalog as many man-beast accounts and legends from Devon and Cornwall that he could find in an attempt to resolve the mystery. More than three decades on, he had a lot of data and one singularly intriguing answer.

At noon he invited us into his study and pulled from a shelf three files all titled Wild Men—Papers, and labeled 1–3. As he opened the first, we were startled to see that it contained a massive amount of letters, documents, clippings, and a personal diary of his investigations. It also contained a number of old and fading papers—including an original handwritten letter from the eighteenth century concerning the activities of what were known as the Cannibals of Clovelly and that Alfred now believed were directly linked with today's accounts of wild men and man-beasts in the U.K.

Preserved in an eight-page book in a collection at Bideford is a story of one John Gregg and his assorted family of murderers and thieves. The text is estimated to date from the latter part of the eighteenth century and it recounts the story of how the Gregg family took up residence in a cave near Clovelly on the north coast of Devon in the 1700s and from where they were to live for an astonishing twenty-five years.

So the legend goes, during this period they passed their time by robbing more than a thousand unfortunates, and merrily devoured the corpses of all those they robbed. Such was the horror the story generated that even the king himself—along with four hundred men—allegedly resolved to bring to an end their prehistoric-like and abominable existence. The cave was supposedly discovered and reportedly contained, according to the book, "such a multitude of arms, legs, thighs, hands and feet, of men, women and children hung up in rows, like dry'd beef and a great many lying in pickle."

Gregg's distinctly-less-than-charming family was found to consist of a wife, eight sons, six daughters, eighteen grandsons, and fourteen granddaughters all begotten by incest—and many as mad as hatters—and all of whom were taken to Exeter and on the following day executed at Plymouth without trial.

It had been suggested very convincingly by A. D. Hippisley-Coxe, in his 1981 book *The Cannibals of Clovelly: Fact or Fiction?*, that this bizarre and horrific tale was simply that: a tale, and was created to ensure that the superstitious locals kept away from the myriad local caves used by smugglers at the time. And, indeed, the area around Bideford and Clovelly *was* a hotbed for smuggling.

Precisely the same legend appears in a number of other books— such as *The Legend of Sawney Beane,* that places the scene of the action in Galloway, Scotland. The tale of Sawney Beane was first recorded in 1734 in *A General and True History of the Lives and Actions of the Most Famous Highwaymen* by Captain Charles Johnson, a pseudonym of none other than Daniel Defoe, who had visited north Devon in his *Tour Through the Whole Island of Great Britain* and from where, in 1714, he reported that he "could not find any foreign commerce, except it be what we call smuggling."[1] So much for the legend, but what of the truth? Alfred had a few ideas.

"Defoe, we know, definitely visited the area and heard the tales of people living in the Devon caves and dining upon the flesh of visitors to the area. Now, even though the Sawney Beane and the Clovelly stories are fiction, it *is* true that Defoe *did* hear these and similar tales; and, as you know, there is always a little bit of fact in tales like this," said Alfred.

"We also know that, according to legend, these people had exclusively inbred for at least four generations, which would certainly have resulted in massive genetic defects. They may even have suffered from hypertrichosis, which causes the body to develop an excessive amount of hair.

"I can tell you that having worked at the Royal Western Counties Hospital for decades, I saw some appalling cases of deformities of the type that today we seldom—if indeed ever—see now, thankfully, that *were* in some cases due to repeated inbreeding." Jon nodded silently in agreement and would later tell Richard and myself of how he, too, had seen at the hospital tragic cases of physical deformity of a type that would make a grown man shudder.

Alfred poured us all a glass of sherry and Robert brought into the room a plentiful supply of cheese sandwiches, along with all manner of pickle and sauce. Alfred continued. "Now, as I said, there is always a little truth behind any legend, even if it is far more sober than might initially be believed. I have countless reports in my files—as I'll show you in a moment—that lead me to believe, and I earnestly believe that I will be vindicated on this matter, that at least as far back as the 1600s there were people living in Devon, Cornwall, and possibly as far as Somerset, who had descended into a wild lifestyle of the type depicted in the tales of John Gregg and Sawney Beane.

"That is to say, they lived in the many caves that, as you know yourself, Jon, pepper this part of the country. Over the course of several generations, genetic defects began to afflict the population—to the extent that mental aberrations would have been the norm, as would an altered physical appearance—and they adopted a cannibalistic lifestyle that, again, Defoe had heard was so."

Alfred smiled at us. "It now gets a little controversial. I don't doubt that a small population of this type *could* have existed through the 1600s and the 1700s. But imagine if a relic—and almost certainly relatively small—population of such people had survived beyond that time and that things did not come to a close with the legend of John Gregg. Suppose that these people—devolved people, I like to call them—survived, keeping themselves hidden from society, living in the caves and the old tin mines and only surfacing out of their lair at night for food. Imagine, too, if the ragged remnants of this group managed—and I grant that this *is* speculative—to drag themselves into the mid-twentieth century."

"And ended their days at the Royal Western?" interjected Jon.

"Exactly," replied Alfred, resting his chin on his fingers. "Would this not account for the many accounts of wild men in Britain? Suppose they spread elsewhere: Snowdonia, some of the larger forests in Kent and central England, the Lake District and Scotland. The possibilities are endless. Perhaps the accounts of hairy men of the type that you have investigated, Jon, are in fact wild men of the type that I am postulating and that were wrapped in animal fur or were afflicted by hypertrichosis."

"And they're still living, now, in the twenty-first century, in England, hidden from us in forests and mountains?" I asked slightly incredulously.

Detecting an air of skepticism in my voice, Alfred added, "Granted, this is a theory and nothing more. But I come back to the fact that there are persistent legends in this area of wild men descending into cannibalism and inbreeding that were investigated by notable personalities such as Daniel Defoe. And there is another factor, too. I do wonder if the reason for the wild man that I saw and the one that was supposedly captured in 1944 was because they were the last of their kind—at least, in this area. Imagine if that *was* the case, that after the passing of numerous generations and incessant inbreeding, the line finally came to a close and that these two were the last. Perhaps it would be only then that they would come out of hiding, out of the old mines, and craving some form of human contact, and that it was this that led to their capture."

It was without a doubt an ingenious theory. And as Alfred noted, too, the overwhelming secrecy that accompanied the 1948 capture was also understandable. Who in a position of authority would want to reveal to the public at large that a relict colony of inbred cannibals had for centuries existed in stealth in the wilder parts of Dartmoor and had now possibly spread elsewhere in the U.K.?

"Do you know how many people go missing every year?" Alfred

asked knowingly. "I'm not talking about serial killers or people left for dead but people who just vanish? I suggest my theory now offers some of the answers as to why."

"You're suggesting that these missing people have been used as food?" asked Richard with an evil grin on his face.

Alfred sat back in his chair, pointed the index finger of his right hand at Richard, and replied in a quiet voice: "That is *exactly* what I am saying."

"Cool!" exclaimed Richard.

⁘ ⁙ ⁘

After first returning to Widecombe-in-the-Moor for a brief and final look at the old church, the rest of our day was spent poring over Alfred's vast collection of files, including the additional data and witness testimony relating to sightings of caveman-style creatures seen in the vicinity of the old earthworks at Lustleigh Cleave on Dartmoor in the 1950s. According to one piece of testimony, three men driving across the moors late at night in March 1957 had seen four such creatures— described as hairy and wild-looking—run across the road in the direction of the earthworks. Naturally scared out of their wits, the men did not even consider stopping their vehicle and turning around. Instead they continued on their journey and remained resolutely silent on the matter until one of them had approached Alfred in 1978, after being directed to him by a mutual friend.

While reports of this caliber certainly gelled with his theory, said Alfred, there were several that did not. Certainly the most bizarre dated from 1789 and was referenced in an old document that came from the private collection of a noted family of landowners in Cornwall. It concerned an immense monkeylike creature seen on several occasions at Crowlas, near Penzance.

The creature was seen by local folk late at night on at least three occasions and was described as being around eight feet in height and would make a strange whistling noise that was interpreted as a call. Most notable of all was the fact that when the creature was last seen, it literally disappeared in an almighty flash of light during a thunderstorm—something that echoed the ghostly black dog legend of Bungay, Suffolk.

"I have no answer for cases of this type," said Alfred, "and I suggest that they fall more into your sphere of investigation, Jon. But, I am not saying that I can supply you with *all* of the answers. I can only tell you that it is my firm conviction that at least *some* of the man-beast legends and sightings of the last few centuries do, I believe, have their origins in whatever was taking place on Dartmoor in the 1600s and 1700s."

Later that evening, Alfred had to go out to visit an old friend and that left Jon, Richard, and myself the opportunity to muse upon Alfred's remarkable tale. "Do you believe him?" I asked Jon, as we sat around the table devouring a turkey dinner and several bottles of the finest wine. "He seems okay, but the guy is just obsessed by all this. It's not an interest: it's his whole life."

"You're right," Jon nodded. "You know, I was unsure what to make of it all when Alfred told me all this back in 1982 and I'm just as unsure now. He seems reasonable, he's a fellow of good standing, and I can't think of any reason on earth why he would want to invent something like this. And it's obvious from his files that he cares passionately about it.

"I have to say, too, that his theory, and the way it blends in with the story of the Cannibals of Clovelly, is ingenious. But mutated cannibals hiding out in caves and mines and stalking the countryside at night—*and* in the twentieth century? If we could prove *that*, it would be the story of the millennium. I don't know. I just don't know."

But, as Jon rightly pointed out, there were numerous accounts of large predatory cats, such as pumas and panthers, prowling the British countryside by night that were taken very seriously by the authorities. Was Alfred's tale, he asked us, really that much different? At around eleven o'clock we heard the front door close loudly. Alfred had returned home. We were still at the dining table and still discussing the day's events when he entered.

"Gentlemen," he began, addressing us all with a concerned expression on his face, "I have to apologize to you but I must ask you to leave tonight. Now." For a moment Richard, Jon, and myself looked at each other in a stunned fashion.

"Have we offended you in some way?" asked Jon in a worried voice.

"No, not at all. It has been delightful to have had your company," Alfred replied. "I must just ask you to leave, though." And so—in an atmosphere that was so thick you would have needed a chain saw to cut it—we exited the room, headed for our bedrooms, packed, descended the staircase, and made our way to the front door.

"Again, you have my apologies," said Alfred as we headed down the small flight of steps from the main door to the driveway. We walked over to the Mystery Machine, loaded our belongings, and climbed into the cab.

"Now what the hell was all *that* about?" I asked, looking in Richard's direction.

"Mad. Bloody mad," he replied, shaking his head.

"Screw this. Let's go to Lustleigh Cleave," I said and turned on the ignition. We had barely traveled for five minutes when two police cars screeched past us on the opposite side of the lonely road and in the direction of Alfred's home.

"Now, where do you think they're going?" shouted Richard. "Let's get after 'em!"

"Er, Richard, that may not be the best idea," said a concerned Jon. "I do *not* want to find myself sharing a jail cell for the night with a guy named Big Charlie who wants me as his bitch."

"Hang on!" I cried as we speedily approached a crossroads and where there was ample room for me to maneuver. I floored the brakes, swung the vehicle around, and only minutes after we had been practically thrown out of Alfred's home, we were on our way back there. We pulled up outside the gates and I turned off the headlights on the Mystery Machine, put it into low gear, and edged the vehicle as carefully and as quietly as was humanly possible into the grounds. As we were still some distance from the house it was unlikely that our actions would have been noticed.

"Well, *now* what?" said Jon. "Tell me, please, we are not walking to the house from here?"

"Come on, mate," I responded. "It'll be okay."

"Yes, like the cellar affair, no doubt," he shot back.

"Yes, exactly," I assured him, or perhaps not. As we began the stealthy walk of several hundred yards along the graveled driveway, the crunching under our feet seemed to get ever louder as we got nearer the house and we took care to remain as close to the thick bushes as possible for cover.

"God, I hope he doesn't have a pack of Rotweillers or pit bulls around," I whispered.

"Nicholas! I do *not* need to hear things like that!" seethed an ever more nervous Jon. We reached the house and there, sure enough, parked directly in front of the steps that we had descended only a brief time before, were the same two police cars. We began to carefully and quietly walk around the house and took every opportunity to try to peer through the curtains of each and every room.

Regrettably, most were in pitch darkness and only two downstairs rooms had lights on. One, we recognized as the kitchen, but through the small crack in the curtains we could see no one. The other room was to the immediate left of the front door. In turn all three of us pressed our ears to the window but could detect nothing beyond muffled voices. What was going on?

We quickly developed a plan to knock on the door and claim that we had left something in one of the bedrooms. That, at least, would afford us the opportunity to reenter the house and perhaps learn something about Alfred's late-night visit from Her Majesty's finest. Before we had the chance to do so, however, the front door opened and to our horror two uniformed policemen and a guy in plainclothes descended the steps. We dove for cover into the foliage and peered through the bushes.

"Oh, shit!" exclaimed Richard. "They're gonna see the camper when they go down the drive."

"Tell me about it," I said, already wondering how I was going to explain to Dave that his beloved vehicle had been impounded. We could only watch helplessly as the two police cars headed down the driveway, stopped by the Mystery Machine for thirty seconds or so—

seconds that seemed like a veritable lifetime—and then headed on their merry way.

"Nicholas, I suggest we get back to the camper and get out of here before the constabulary return with a posse to round up both it and us," Jon said.

We quickly headed down the driveway, glancing back as we did so—partly in the hope of learning something more in our final moments on Alfred's estate and partly to ensure that no one had seen us lurking around. Although he did not mention it until we were safely on our way out of the gates, Richard would tell Jon and me that for a moment he thought he had seen the silhouette of a woman looking down at us from an upstairs window in a fashion that, he added, reminded him of the classic film *Psycho*, when a deranged Norman Bates—dressed as his long-dead mother—peered down from their old, dark house toward the infamous Bates Motel. And what if Alfred, too, was an insane, knife-wielding cross-dresser who was hiding in the back of the Mystery Machine and was just waiting for the chance to slit our throats? asked Richard helpfully.

"Please, Richard," wailed Jon, "do *not* torture me anymore!"

"Okay, *now* let's get down to Lustleigh," I said, laughing, as Jon's tormented brain threatened to explode into tiny pieces.

For the first few miles, the journey from Alfred's was rather tense, as every headlight that appeared in our rearview mirror was potentially a police car and none of us wanted to be confronted by those most dreaded of words: "Step out of the vehicle, please, sir."

The worst-case scenario did not come to pass, however, and we made our way toward Lustleigh without incident and parked the vehicle in a rest stop some miles from the village. Despite the fact that we were sure that Richard had only meant it in jest, Jon and I cast a cautious eye around the camper's sleeping compartment just in case Britain's answer to Norman Bates came looming out of the darkness amid a torrent of screeching music. But it was not to be. We settled comfortably into the beds and within moments all three of us were sound asleep—as if the bizarre events of the last two days had never occurred.

7

GOING UNDERGROUND

**Come out the ground not making a sound,
the smell of death is all around.**

"PET SEMATARY," THE RAMONES

As Jon had told Richard and me just before we embarked on
our adventure, the Devon folklorist Theo Brown had collected a
number of stories of unusual goings-on in the vicinity of the village of
Lustleigh (as had Alfred himself), including one chilling recollection
from a friend of hers. She had been walking alone at dusk near the
Neolithic earthworks at the top of Lustleigh Cleave on the extreme
eastern side of Dartmoor when she had seen a family of "cavemen,"
either naked and covered in hair or wrapped in the shaggy pelts of
some wild animal, shambling around the stone circle at the top of the
Cleave. Could these have been the last remnants of Alfred's tribe of
cannibals? After breakfast we elected to try to find out and headed
for the village itself.

As an aside, Jon noted that this was not the only earthworks associated with sightings of people out of time. The respected authority
on prehistory, R. C. C. Clay, had just such an encounter while driving
at Bottlebush Down, Dorset, an area strewn with earthworks, during
the winter of 1927, Jon elaborated. A horseman was riding on the
Downs in the same direction as Clay. On slowing his car, Clay clearly
saw that the horseman's legs were bare and that he wore a long, loose

cloak. The horseman turned his face toward Clay and waved a large weapon threateningly above his head. Clay then realized to his complete astonishment that he was looking at nothing less than a prehistoric man. Horse and rider abruptly disappeared. Shepherds who used Bottlebush Down had seen a similar spectral figure there, said Jon. Was this, he wondered, another example of an encounter with a wild man similar to that which appeared in Alfred's tale? Or was this, incredibly, an example of two different time zones briefly and inexplicably crossing? Realizing that bringing theories pertaining to time travel into the story was going to complicate matters even further, we decided to press on with our preplanned arrangements.[1]

Nestling in the Dartmoor foothills, Lustleigh is considered to be one of the most picturesque of Devonshire villages; its thatched cottages, village green, and churchyard echo back to an England that is—sadly—diminishing day by day. We scoured the area and walked up to the earthworks, but found precisely nothing. After speaking about Theo Brown's story with numerous villagers who responded with looks that ranged from bemused to amused and from wary to downright petrified, we did the only thing that we could do. We headed for the local pub.

The Cleave is a fifteenth-century thatched inn with two bars—a cozy lounge bar with granite walls and a vast inglenook fireplace, and a more spacious Victorian bar that contains an impressive array of musical instruments. The inn's name is taken from the steep, wooded escarpment that rises up behind Lustleigh, known as The Cleave. A popular place for walkers, it boasts magnificent views over the moor toward Hound Tor and Haytor, and to the north are the well-known moorland towns of Moretonhampstead and Chagford. A little way beyond is Lutyen's magnificent Castle Drogo and to the south is the town of Bovey Tracey, where the Devon Guild of Craftsmen has its gallery and shop, and from where the Beck Falls are only minutes away.

We entered the lounge bar, ordered three pints of lager and sat down. By now it was getting close to lunchtime and we were hungry after our morning excursions and ordered food. Since no one seemed to have heard any Theo Brown–like stories, we elected to spend the rest of the day trying to analyze Alfred's bizarre tale. Was it real? Was he a fantasist and an obsessive? Or did the truth lie somewhere in between?

Within minutes our meal had arrived. Jon had chosen prawns in sauce, Richard—in a monumentally surprising move for someone who professed to hate anything other than "solid Northern grub"—ordered homemade chicken liver and brandy paté; I went for the tomato and mozzarella salad.

As we sat and discussed the events of the last few days, we tried to make some semblance out of what we had learned and seen. It was clear, Jon said, that the tale Alfred had related to us was essentially the same as the one Alfred had related to him in 1982. In other words, Alfred had not elaborated on his account, as fakers often do trying to peddle their ever-escalating fantasies.

Alfred was also a man of good standing in the community and seemingly had no reason to lie or to invent bizarre tales for his—or indeed our—amusement. More importantly, the fact that he had three large files on man-beast and wild-man encounters in the West Country was evidence that this was a subject that he cared passionately about and had done so for decades. Then, of course, there were the mysterious chains in the cellar and the weird affair of the previous night when we were asked to leave the house shortly before the police arrived—all of which were suggestive of *something* unusual.

And from a historical perspective, the studies of Daniel Defoe and the stories of Sawney Bean and the Cannibals of Clovelly served as an indication that wild men of the type that Alfred was talking about possibly *did*, at some point in centuries past, inhabit the more remote parts of Dartmoor. But as is often the case in accounts such as these, there were problems, too. As a firm devotee of novels and films on werewolves and lycanthropy, I was concerned by the fact that Alfred's story bore an uncanny resemblance to a classic werewolf film based in the West Country and released in the early 1940s—just a matter of years before the alleged capture of a wild man on Dartmoor.

"Savage! Sinister! Supernatural! The black fury of a werewolf—sacrificing life and love to the maddening evil that drove him to the most monstrous murders man ever committed!" This was the advertising blurb that accompanied 20th Century-Fox's 1942 production, *The Undying Monster.*

Produced largely in response to Universal's phenomenally successful *The Wolfman* of 1941, *The Undying Monster* is set in an isolated and sinister mansion on a cliff edge in a remote corner of Cornwall. Walton the butler, and his wife, the maid, narrate the history of Hammond Hall and of the legendary monster that plagues the Hammond family, as is referred to in an ancient curse: "When the stars are bright on a frosty night, beware thy bane on the rocky lane."

Awaiting the arrival of her brother Oliver, Helga Hammond and Walton experience a strange howling accompanied by a woman's scream that seems close by. Upon investigation, they find Oliver close to death and a woman from the village slaughtered by an unholy assailant. Robert Curtis and Cornelia Christopher, both forensic scientists for Scotland Yard, are called in to investigate the mysterious events. The legend goes on to explain that one of the Hammond ancestors sold his soul to the Devil and still lives in a secret room at the house, only venturing forth occasionally to take a human life to prolong his own, which prompts Oliver, with his acquaintance Dr. Jeff Corbert, to inspect the darkest recesses of the house and the family crypt.

Shortly thereafter a scream is heard and a figure is seen carrying Helga Hammond away. Several policemen, Curtis, and Dr. Cobert give chase and follow the figure to the rocky shore. As the culprit clambers to the top of the cliff, the police aim their guns at the suspect, whose face is revealed to be Oliver Hammond as a werewolf. The creature falls to its death on the rocks below, its face once again changing back to the human form of Oliver Hammond.[2]

In essence, that is the story of the cinematic masterpiece that is *The Undying Monster.* Ironically, it had been a favorite of mine since my early teens, but I never dreamed that it would come to play a role in my life more than twenty years later. As Jon, Richard, and I recognized, there were several aspects of *The Undying Monster* that paralleled Alfred's tale. First, the film was set in Cornwall and only a relatively short distance from the wilds of Dartmoor. Second, the story was centered upon an old mansion not unlike Alfred's home.

Third, the film alludes to an unholy creature hidden in a secret room at the house—or perhaps in the family crypt—and which eerily paralleled our "cellar saga," as Richard liked to refer to it. Fourth, there were the references in both the film and in Alfred's account to Scotland Yard and the attempts of the local police to end the creature's reign of terror. And finally, the film was released only two years before tales of wild men being found on Dartmoor began to circulate at the Royal Western Counties Hospital in Starcross, and only six years before Alfred's own alleged experience. And there was more, too.

Recall that, according to Alfred, the wild man was taken to a secure location somewhere in the mass of tunnels that make up the London Underground. Of course, tales of strange creatures inhabiting the darker depths of the London Underground subway system abound and have done so for years—and in fictional format were most famously portrayed in the 1981 film, *An American Werewolf in London*, and most recently in the 2002 film *Reign of Fire*. The writer Michael Goss—who is highly skeptical about such tales, I should stress—describes the legends thus:

"The London subterraneans are real troglodytes, born and bred down below and seldom if ever coming to the surface. They are an evolved or perhaps devolved species: foul, secretive, stunted, ruinous. They've probably forgotten how to speak English; it's even likely that they've developed their own guttural and ghastly language by now— if they have been under London for as long as popular lore avers.

"I have never seen one of these subterraneans, nor so much as met a person who has seen one. These troglodytes exist in that nebulous quasi-material form that is part-rumour, part-legend (or, as some folklorists say, 'rumour legend').

"The subterraneans seems a deceptively playful kind of London legend, the sort which narrators repeat with disparaging amusement, but which cries out to be believed. It is fairly consistent as such legends go. They prowl the sewers and railway tunnels showing themselves as little as possible. They might be pitied, except that (tacitly or explicitly) the legends make them ferociously antagonistic towards us. They probably eat the sandwiches and burgers we discard and it is 'widely believed' that they also eat tramps, drunks and other isolated late-night commuters. Now you have another good reason for avoiding the Northern Line after rush hour."[3]

Indeed, some of these legends were incorporated into a seldom-screened film of the 1970s titled *Death Line,* starring Christopher Lee and Donald Pleasance. The film begins in the late 1890s, and tells the story of a cave-in at a new line and station being constructed at Russell Square where several Irish laborers, both men and women, are killed. The construction company subsequently goes bankrupt and cannot afford to dig out the bodies.

As might be guessed, however, the laborers *don't* die but instead survive and reproduce, and, eighty years later, their descendants—who live deep within the underground tunnels—are replenishing their food supply from the platform at Russell Square. As the publicity blurb that accompanied *Death Line* on its release stated: "Beneath modern London buried alive in its plague-ridden tunnels lives a tribe of once humans. Neither men nor women, they were less than animals . . . they are the raw meat of the human race."

While such tales are almost certainly apocryphal, I was intrigued that in some ways they paralleled the account that I had been told by the "alien abductee" who informed me of a vision that she had of a post-holocaust London where the starving and irradiated survivors were forced to do battle for food with strange creatures that would emerge from the Underground tunnels late at night. And it is a matter of record that there *have* been other unexplained and dark goings-on in the depths of the London Underground.

⠿ ⠿ ⠿

British Museum Station closed on September 25, 1933, and for many years a local myth circulated to the effect that the ghost of an ancient Egyptian haunted the station. Dressed in a loincloth and headdress, the figure would emerge late at night into the labyrinth of tunnels. Indeed, the rumor grew so strong that a London newspaper offered a reward to anyone who would spend the night there. Somewhat surprisingly, no one took the newspaper up on its offer.

However, the story takes a stranger turn after the closure of the station. The comedy thriller, *Bulldog Jack,* which was released in 1935, included in its story a secret tunnel that ran from the station to the Egyptian Room at the Museum. The station in the film is known as Bloomsbury, and in all likelihood was a stage set, but it *was* based on the ghost story of British Museum Station. Oddly enough, on the same night that the film was released, two women disappeared from the platform at Holborn—the next station along from the British Museum. Strange marks were later found on the walls of the closed station and more sightings of the ghost were reported, along with weird moaning noises coming from behind the walls of the tunnels.

London Underground officials, however, repeatedly played down the story and there has always been a blanket denial of the existence of a tunnel from the station to the Egyptian Room. Nevertheless, the story was resurrected in Keith Lowe's novel *Tunnel Vision,* in which the lead character states, while trying to both impress and scare his girlfriend, "If you listen carefully when you're standing at the platform at Holborn, sometimes—just sometimes—you can hear the wailing of Egyptian voices floating down the tunnel towards you."[4]

While this little-known account has no direct bearing on whether or not devolved people or strange creatures really *do* prowl the deepest depths of the London Underground and the maze of tunnels that extend under the heart of the nation's capital, it does serve to show that only a few hundred feet below the bustling streets of London, the world is perceived to be a very different place.

But was Alfred's tale simply that: a tale? Or was there a semblance of truth to it? Or were my, Jon's and Richard's collective imaginations simply spiraling out of control thanks to the wild stories of a cunning old prankster? It has to be said that as we sat there in The Cleave mulling over the many and varied scenarios, our thoughts and opinions constantly changed. Every time we came up with something that added credence to Alfred's tale, along would come something from the world of fiction that would make us reevaluate our position.

But there was one other piece of evidence in favor of Alfred's tale: that of the so-called feral children. For literally centuries tales have circulated concerning children brought up in the wild by animals such as wolves, apes, and even sheep. Many have been found to be apocryphal or outright hoaxes. However, a number of such accounts *have* stood the test of time and *do* indicate that people can revert—and, indeed, *have* reverted—to a wild form of lifestyle of the type that Alfred maintained had occurred on darkest Dartmoor over the course of the last four or five centuries.

Sir Kenelm Digby, one of the Royal Society's founders, was the first to mention the case of Jean de Liège in 1644, having interviewed at length those who had met him a few years earlier. As a five-year-old boy during the religious wars, Jean took to the woods with fellow villagers. When the fighting moved elsewhere, the villagers returned home; however, Jean remained in hiding and out of human contact for sixteen years. In the wild, his senses sharpened to an astonishing degree. He could smell "wholesome fruits or roots" at an incredible distance and when he was captured at the age of about twenty-one, he was naked, "all overgrown with hair," and incapable of speech. Later, after having been reintegrated into human society, he learned to talk, but unfortunately lost his acute sense of smell.

Similarly, Nicholaus Tulp, the Dutch doctor portrayed by Rembrandt in *The Anatomy Lesson,* described an Irish "sheep-boy" in 1672. "There was brought to Amsterdam a youth of 16 years, who being lost perhaps by his parents and brought up from his cradle amongst the wild sheep of Ireland, had acquired a sort of ovine nature," recorded Tulp. "He was rapid in body, nimble of foot, of fierce countenance, firm flesh, scorched skin, rigid limbs, with retreating and depressed forehead, but convex and knotty occiput, rude, rash, ignorant of fear, and destitute of all softness. In other respects sound, and in good health. Being without human voice he bleated like a sheep, and being averse to the food and drink we are accustomed to, he chewed grass only and hay, and that with the same choice as the most particular sheep."

Across the Atlantic, according to legend, in the early part of the nineteenth century, a wolf girl roamed the banks of the Devil's River near Del Rio in southwest Texas. The girl's mother had died in childbirth, and her father, John Dent, was killed in a thunderstorm while riding for help. "The child was never found, and the presumption was that she had been eaten by wolves near the Dents' isolated cabin," wrote Barry Lopez in his book *Of Wolves and Men*.

Lopez said that a boy living at San Felipe Springs in 1845 had reported seeing several wolves and "a creature, with long hair covering its features, that looked like a naked girl," attacking a herd of goats. Others made similar reports the following year and Apache Indians told several times of finding a child's footprints among those of the local wolf population.

A hunt commenced and on the third day the girl was duly cornered in a canyon. A wolf with her was driven off and finally shot when it attacked the hunting party. The girl was then bound and taken to the nearest ranch, where she was untied and locked in a room. That evening, however, a large number of wolves, apparently attracted by the girl's loud, mournful, and incessant howling, approached the ranch. The domestic stock subsequently panicked, and in the confusion the girl succeeded in making good her escape. According to Lopez, the girl was not seen again for seven years. In 1852, a surveying crew exploring a new route to El Paso allegedly saw her on a sand bar on the Rio Grande, far above its confluence with Devil's River. "She was with two pups. After that, she was never seen again."[5]

As these accounts—that are supported by literally dozens of similar reports—suggest, the idea that true wild men (and women) have existed in times past and may continue to exist to this day, was one that none of us could completely dismiss. After spending several hours at The Cleave considering the evidence, valiantly trying to drain the pub's cellar of beer, and making three unsuccessful telephone calls to Alfred's residence in an attempt to speak with him (all of which were thwarted by his staff), we decided that, for now at least, the best course of action was to simply file away Alfred's story and continue on our travels to our next location and our next interviewee: a witch from Cornwall whom Jon had known since the late 1970s and who, he said, was going to take us on a roller coaster of a journey into the unknown.

8

FULL MOON MADNESS

I'm howling at the moon.

"HOWLING AT THE MOON," THE RAMONES

Although our interview with Jon's witch friend, who went by the suspiciously fake-sounding name of Mother Sarah Graymalkin, had been firmly arranged, her schedule meant that we were unable to meet with her for another four days, and so we spent the intervening period hooking up with old friends and acquaintances. One was known as Billy Two-Barrels, a genial ex-gangster originally from Glasgow, who was now living out his retirement in a pleasant Dartmoor cottage and who had a deep passion for the Loch Ness Monster. Another was a distinctly bizarre couple named Clive and Susan, who lived near the town of Moretonhampstead, and who claimed to have knowledge of an alien base buried deep below the South Pole.

Billy was a nice guy, providing that you didn't press him too closely about his Al Capone–like past. Clive and Susan, however, were utterly mad and regaled us with their ingeniously insane theories linking the death of the actress Marilyn Monroe with the notorious Cottingley fairy photographs that so intrigued Sherlock Holmes's creator, Sir Arthur Conan Doyle. Clive, it transpired, had a rather unusual and somewhat disturbing fixation with Marilyn Monroe and would spend hours surfing the internet in pursuit of anything and everything remotely connected with the long-deceased actress.

On one particular evening, said Clive, he had found a site that provided numerous rare photographs of Hollywood's most famous glamour girl. Looking at one such photograph he noticed an anomaly in the structure of her hand that reminded him of the hands of one of the creatures portrayed in the Cottingley fairy photographs. Since Clive was convinced that the Cottingley fairies were, in fact, aliens from the far side of the moon, he concluded that Marilyn Monroe—along with many other Hollywood stars—was in reality a hostile alien that had infiltrated California. The U.S. government secretly knew this, said Clive, and a covert team of alien hunters was dispatched from Area 51 to kill the actress. Needless to say, all three of us took a look at the photograph. The "anomaly" was undoubtedly a trick of the light and Clive was undoubtedly insane—but highly entertaining, too.

We had welcomed this diversion from our main task, particularly after our bizarre experience at Castle Alfred. But after four days of relative normality (for us, at least) spent with an ex-gangster and a couple that seemed to have stepped right out of a particularly bad episode of *The X-Files*, we were ready to take up our mighty challenge again.

We waved out of the windows of the Mystery Machine to the ever-smiling Clive and Susan as we departed from their home and headed for our next location: the cottage of Mother Sarah Graymalkin, in Ponsanooth, near Falmouth. We had only been driving for approximately twenty minutes, however, when Jon's mobile telephone rang.

"Downes speaking," he bellowed into its mouthpiece in an amusingly pompous fashion. It was Mother Sarah. Could we postpone the interview until the following day? We could. And so with another day and night at our disposal we decided to spend it wisely: at one of the many taverns that peppered the landscape on our journey to Ponsanooth.

After a seriously amusing three-hour-long conversation about monsters and UFOs with the distinctly skeptical owner of the pub, we decided to park for the evening near the Carnon Downs to review our plan of action. Jon, however, had other things on his mind. As we stretched out on the seats of the camper, opened a bottle of red wine and surveyed the pleasant summer's evening through the windows, Jon revealed all—metaphorically speaking, that is.

He had, he said, been reluctant to discuss what he was about to tell us because it would inevitably lead back to a traumatic time from his childhood. Nevertheless, he felt that in the interests of ensuring that our quest was as profitable as possible, it was time he shared some long-buried memories with us. Jon was, he began, intrigued by the story that I had related to him and Richard that noted the suspicious links between the story told to us by Alfred and that of the 1942 production, *The Undying Monster*.

"But, Nicky," added Jon, "*I* have a problem with *your* problem."

"Speak English, Jon," I said.

"Well," he added after giving us both long and thoughtful looks, "it's like this. You say that Alfred's tale is suspicious because you believe that its roots can be traced back to *The Undying Monster*."

"Yeah, that's right," I replied.

"But, what you may not know is that the film itself, and Jessie Douglas Kerruish's book that the film was based on, were almost certainly based on preexisting accounts of werewolves and man-beasts that have circulated in both Devon and Cornwall for centuries.

"So," Jon elaborated, "it's kind of like the chicken and the egg syndrome. Which came first? Was Alfred's tale built upon him seeing the film? Or were the film and the book based on legends and stories similar to that told by Alfred?"

"So we may not be any clearer, anyway?" I asked.

"I fear not," Jon replied with a look of apology on his face. Jon was now ready to tell his tale. However, we had a few things to do beforehand and by the time Richard and I were ready to listen, the sun had set, the creatures of the night—such as the owls and the foxes—had surfaced, and total darkness had descended upon the Mystery Machine.

"Not another bloody candle, mate," said Richard as Jon went to light up.

"Richard, I am shocked, dear boy. It makes for a much better atmosphere."

"Alright," he grumbled. "But if some big, bloody bird comes flying through the window again, you better know where the lights are."

As we sat back and listened, Jon began. He revealed to us that throughout much of Devon and Cornwall there were numerous rumors and legends pertaining to shape-shifting man-beasts such as werewolves. Perhaps they were really misidentifications and distorted legends based on the tales of the Cannibals of Clovelly. Or, Jon said, perhaps they were far more than that.

He had learned that when the British folklorist Ruth St. Ledger Gordon had visited a small village on Dartmoor in 1961, she was asked, quite seriously, by the locals whether she had heard stories of animals on the moor "not being quite what they seemed." It transpired that St. Ledger Gordon was told of old moor men who knew from the behavior or the appearance of some particular sheep, bullock, or pony that it was "not a true beast," but only a semblance of one. The idea seemed to be that some elemental or malignant spirit had temporarily assumed the form of the animal in question and was grazing with the herd or the flock.

Jon added, "I'm not going to come out with any of the old clichés about life imitating art, but the whole affair is curious because there is a long and sordid history of lycanthropes and shape-shifting from man to animal in Devonshire."

The earliest account that Jon was aware of came from the Valley of the Rocks near Lynton in North Devon and was related by the author Elliot O'Donnell, who wrote:

"A woman I met in Tavistock told me she had seen a ghost which she believed to be that of a werewolf, in the Valley of the Doones, Exmoor. She was walking home alone, late one evening, when she saw on the path directly in front of her the tall gray figure of a man with a wolf's head. Advancing stealthily forward, this creature was preparing to spring on a large rabbit that was crouching on the ground, apparently too terror stricken to move, when the abrupt appearance of a stag bursting through the bushes caused it to vanish."[1]

And there were more reports, too. The researcher Andy Roberts had written about a strange creature that had been seen in the vicinity of Flixton in the north of England in A.D. 940. The beast, said Andy, appeared to have been a combination of a black dog, a phantom felid, and a werewolf. It was popularly described as possessing abnormally large eyes that glowed in the dark, had a long tail, and exuded a terrible stench. The creature also attacked and mutilated livestock, dogs, and even people; and it was said at the time the beast was being manipulated by a magician. The fog of time has effectively ensured that the full facts pertaining to the Flixton werewolf will continue to remain a mystery. And yet the components of the tale, such as the nature of the beast and the presence of a magician, paralleled a remarkable tale we would later hear about.[2]

Similarly, the writer Tom Slemen had published details of a werewolf legend that centered on the North Wales town of Denbigh. Supposedly in the latter part of the 1700s such a creature stalked the area, killing both man and beast over a period of several years. Interestingly, the town of Denbigh owes its name to a species of dragon— a fire-breathing winged serpent, to be precise. This beast, according to legend, haunted the vicinity and scared away the whole populace, until it was slain by the twelve-fingered "Sir John of the Thumbs" of the Salisbury family who "hewed off its head." All the people thereupon cried "Dim Bych," or "no more dragon," which is the derivation of the name of the town. So here was a relatively innocuous town in Wales that was home to legends pertaining to two forms of beast: werewolf and dragon. Whether or not the twelve-fingered and fearless Sir John had a connection with the diabolical great-grandmother (also of multidigits) who was rumored to inhabit Jon's attic was an issue that I, perhaps wisely, avoided addressing.[3]

Another account from Devonshire had come to Jon's attention from the Devon naturalist and folklorist Trevor Beer. "The story goes back to the late fifties when the writer was out rabbiting with his dog. Climbing a hedge, he stumbled upon an animal ravaging a flock of sheep and taking careful aim he shot it, knowing that he had wounded the animal, the beast rearing onto its hind legs to run off in this fashion into the woods. The dog followed the animal into the trees where there was much hideous snarling, unlike any creature he had ever heard before. Suddenly the dog came dashing out of the woods and bolted past its master who, firing a second shot into the trees, also ran for home in great fear.

"The writer went on to explain his later studies of matters concerning the occult and his realization that the animal he had shot was a werewolf and a member of a well-known local family. The writer states further that he knows the family involved and that they called in help from the Church over a decade ago but that they had to withdraw because of the terrible phenomena beyond their comprehension. Now the problem is at a stalemate, the family being aware of the nature of his character and chaining him and locking him behind barred doors every night."[4]

Turning away from Trevor Beer's account, Jon began his tale in earnest. "When I was at school in Bideford in the early 1970s a similar story was told about one of the older houses on the outskirts of the village of Abbotsham, a few miles outside Bideford and where a werewolf was supposed to reside. It was very much a friend-of-a-friend tale—everyone knew about 'the beast' and its predations, which were supposed to be on sheep."

Needless to say, Jon added, no one ever admitted to having actually had firsthand experience of the werewolf, but he is certain that the story is still discussed in whispered tones in the memories of a whole generation from the Bideford Grammar School.

We cracked open bottle number two and Jon continued. "The stories I had heard as a young teenager impressed me enough to want to investigate more. I was twelve or thirteen and at that time I was convinced that I could outrun any old werewolf. I was young, brave, intrepid, and my mate, Jim, whose aid I had enlisted in this noble expedition, had an air pistol. So I knew everything was going to be alright.

"At that time I lived in a tiny village called Woolfardisworthy, which was about nine miles from Bideford. But I visited my friend Jim regularly and on one June weekend we conspired together to go werewolf hunting."

The intrepid pals set off soon after breakfast and cheerfully walked along Abbotsham Road, past the old school gates and toward the village where the werewolf was alleged to have its dwelling. To this day, said Jon, he can still recall the hedgerows being alight with mayflowers and honeysuckle, but as he and Jim approached the village of Abbotsham, and the coast path that led toward Abbotsham Cliffs, the pleasant surroundings were replaced by gorse and furze.

"Climbing over a field gate at a predetermined point, our expedition became an illegal one," Jon reminisced, "as we shamelessly trespassed across farmers' fields toward our destination. About a mile and a half from the road that we had left was the beginning of a wood. This was, allegedly at least, our destination, and we started to feel a little uneasy." Sheepishly they entered the wood.

Jon looked at Richard and me for a moment and continued. "In all my life of wandering through woods, forests, thickets, jungles, and rain forests across the world I have *never* come across one that was completely silent. Except for this one.

"Here and there we could see the mangled and dilapidated remains of a rhododendron bush, indicating that once this had been a carefully managed woodland. Now it was just abandoned wilderness. It felt to us like we were the only visitors here for decades, if not longer. There was absolutely no sound except for the crunching noise of twigs and dead leaves scrunching beneath our feet. No birdsong, no buzzing insects, no tiny scurrying animals.

"Then we noticed something else strange. Apart from the occasional dirty gray-green of the sickly rhododendron leaves, there was practically no color. It was midsummer, remember, but all of the trees and bushes at eye level anyway appeared to be dead. If you looked up, you could see the outline of the leafy canopy silhouetted against the blue sky, but down here in the wood itself it was as dead as a morgue."

The boys carried on in silence but both felt uncomfortable and neither wanted to be the first to suggest that discretion should be the better part of valor and that they should get the hell out of there as quickly as possible.

"So we carried on," said Jon. "After what seemed like a lifetime—but was probably only about half an hour—the undergrowth began to thin out and before us we could see a rusty, three-strand, barbed-wire fence. Being the intrepid souls that we were, we didn't hesitate to clamber over. I tore the seat of my jeans to blazes and was soundly scolded by my mother when I got home, but that is another and completely irrelevant story.

"Well, we found a house in the woods alright, but no werewolf. Anyway, we were hungry, there were fifty pence pieces burning holes in our pockets and there was a little shop back on the outskirts of Northam that sold the most delicious pies known to man. We decided to take what we believed was the most direct path through the woods to get to Northam where we could eat those pies, drink lemonade, and relive our adventure of the morning."

Jon and Jim set off in what they believed was the right direction for Northam. And although they were undoubtedly intrepid, direction finding was certainly not one of their strong points and they soon became hopelessly lost. And as they went deeper and deeper into the woods the atmosphere became more and more unpleasant. The woods, Jon explained, were not just quiet, but oppressively silent. It was not just the absence of birdsong or insects that was noticeable, but the absence of *anything*.

Jon and Jim were now running as if their very lives depended on it. Needless to say, they had completely lost interest in the Northam bun shop. Jon explained the situation succinctly. "We just wanted to get the hell out of this accursed wood. Then it hit us. A stench the like of which I have never encountered before, or since, rolled up toward us through the trees.

"Now, I have examined dead animals in the tropics where corpses are reduced to a putrefying mess within hours. I have observed a human autopsy and have conducted dissections of creatures ranging from a woodlouse to a bottle-nosed dolphin. I have seen quite a few dead humans, some in particularly unpleasant conditions. On one occasion I even attempted mouth-to-mouth resuscitation on a corpse that had drowned on her own vomit. I am not a squeamish man, and I was an even less squeamish youth. But this smell was the most disgusting that I have ever encountered."

Then suddenly there it was, added Jon: a dead roebuck. Its head was caught in a barbed-wire fence and its tortured body lay splayed out behind it, bloated with putrefaction and with its intestines spread out beside it.

Jon's voice lowered in tone as he continued his tale. "To this day I am convinced that I know what killed it. In the half-light we could see an amorphous shadow of what appeared to be an enormous black predatory creature crouching over the carcass of the roebuck. If you looked at it directly there was nothing to see, but out of the corners of our eyes it was clearly visible. That was just too much for us. We were explorers no longer and ran like hell until we finally found ourselves on the cliff path that traverses the long journey between Abbotsham and Westward Ho.

"We were back in the sunshine. We were safe. And we never spoke about what had happened again. Sadly, soon afterward our friendship disintegrated in the way that adolescent friendships often do. We never fell out but simply grew apart."

Jon took a mouthful of wine and added: "To this day I am convinced that we encountered the Abbotsham werewolf."

The last word on the North Devon werewolves, Jon said, came from a telephone call to BBC Radio Devon in Exeter following on one of his weekly *Weird about the West* radio shows that he regularly hosted until the *X-Files* mania of the 1990s disappeared up its own orifice. The call was from a young man named Chris who asked not to be identified further and who had been visiting the Valley of the Rocks near Lynton the previous Sunday when he saw what he described as a strange creature like "a man on all fours but covered in black shaggy hair" rushing across a field about a hundred yards away from him. There were sheep in the field but they appeared to ignore the creature, which made no noise, and it soon vanished from sight. Oddly, afterward, Chris realized that the creature had been moving several feet *above* the surface of the ground.

However, accounts of real-life werewolves and man-beasts prowling the British countryside did not begin and end in Devonshire, said Jon, referring to the account of one Andrew Warren, the grandson of a Kirk elder from the Hebrides.

According to the researcher and writer Graham McEwan, Warren's grandfather was keenly interested in natural history and geology and his house was filled with rocks and fossils that he had found in the surrounding countryside. One morning he came home very excited and told the boy to come and look at some curious remains he had found in a dried-up mountain lake. It looked to be a human skeleton with a wolflike head and the boy subsequently helped his grandfather carry the bones back home. That evening Warren was alone in the house, his grandfather and other members of the family having gone to church. Sitting reading, he heard a noise at the back of the house and got up to investigate, but found all secure and no signs of an intruder. He sat at the kitchen table, where the strange bones had been laid and listened to see if the noises would recommence. He was staring down at the floor, his mind blank, when he heard a loud rapping of knuckles on the windowpane.

Warren's own account continued: "I immediately turned in the direction of the noise and saw a dark face looking in at me. At first dim and indistinct, it became more and more complete, until it developed into a perfectly defined head of a wolf terminating in the neck of a human being. Though greatly shocked, my first act was to look in every direction for a possible reflection—but in vain. There was no light, either without or within, other than that from the setting sun—nothing that could in any way have produced an illusion.

"I looked at the face and marked each feature intently. It was unmistakably a wolf's face, the jaws slightly distended, the lips wreathed in a savage snarl, the teeth sharp and white, the eyes light green, the ears pointed."

McEwan then concluded his grim tale: "The boy could only stare, horrified, at the creature, which raised a slender humanlike hand with long, curved fingernails. Fearing that it was going to smash the window, he ran out of the kitchen, locking the door behind him, and stayed in the hall until the family returned, by which time the creature had departed. The following day the boy and his grandfather returned the bones to the place where they had been found. The creature was seen no more."[5]

But for what is certainly one of the strangest werewolf stories of all, we have to turn to the tale of the Hexham Heads—a macabre account that all three of us were already well acquainted with. It all began in February 1972, when an eleven-year-old boy and his younger brother were weeding their parents' garden in Hexham, Northumberland, and unearthed two carved stone heads, slightly smaller than a tennis ball and very heavy in weight. Crudely carved and weathered-looking, one resembled a skull-like masculine head and the other a slightly smaller female head with what were said to be witchlike qualities.

Shortly after the boys had taken the heads into their house, a number of peculiar incidents occurred in the family home. The heads would move by themselves. Household objects were found inexplicably broken. And at one point the boys' sister found her bed showered with glass. However, it was the next-door neighbors who would experience the most bizarre phenomena.

A few nights after the discovery of the heads, a mother living in the neighboring house, Ellen Dodd, was sitting up late with her daughter, who was suffering from toothache, when both saw what they described as a hellish "half man, half beast" enter the room. Naturally, they both screamed for their lives and a breathless husband came running from another room to see what the commotion was about.

By this stage, however, the beast had fled the room and could reportedly be heard "padding down the stairs as if on its hind legs." The front door was later found wide open and it was presumed that the creature had left the house in haste.

Soon after this incident, one Anne Ross—a doctor who had studied the Celtic culture and had written several books on the subject—took possession of the stone heads to study them. She already had in her possession several similar heads and she was certain that the Hexham heads were Celtic and nearly two thousand years old. The doctor, who lived in Southampton and about 150 miles from Hexham, had heard nothing of the strange goings-on encountered by the previous owners of the heads.

However, having put the two stone heads with the rest of her collection, Dr. Ross, too, encountered the mysterious creature a few nights later. She awoke from her sleep feeling cold and frightened and, on looking up, found herself confronted by a horrific man-beast identical to that seen at Hexham.

"It was about six feet high," Dr. Ross recalled, "slightly stooping, and it was black, against the white door, and it was half animal and half man. The upper part, I would have said, was a wolf, and the lower part was human and, I would have again said, that it was covered with a kind of black, very dark fur. It went out and I just saw it clearly, and then it disappeared, and something made me run after it, a thing I wouldn't normally have done, but I felt compelled to run after it. I got out of bed and I ran, and I could hear it going down the stairs, then it disappeared toward the back of the house."

After this startling and terrifying event, the doctor and her family saw on several occasions what they described as a huge black creature, not unlike a werewolf, materialize within the confines of the house. It invariably appeared on the stairs, said the doctor, and would then jump over the banisters to land in the hall, whereupon it would exit at speed on padded feet. And at other times, it could be heard padding around unseen and doors would fly open seemingly for no reason.

According to the doctor, there was "an evil presence about the house" and she eventually decided that the stone heads were the source of the problem and got rid of the entire collection. The two Hexham heads subsequently passed into the hands of other collectors, none of whom apparently experienced any werewolf-like encounters. Some, however, did report that the sense of pure evil, which seemed to emit from the witchlike head, made them feel extremely uncomfortable. Eventually the heads were lost and their current whereabouts are unknown.

Interestingly, the previous owner of the house in Hexham, where the heads were discovered, claims that he had in fact carved the heads as toys for his children in the 1950s and that they had been lost in the garden. Although tests were undertaken at Southampton and

Newcastle Universities to try to confirm the age of the heads, the results of those tests remain unknown.[6]

After having discussed the case of the Hexham heads, the wolf-man of the Hebrides, and Jon's very own encounter as a young boy, I wondered if he really believed that bloodthirsty werewolves were prowling the British countryside by night and howling at the full moon.

"Well, Nicky," Jon smiled, "that's where Mother Sarah comes into play. She will, I suspect, have more than a few things to tell us," he added, with a knowing wink. It was at 12:30 P.M. the next day that we finally got to meet with Mother Sarah Graymalkin at the Seven Stars public house in Falmouth. A regular hangout of Jon's, this was where on numerous occasions he had interviewed the notorious Tony "Doc" Shiels, a legendary character in monster-hunting circles and the key figure in Jon's investigation of the Owlman of Mawnan Woods. Here is Jon's description of the Seven Stars as it appears in his mighty tome, *The Owlman and Others:*

"The Seven Stars in Falmouth is a pub of the sort that you thought didn't exist anymore. . . . As you enter the public bar, the first thing that strikes you is how oddly long and thin it is. The lack of space is accentuated by a large, glass-fronted display cabinet selling cigarettes and sweets which stands on top of much of the bar itself. There are very few actual seats and tables. What there is are covered in 1950's patterned Formica. Behind the bar is a clergyman pulling the pints. There is no piped music—or if there is, it is inaudible beneath the general hubbub of chatter from the dozen or so regular customers sitting at the Formica tables, living out their own exclusive fantasies and drinking pints of bilious yellow lager."[7]

We had been sitting around chatting with the locals for around forty-five minutes and downing copious amounts of the aforementioned bilious yellow lager, when one of the strangest and creepiest-looking people I have ever encountered in my entire life walked—or rather slid—in. Jon said that Sarah Graymalkin was a witch, and by God, he wasn't kidding.

Barely five feet in height and clad in a long black dress that was partially covered by a purple velvet cloak, was an elderly woman with jet-black, waist-length (and obviously dyed) hair who must have weighed close to three hundred pounds. Not only that: She was the spitting image of the proverbial witch—even down to possessing the slightly hooked nose. Indeed, all she was missing was the obligatory broomstick and pointed hat.

"Oh, no," whispered Richard under his breath and with a look of pure dread on his ashen face as she closed in on us. The whole pub went quiet in a fashion that reminded us of the classic scene in the film, *An American Werewolf in London,* where the hapless victims of the wolfman stop off for a pint in a remote public house on the Yorkshire moors and receive a less-than-hospitable welcome from the locals—all of whom are in on the dark secret of the man-beast lurking within their tiny hamlet. She glided toward our table and Richard and I were unable to look away from her steely gaze.

"Jonnnnn," she intoned in a thick Irish accent that emphasized the "n" in his name for what seemed like an absolute eternity. Even Jon, who had known Mother Sarah for years, looked apprehensive.

"How are you, Mother Sarah?" he asked nervously, and swallowed hard.

"I'm well. I'm *very* well," she whispered in response as Jon motioned her toward a chair. On sitting down, Mother Sarah's eyes flashed back and forth across our faces and she proceeded to smile the smile of a deranged ax murderer. Quick as a flash she grabbed my right hand and Richard's left and gripped them tightly. Her fleshy fingers were ice cold and a shudder penetrated my bones. In a manner that on reflection is now very funny, Richard let out a loud cry and Mother Sarah cackled in a fashion that only someone well acquainted with the dark side can.

"You want to know about the beasts, don't you?" It was more of a statement than a question. Richard and I nodded.

"Bring them," she said sharply to Jon.

Mother Sarah glided back to the door of the Seven Stars that she had entered only a minute or so earlier and the three of us stood up and downed the last of our beer.

"Where are we going?" asked Jon, less than cheerfully, as the locals looked at us as if we were heading for execution.

"We're going to my home," she replied with a look of evil mischievousness on her face. "You will stay the night. We have much to discuss. You know where I live, Jon. I will see you at the house."

"Here we go again," said Richard apprehensively as we exited the pub and the eyes of the silent crowd burned into the backs of our heads.

9

I WANT TO BELIEVE

I'm looking for something to believe in.

"SOMETHING TO BELIEVE IN," THE RAMONES

"**B**loody hell!" Richard exclaimed to Jon as we climbed back into the Mystery Machine. "Where did you dig her up from?"

"Richard, don't go making jokes about her whatever you do," Jon replied with unease in his voice. "She is very powerful."

"Is Sarah Graymalkin her real name?" I asked. "Sounds a bit too contrived, doesn't it?"

"Ha!" Jon laughed. "Do *you* want to ask her if it's her real name or if she's a bare-faced liar?" No. I did not. I most definitely did not.

"Yeah, she'd probably put a bloody hex on me," I said.

"You know, Nicky, she probably would," Jon replied in all seriousness.

Shortly afterward, we arrived at Mother Sarah's home, a spacious eighteenth-century cottage. Like Mother Sarah, the furniture, carpets, and drapes were made up of a combination of mostly blacks, purples, and deep reds. Magical symbols were chalked on the walls of every room and rune stones, tarot cards, old Celtic statuettes, and more filled every last inch of space. Her aged and dusty bookshelves were dominated by centuries-old titles dealing with the summoning up of demons and the denizens of the underworld. Even the air seemed oppressive.

The house felt somehow "wrong." An atmosphere of pure evil emanated from every last inch of the building. In addition to that, over the centuries the foundation of the house had clearly moved and the fact that this resulted in each room looking slightly tilted, led to a curious sensation that I can only describe as a combination of drunkenness and vertigo.

Mother Sarah flung off her cape and ushered the three of us to the luxuriant couch. "You will drink tea," she said in what was once again a voice that suggested a command rather than a question.

"So where's the black cat, then?" I asked Richard while Mother Sarah was in the kitchen. "And how does she manage that walk?" I added in reference to her strange steps, which were not unlike Michael Jackson's "moonwalk"—in reverse.

We both laughed while Jon nervously berated us. In a few minutes she returned with four cups of what proved to be the foulest-tasting green-colored brew that it has ever been my misfortune to ingest, and a large homemade fruit pie.

"You don't have Typhoo tea, do you, with milk and a couple of sugars?" I asked.

Mother Sarah glared at me and I took it that her answer was a firm and conclusive no. Afterward, Richard would ask me if we had been drinking tea or pee and I truly was unable to answer him with any degree of certainty. Despite the fact that drinking the tea was a real effort, the pie was superb; and the three of us ate and drank in complete silence for the next fifteen minutes, acutely aware of the fact that Mother Sarah's bulging eyes seemed to penetrate into the heart of our collective souls.

"The key to understanding the beasts is belief," said Mother Sarah, quite out of the blue as we finished our second platefuls of pie. "They coexist with us because we want them to exist with us and for no other reason."

"So people are imagining that they are seeing these things, then?" I asked.

"Not at all, lad, not at all. Do you know what a Tulpa is?" she asked me. I did. And now it was all becoming clear to me. To uncover the truth, said Mother Sarah, we had to focus our attention first on one key individual: Alexandra David-Neel. Born on October 24, 1868, in France, Alexandra David-Neel was the first woman to be granted the title of a Lama in Tibet. Throughout her century-long life David-Neel traveled widely across Asia, was particularly drawn to the Himalayas, and in 1932 wrote a truly remarkable book about her travels called *Magic and Mystery in Tibet*.

"You might recall, Nicky, that I wrote about David-Neel quite a bit in my book *The Rising of the Moon*," said Jon. "Mother Sarah and I share a lot of similar ideas about Tulpas and—"

"Silence, Jon. This is my story to tell," the witch hissed firmly. Jon wisely did as he was told and meekly sank back into his seat without uttering another word. "Now, to the Tulpas," said Mother Sarah, glaring intently at Jon after his unwelcome interruption. The word Tulpa, said the hag, can be traced back to the Tibetan language and refers specifically to an entity that attains a form of reality after being created solely in the imagination. The process requires an immense amount of skill, she elaborated, but those trained in the ancient art of the Tulpa can draw their creations out of the confines of their minds and into the world of the physical. More problematic, though, added Mother Sarah, were those occasions when a Tulpa had succeeded in crossing from imagination to reality of its own volition or when a Tulpa began working against the will of its creator.

"That's a bit like the scene in *Ghostbusters* when Dan Aykroyd conjures up the Puff-Pastry Man to destroy New York," Richard interjected.

"Be silent! I will tolerate no more interruptions!" screamed Mother Sarah. For a moment the witch breathed heavily, held her arms aloft and an eerie sense of foreboding filled the room. We braced ourselves for whatever calamity was to come but instead Mother Sarah suddenly let her arms drop and continued her story. We all breathed an audible sigh of relief. David-Neel, it transpired, had become fascinated and obsessed by the mystery of the Tulpa and elected to try to create one herself, Mother Sarah continued.

David-Neel chose to visualize a fat and jolly little monk—not unlike the Friar Tuck character in the legend of Robin Hood. The process of trying to create within her imagination the image of the monk was both long and arduous; but, in time, David-Neel was able to view the creation not only in her mind but in the real world, too. A new kind of spectral life-form was coming into being.

In time the vision grew in clarity and substance until it was indistinguishable from physical reality. But the day came when the hallucination slipped from David-Neel's conscious control. She discovered to her horror that the monk would appear on occasions when she had not willed it. Furthermore, her friendly little figure was changing in appearance and was becoming ever more sinister.

"I proceeded to perform the prescribed concentration of thought and other rites," wrote David-Neel. "After a few months the phantom monk was formed. His form grew gradually fixed and lifelike. He became a kind of guest, living in my apartment. I then broke my seclusion and started for a tour with my servants and tents.

"The monk included himself in the party. Though I lived in the open riding on horseback for miles each day, the illusion persisted. It was not necessary for me to think of him to make him appear. The phantom performed various actions of the kind that are natural to travelers and that I had not commanded. For instance, he walked, stopped, looked around him. The illusion was mostly visual, but sometimes I felt as if a robe was lightly rubbing against me, and once a hand seemed to touch my shoulder.

"The features which I had imagined, when building my phantom, gradually underwent a change. The fat, chubby-cheeked fellow grew leaner; his face assumed a vaguely mocking, sly, malignant look. He became more troublesome and bold. In brief, he escaped my control."

At this juncture, David-Neel decided that things had gone much too far and she applied a whole variety of ancient techniques of Lamaism to try to reabsorb the creature into her own mind. Needless to say, the Tulpa was most unwilling to face destruction and the whole process took several weeks to complete.

"I ought to have let the phenomenon follow its course," David

Neel noted, "but the presence of that unwanted companion began to prove trying to my nerves; it turned into a 'daynightmare.' I decided to dissolve the phantom. I succeeded, but only after six months of hard struggle. My mind-creature was tenacious of life."

According to Mother Sarah, a Tulpa begins to act independently of its creator when it is endowed with sufficient vitality and energy to take on some semblance of reality. Alexandra David-Neel, the witch said, was informed by Tibetan occultists that this is an almost inevitable part of the overall process and is not unlike the natural birthing process that occurs between mother and child. Indeed, this was something elaborated upon by David-Neel herself: "Sometimes the phantom becomes a rebellious son and one hears of uncanny struggles that have taken place between magicians and their creatures, the former being severely hurt or even killed by the latter."

Tibetan magicians had also informed David-Neel of cases involving Tulpas that had been dispatched to fulfill a specific mission or task, but subsequently failed to do so and instead began following their own "dangerously mischievous" agendas. The same thing, Mother Sarah elaborated, can happen if the creator of the Tulpa dies before having successfully destroyed it. Generally, however, the ghostlike creation would also expire at the moment of its creator's death—but not always. In addition to the Tulpa, there existed something known as the Tulku: a similar entity that was specifically created to outlive its creator and that was designed to have independent existence.[1]

Mother Sarah then abruptly went off at a tangent and turned her attention to the life and work of one Franek Kluski. "Now I'll tell ye something that'll fire up your bellies," she chuckled in an unholy fashion.

Born in 1873, Kluski (whose real name was Teofil Modrzejewski) had a long history of paranormal experiences that began in childhood. He would, for example, recall seeing dead relatives, long-deceased pets, and other phantomlike animals. But it was not until 1918, after a séance with Jean Guzik, that Kluski's mediumistic potential was finally recognized and a series of truly mind-blowing séances began in earnest. Indeed, such was Kluski's reputation that the number of those attending Kluski's sittings ran into the hundreds and included a host of people from all walks of society, including professors, soldiers, professional magicians, and parapsychologists.

Throughout the period of Kluski's activities, he claimed over eight hundred successful visitations, with sitters recognizing some of these as people who had died. But most intriguing—and most relevant perhaps to the subject at hand—were the materializations that occurred during Franek's séances. These, said Mother Sarah, included a huge dog, a spectral bird, a giant cat that resembled a lion, and a large ape-like creature. According to Gustave Geley, M.D., who participated in Kluski's séances at the Paris Institut Metapsychique International, "All these phantoms give the impression of being alive."

But according to Mother Sarah, she was convinced that these apparitions were not from the realm of the dead. Rather, she believed that they were Tulpa-like manifestations summoned from within the depths of Kluski's own subconscious. In support of this notion, she informed us of the way in which these quasi-real creatures would also materialize in front of Kluski in his own abode on occasions when he was not performing his séances. In other words, the giant cat, the phantom dog, and the spectral monkey-beast had taken on independent existences.[2]

Mother Sarah then leaned forward in her chair and an evil smile came over her face. The three of us edged back into the farthest corners of the couch. "This is the key to the beasts. The key, I tell you!" she screamed and pointed a fleshy finger at us. I looked to my left and Richard's mouth was hanging wide open and his eyes threatened to bulge right out of his head. To my right, Jon had a similar expression on his face and I suddenly realized that I did, too. We were hanging on every word of the accursed witch.

"I will tell you the real secret now," she hissed in lowered tones. "When I say that the Tulpa is a product of the imagination, that is only partly true. Yes, they have to be summoned up from the imagination, but that is not their point of origin. For thousands of years our ancestors possessed the power to invoke a presence known as the

Cormons—a word you will very seldom hear uttered. These creatures are not created by us. The Cormons are the denizens of a realm that coexists with us and that always has. It is the realm of the pixie, the fairy, the elf, the dragon, and the mermaid. And at times our worlds can merge as one. The skill to enter that world is possessed by few of us today, and practically none at a conscious level, but there were those within the villages of old England who had this power. These people were part of a dark order that practiced archaic rituals and followed the teachings of the old earth gods. A thousand years ago Britain was a very different place to that of today."

"Yeah, no TV!" Richard butted in.

"Lad," Mother Sarah said in a low voice that seemed to echo throughout our bodies, "do not test me. Do *not* test me." I could hear Jon nervously licking his suddenly dry lips and Richard grudgingly mumbled a barely audible word of apology.

"You will find the answers you are looking for in the woods and forests of old," she added. At that moment Mother Sarah stood up, left the room for a moment and returned with a large leather-bound book adorned with the image of a goat-headed man and a giant wormlike creature wrapped around an oak tree on its front cover. It turned out to be a book that had been passed down through the Graymalkin family for generations. Mother Sarah sat down and carefully began to turn its well-preserved pages. The book told the story of how a group known as the Nine (that was not a reference to the size of its membership), from a time estimated to be the latter part of the eighth century, had uncovered the secret of how to interact with, and invoke, the phenomenon that was the Cormons. It was the intent of this elite order of men and women to bring into our world a veritable menagerie of creatures that could be put to good use by what was then a very small and—in part—less-than-civilized population of what would later become Great Britain. A plan was hatched that would ensure Britain never again found itself overrun by marauding tribes of invading forces, such as the Romans.

The Nine worked closely, Mother Sarah elaborated, with a group of powerful Irish occultists that had succeeded in invoking the presence of the Morrigan—a goddess of battle from Celtic legend that often appears in the guise of a hooded crow and whose name translates as Phantom Queen. The Morrigan's role in Irish legend is relatively simple: to use magic to cast fetters on warriors and determine who dies on the battlefield and who is spared. I wondered if the crow that crashed through Jon's kitchen window only days earlier was a less than subtle message from the Morrigan that we were going to be its next victims.[3]

The Nine, said Mother Sarah, quoting from the text, would use their powers to create five specific types of Cormon and invoke the fearsome and fearless Morrigan, who would lead them into battle. There would be large and menacing sea beasts that would swim the high seas and terrify anyone who dared approach the British coastline. And if an invading armada were successful in reaching land, similar animals would rear up from the depths of the many lakes and lochs that peppered the country to do battle with the enemy. Deep within the dense woods and forests that covered much of the country at the time, mighty man-beasts (perhaps created out of a collective and subconscious memory of our ancestors, suggested Mother Sarah) would roam and act as guardians of the land. Powerful and fleet of foot, cats would prowl the landscape, spying on the enemy; monstrous dogs with no understanding of fear would engage the foe in mortal combat; and unholy, gargoyle-like creatures would soar across the skies seeking out any evidence of unwelcome visitors.

The Nine were scattered across the length and breadth of the country but came together at a designated time and place to initiate their plans. The exact date was unknown and had been lost to the fog of time. The location, however, was an ancient circle of standing stones on Dartmoor. For weeks, the Nine would sit under the moonlit sky and ingest natural herbs and powerful psychedelics to enhance their psychic skills and to open a doorway to the twilight worlds of the Cormon and the Morrigan. Then something truly disturbing happened: At daybreak on one particular morning, each and every one of the Nine were found slaughtered, hideously mutilated by forces unknown. However, in the days and weeks that followed, evidence began to emerge that their efforts had not been in vain.

Word began to circulate among disciples of the Nine in the populated areas of the country of sightings of giant hairy men, of strange long-necked animals sailing the high seas, of giant cats and dogs that would appear and disappear at will, and of vile-looking winged creatures that could best be described as being half-man and half-bat. The Nine had been successful. They had opened the door to another world. But they had also brought something back with them.

A large and disturbing problem was beginning to rear its head. The deaths of the Nine meant that there was no one to ensure that the Cormons acted according to the wishes of their masters. In other words, Britain was now home to an untold number of unnatural beasts from another realm that had the ability to appear and disappear at will, that were unhindered by the physical world of mere mortals, and that were now rampaging around the countryside, free of whatever restrictions had tied them to their previous plane of existence.

Mother Sarah told us that suspicions had been passed down through the Graymalkin family that the very creatures the Nine had brought into our world were the same ones that had ensured they met a grisly end. Freed from their strange realm of existence where reality was whatever you wanted it to be and where time was a nonexistent factor, the beasts relished the power that their presence in our world gave them.

But, said Mother Sarah, the ability of the creatures to exist in our environment was directly linked with our ability to perceive them. Where we feed on animal, fruit, and vegetable, they feed on emotion: fear, hatred, and love (or whatever we felt for them). This sustains their very being in our world. However, the action that had led to their presence was also the one action that led to their downfall. By killing each and every one of the Nine, the number of people who possessed the psychic ability to see the beasts on a regular basis and in their full glory was drastically cut and the still-surviving and terrified disciples of the Nine took flight, understandably not willing to succumb to the fate of their comrades.

As a result, over time belief in the beasts, and an emotional response to their presence, began to diminish. And as that belief and emotional response to their presence shrunk to the point where they were seen as little more than myths and legends, so their power and presence in our environment diminished also. Thus they became little more than specters without true form, forever doomed to an ethereal existence that tied them to both this world and their own but, paradoxically, to neither.

Mother Sarah continued and stated that this is precisely why, for example, when a sighting occurs today of one of the phantom big cats in England or of Bigfoot in the U.S. Pacific Northwest, there are numerous follow-up encounters. She explained that someone who has latent psychic abilities (whether they are aware of it or not) always makes the initial sighting and that this allows the creatures (which are always around us in some form, at least) to be seen and interact with us to a degree. Indeed, she continued, the creatures actively seek out those with psychic abilities to ensure a strong emotional feeding. And as the beast then feeds on the emotions of the witness—who subsequently gives it added strength and life—its ability to be seen in our world in full physical form is extended. Inevitably this added opportunity for the creature to coexist with us physically for a longer period of time means a greater likelihood of being spotted by others, and by this it gains yet more emotional strength for further encounters.

Thus a cycle is created where one sighting leads to another, belief in the possible existence of the creature is bolstered via the media and word of mouth, the beast secures an ever-increasing foothold in our world as emotions run high, sightings escalate, and the creature's emotional food supply reaches mammoth proportions. In some cases, speculated Mother Sarah, belief may be so strong that some of these creatures (such as the lake monsters of Scotland, Bigfoot, the Yeti, and the phantom felids and devil dogs) have now secured a permanent foothold in our world and can traverse from one plane of existence to another as they seek out their food of the mind.

This was also the reason, according to Mother Sarah, why creatures fitting the classic description of Bigfoot can be seen in absurdly out-of-place locations such as England. But there was more. For reasons that Mother Sarah could not explain, when the beasts were fully sated by their emotional feeding, they would vanish as mysteriously as they had arrived and would then begin the process all over again, perhaps weeks later and in an entirely different location.

"When they get hungry for their next emotional feeding?" I suggested.

"That is correct. That is why sightings of these creatures begin suddenly, continue for weeks at a time, and then come to a halt as mysteriously as they had begun. This is also the reason why investigators of these phenomena find themselves in such bizarre situations. That's also why they—and you—I would be willing to bet, experience a higher degree of synchronicities than most folk."

We nodded silently. "That is because these creatures are using you," Mother Sarah said bluntly. Looking at us with a mixture of pity and scorn, she continued: "You don't realize that while you are looking for these things, believing in them and telling others about them who also become emotionally charged believers, they are manipulating you and your followers as their food source. That is all you are: a source of emotional food for the beasts. That is why people who investigate things such as this have these synchronicities: You are being emotionally manipulated and bled dry by them. You are puppets on a string and that is all you will ever be." Once again, she let out a Harpy-like cackle.

"So, by writing about and investigating these things, we inadvertently cause people to believe in them?" I inquired. "And this belief then gives them the emotional output that they need to live?"

Mother Sarah nodded her head slowly in my direction, and fixed her staring eyes on mine. I pressed on. "But that would mean that reality isn't what we think it is. And if we're being manipulated as part of this emotional feeding on their part, how much else of our reality is being manipulated by them?"

Mother Sarah smiled grimly. "That is the bigger question. Perhaps our entire lives and our whole existence is but a dream or a nightmare created by these emotional parasites and that reality is not what we see around us. Imagine the emotional output throughout the planet on a daily basis: the managing director stuck in a traffic jam on his way to work; the mother pleading with her newborn baby to stop crying; the soldier facing death on the battlefield. The collective emotions of the human species are huge. But just imagine if this is but an image, a mirage of the truth designed to allow these things to bleed us dry. And everyone has experienced synchronicities and coincidences to the extent that they have wondered at some time if there is some hidden force manipulating and driving us." Mother Sarah looked at all three of us closely and carefully. "Perhaps there is," she whispered.

"But if the Cormons were created in Britain," asked Richard, "why are similar creatures seen all around the world?"

"That is simple, boy," Mother Sarah replied. "The Nine were but a small part of a much larger and broader group whose tentacles extended across the planet. I cannot prove it, but there is no doubt in my mind that similar practices to invoke the presence of the Cormons had been going on for centuries before the events in England even began. Yet the result is always the same, and whether the location is Britain, Scandinavia, Africa, South America, or North America, the beasts escape the control of the people who invoke their presence and establish a foothold in our reality that they are unwilling to give up."

Mother Sarah then stood up, came over to me, and put her icy hands on my shoulders. Given the fact that she was hardly a giant in stature and I am six feet two inches tall in my Doc Martens, I found myself looking directly at her yellowed teeth. I could sense Jon trying to edge even farther—if that were possible—into the corner of the couch.

"You're the one that writes the UFO books, aren't you?"

"Yeah, I am."

"And you believe that these things are alien in origin?"

"Well, some I do, yes, or suspect that they are."

"Well, you're wrong, lad. You're wrong, wrong, wrong!" she screamed and laughed in a fashion that bordered upon insanity. As she shook my shoulders vigorously, I saw Jon wipe his sweat-soaked palms on the edge of the couch.

After her manic cackling had subsided and she released her vise-like grip on me, Mother Sarah returned to her seat and continued to berate my belief in aliens. "There are no aliens, none at all, at least not in the sense that you would have it, boy. The aliens of today are no different from the fairies, the elves, and the pixies of yesteryear. Quite simply, the aliens, as you describe them, are but another form of Cormon. In centuries past, they would present themselves in the form of the little folk of the woods. But, again, as time passed and society changed, belief in such creatures diminished—although they are still seen in parts of Cornwall and Devon where acceptance of the old traditions remains. And so, with belief diminishing, society changing, and technology developing, this breed of Cormon recognized that the creation of a new belief system on their part was required for their emotional feeding. And for a civilization that was beginning to venture forth into outer space, there was no better way for the Cormons to present themselves than as the aliens that we were beginning to realize might be out there. It was seen as acceptable by us and, more importantly to the survival and presence of the Cormons, as believable on our part.

"And so, this breed of Cormon, whose presence had for so long waned and existed in a state of semilimbo after the fairy tradition faded, began to become ever more powerful as belief in the alien image and motif increased. Do you know why so many so-called alien abductees are shown images of a destroyed world and a dark and frightening future? It is not because we have aliens among us who are concerned by our warlike ways, as UFO researchers would have us believe. Not at all. They do this because this imagery provokes a strong emotional response from us and this is their nectar.

"Now, do not think that the fact that these are not aliens from the other side of the galaxy means that they are not alien. Far from it. They *are* alien in the true sense of the word, but from a realm that is far closer to home."

"You mentioned that the answers can be found to many of these mysteries in the woods and forests," Richard butted in. "What do you mean by that?"

"The world today is a very sterile one," the witch explained. "But when we venture out into the woods, the forests, the jungles, or anywhere that takes us away from civilization, we are consciously or unconsciously more in tune with the way things were in the old days. And it is in the places where we are away from our technologically filled world and back among the primitive that the Cormons are at their strongest.

"Again, that is why beasts such as Bigfoot are seen in forests: not because that is their natural habitat, but because the primal nature of ancient woodlands and hostile mountain ranges provokes an emotional and primitive response in us that gives these creatures added power. So, they live where they have the greatest ability to feed."

At that moment Mother Sarah clapped her hands, and despite the fact that we had been listening intently to what she had to say, it was—to all three of us—as if we had awakened from some half slumber and we were suddenly thrown back into the real world. I stretched my arms and both Jon and Richard had wide yawns on their faces. The witch grinned maliciously.

"We will eat now," she said.

Jon looked at his watch and I saw a puzzled expression appear on his face. "Have you seen the time?" he said quietly, after Mother Sarah had departed for the kitchen. "It's nearly eight o'clock."

"What?" Richard said. "It can't be!"

"Shit. It is, mate," I replied, showing him my own watch face. "What the hell happened? We can't have sat here that long, surely?"

Jon had a look of concern and fear on his face: "Something's happened."

"What do you mean: Something's happened?" asked Richard, trying to make light of the situation.

"I don't know, Richard, but we are not staying here tonight, I can tell you that. And we are leaving right now, unless, that is, you can account for the fact that we spoke, by my estimation, for about two hours with her and we started at about three o'clock. That should make it around five or five-thirty. Where's the last three hours gone?"

"Oh, no," moaned Richard.

"Let's get out of here," Jon whispered in a shaky voice.

"Now? Just like that?" I asked.

"Come on. Quickly, while she's cooking up whatever the hell she's got in store for us," Jon responded. We reached the door as the wizened old hag returned from the kitchen.

"Oh, leaving are you?" she said in icy and mocking tones. What could we say? We were caught in the act like kids with their hands in the cookie jar. Suddenly Mother Sarah's manner changed and a sense of pure evil filled every inch of the room. "Then get out! Get out now! And don't ever darken my door again! If I see any of ye again, you'll regret it."

We piled out of the door, only stopping for Richard to give her the middle finger.

"You've done it now!" she screamed as we ran down her driveway and toward the Mystery Machine. "You have just guaranteed yourselves a world of pain. Mark my words! The Cormons will come for all of you!" Then, for the last time, she emitted a loud and sinister cackle and slammed the door.

"Get this thing moving!" Jon bellowed as we clambered into the cab and slammed and locked the doors. The rumble of the engine was a welcoming sound. I hit the accelerator and we disappeared into the night and headed back to our refuge on the Carnon Downs. As we departed with a screech from the witch's abode, I emitted a loud laugh and a grinning Richard and I gave each other a high five.

"Nicholas, this is no time for frivolities. And, Richard, giving her the middle finger was not, I fear, a wise move." said a worried Jon. "That woman is very powerful." He rubbed his forehead and said woefully: "We are in for a world of trouble. I know it, I just know it. Dear God, what have we done? What *have* we done? I knew I should have stayed at home. I could be watching *The Simpsons* right now."

"Oh, calm down, mate," I replied. "Anyway, we're having a great adventure. Where's the harm in that?" Inwardly, however, I did wonder if dark forces from some unholy realm were about to be unleashed upon us. I looked at Richard and his grin had vanished; he appeared to have the weight of the world on his shoulders.

To try to restore some semblance of normality to our activities—which were already spiraling wildly out of control and were firmly rooted in the worlds of the bizarre, the surreal, and the nightmarish—we stopped at a public house for much-needed liquid refreshment. We finally reached the Carnon Downs around midnight. By this time we were all truly exhausted and on retiring to our beds, were asleep within minutes. However, during the dark hours I would have a nightmare the like of which I had never had before—or, indeed, since.

In my dream, we were sitting on Mother Sarah's couch, as we had been earlier in the day. Suddenly, I heard Richard say, "I don't feel very well." I looked at him and he was gripping the edge of the couch with his left hand and staring curiously at his right hand as his fingers twitched uncontrollably like some form of rabid, five-headed serpent. Meanwhile, Jon had begun to laugh hysterically and I found myself staring at the carpet as woodland creatures such as foxes and squirrels seemed to come to life out of its fabric, leaping toward me and exploding in a cascade of light and color. We had been drugged and the evil old hag sitting opposite us was the culprit.

"Do ye see them, boys? Do ye see them?" she screamed and wailed as images of animals and strange-looking birds flooded my mind.

"You fucking bitch!" Richard shouted. "What have you done?"

Or *was* he shouting? His words *seemed* real enough, but I had the curious feeling that no one could hear him but me. I then found myself sucked into the depths of the couch, which was mutating into a huge mouth that was itself a bizarre caricature of Mother Sarah's own vile, yellow-toothed orifice. A rushing sound filled my ears, the furniture seemed to change color, the old witch turned into a horrific Harpy-like creature, and I could hear a deep, growling sound coming closer and closer.

By now, I had sunk into the depths of what was undoubtedly a deep hallucinatory state—as had Jon and Richard, it transpired—and

I glimpsed images of shadowy, ape- and catlike figures stalking the darkest corners of the room. I could hear vague and unintelligible voices shouting, and the rhythmic pounding of a drumbeat came closer and closer.

The image of an ancient English fertility goddess known as Sheila-Na-Gig filled my mind and suddenly the room had vanished and before me was a huge forest filled with luscious trees, bushes, and plants. I could see deer and wild boar in a clearing and the outline of a large, lumbering bipedal creature crashing through the thick trees at a distance of around seventy feet. Why, I do not know, but I had the impression that I had been transported back to tenth-century England and I was somewhere within the depths of a vast forest in what is now rural Kent.

The remainder of the dream is lost to me and aside from a few puzzling and fragmentary recollections of seeing an ancient stone circle, I can remember nothing else of what seemed to be an eternity of experiences. In a situation akin to waking up after a particularly heavy dose of anesthetic, or a night on the town, it took what appeared to be a lifetime for us to return to normality. Mother Sarah still sat on the couch, cackling maniacally as my senses began to return. Jon, no doubt due to the fact that his bulky frame was far bigger than mine, had begun to recover quicker and Richard had vomited on the carpet and was leaning against the couch on his hands and knees.

"I'm gonna kill you," I whispered in deadly and shaking tones.

"Are ye now? Are ye really?" Mother Sarah said with a sinister chuckle in her voice as she leapt to her feet in a style that surprised me, given how grossly fat she was. "You wanted to see them and you saw them!" she screamed. "Now get out of my house, all of ye! And if I ever see any of ye again, worse is to come!"

Still not in full possession of our faculties, we struggled to make our way to the front door, cursing the old witch in the process and lashing out in all directions with our boots and fists. Furniture and ornaments crashed to the floor and we staggered through the door into what was a warm afternoon. The oppressive atmosphere at once began to lift and we slowly made our unsteady way toward the Mystery Machine. Not surprisingly, none of us were in the mood to talk and we all found ourselves fighting a sudden and all-powerful urge to sleep. I was able to drive for around ten minutes at the most and after I clumsily brought the vehicle to a standstill in a picnic area, it was all that we could then do to crawl into the back of the camper.

It was then, at around two o'clock in the morning, that I awoke in a cold sweat from my tortured slumber. I scanned the camper quickly, realizing that it had all been a dream. I resisted the urge to wake Jon and Richard and decided that my weird experience could wait until morning. That is, if morning ever comes, I thought.

Fortunately, morning *did* arrive. After washing, dressing, and embracing the fresh morning air and the rising sun, at 8:00 A.M. we headed for a little tea room that was a regular stopping-point for Jon when he was in the area. We ordered three platefuls of food: eggs, bacon, fried bread, sausages, tomatoes and mushrooms, three pots of tea, and a large glass of freshly squeezed orange juice each. An hour later, refreshed and thoroughly refueled, we were ready to continue with our quest. Our next stop was the ancient town of Glastonbury where we were due to meet a man who had seen a gargoyle and who claimed to know the location of the beast's lair.

It was once again a hot and sunny day and we drove with the windows open and the CD player cranked up high. After forty-five minutes of being tortured by Jon's Scott Walker and Cat Stevens CDs, Richard and I could take no more and their wailings were replaced by the chanting of Joey Ramone. "Gabba, gabba, we accept you, we accept you, one of us," cried Joey, just before the electric buzz of guitarist Johnny Ramone's distorted chords kicked in. It was summer, our bellies were full, and the Ramones were blasting their classic tune, "Pinhead," out of the CD player. It doesn't get much better than that.

As we headed for Glastonbury, I told Jon and Richard of my strange dream during the previous night. Richard thought that it sounded like great fun. Jon was more than a little perturbed, to say the least.

"Nicky, I don't know what happened in that room and I don't know what prompted your dream, but we *did* lose three hours somewhere." Jon looked at us both. "You *do* know that, don't you?"

Despite the fact that we were trying to make light of the situation, Richard and I *were* aware that something unusual had occurred at Mother Sarah's. Had we been drugged or perhaps hypnotized in some fashion by someone who followed the teachings of the witches and wizards of old? If so, no lasting harm seemed to have been done, so we pressed on.

As we drove to Glastonbury we discussed the fact that in many ways Mother Sarah's story paralleled that of Robert Holdstock in his fantasy novel, *Mythago Wood*. The book tells how, after the end of the Second World War, one Steve Huxley is brought back to the U.K. upon the news that his father has died. George Huxley had devoted his life to the exploration of the ancient Ryhope Wood that backed up against the family home and kept detailed records of his research into the woods. But Ryhope Wood was unlike any other. It was inhabited by "mythagos," creatures and characters from British folklore and mythology, such as Robin Hood and King Arthur. As with the Cormons, the existence of the mythagos was tied directly to the imaginations and minds of those who pursued them and came into contact with them.[4] The truth, it seemed, was, at the very least, as strange as fiction.

As we continued our journey, and the now late and lamented Joey Ramone sang in the background about mental illness, lost love, cretins, and lobotomies, Richard revealed to me that several years previously he had had his own run-in with a Tulpa. What began as a joke, however, mutated into something far stranger. It was the summer of 1997 and Richard was at the time a student at Leeds University, where he was studying for a degree in zoology. Unlike Alexandra David-Neel, who elected to try to conjure up a Tulpa in the form of a jolly monk, however, Richard had set his sights on creating . . . a giant spider!

At a house party, he and his student friends merrily constructed, in the building's cellar, an altar to Athlac-Nacha, the grotesque spider-god invented in the 1930s by horror writer Clark Ashton-Smith. The singular fact that this hideous entity had never existed outside of Ashton-Smith's dark imagination was of little or no concern to Richard and his friends and they decorated the altar with strange and arcane artifacts, erecting a huge cloth spider's web in the middle of which they placed a mechanical toy spider. Then, being students, they did what some would say students do best: They got uproariously drunk. Alcohol and toy spiders aside, there *was* a serious aspect to this.

Over the next few days the group meditated in front of the altar and visualized in their minds and imaginations a huge, glowing spider. Incredibly, after a few weeks something truly unusual happened. Richard entered the cellar where they had built the altar, and was startled and more than a little horrified to see silhouetted against the darkness of the cellar wall the image of nothing less than a huge spider. It appeared white against a black background ("like a photographic negative," said Richard) and moved along with his gaze as he turned his attention to the other walls of the cellar. Richard edged slowly up the stairs, out of the cellar and slammed the door behind him. He did not see the eight-legged beast again. But the story does not end there.

During the latter part of the summer and the early autumn of 1997, a plague of large spiders occurred across Leeds. Concerned citizens who were worried that the spiders might be poisonous foreign immigrants took a number of specimens to the Environmental Health Office. Much to the relief of everyone, they turned out to be nothing more than spiders common to the area that had grown to a large size as a result of the hot summer weather.

But then, shortly afterward, an employee of a well-known firm of fruit importers, in nearby Wakefield, was bitten by a giant spider as he was unpacking a case of bananas. He was rushed to hospital where he was told that there was no antivenin available and that the only way of finding out whether the animal that had bitten him was poisonous or not was by seeing if he was still alive eight hours later! He did indeed survive the ordeal unscathed, but the man was determined to exact revenge and planned to take legal action against his employers.

While the man's plan ultimately proved fruitless, Richard had taken more than a passing interest in these events and hatched an ingenious plot to claim responsibility not just for the plague of giant spiders that had descended upon Leeds but also for the presence of the tropical spider at the warehouse.

Jon, having been informed of Richard's plan, and never one to miss the opportunity to make himself some money out of a bizarre and outlandish situation, offered to try to sell the tale to the national press. The movers and shakers on Fleet Street loved it. And were it not for the fact that a tedious story involving one of the Spice Girls burst forth at precisely the same time, the country would have woken up the next day to images in their newspapers of Richard and a spectacularly attractive Goth chick (dressed in a long black robe and wielding a ritualistic sword) standing beneath a giant mechanical spider. Goth Apologizes for Spider Plague was the planned headline for the story-that-never-was. And to this day, Richard continues to curse the fact that he was beaten to the winning post by the mighty selling-power of Scary, Posh, Sporty, Ginger, and Baby.[5]

Of course, in reality, Richard's connection to the whole affair was tenuous at best, but he was genuinely spooked by the apparitional appearance of the huge spider and to this day believes that he and his friends *did* succeed in creating a Tulpa-like entity—albeit briefly. But that was not Richard's only exposure to the world of the Tulpa.

As I mentioned earlier, for years Jon had been pursuing a devilish entity known as the Owlman that was rumored to haunt the woods and burial ground of Mawnan Old Church in darkest Cornwall. Described by witnesses (mostly young girls, curiously) as an unholy combination of man and owl, with hindsight the beast sounded not unlike the grotesque, batlike gargoyles that Mother Sarah asserted had been summoned up from the realm of the Cormons by the Nine a millennium ago. And every time Jon immersed himself in the mystery of the Owlman he would find himself plagued by disaster, misery, and misfortune (which suggested that Mother Sarah's claim that the Cormons could manipulate the human species to create high and distressing emotional states that they could then feed upon, was correct). Nevertheless, and by his own admission, Jon couldn't and wouldn't let the matter drop.

As a result, in 2000, Richard, Jon, and several other colleagues, including a fellow by the name of Phil who insisted on being referred to as (and dressing as a) "Jester," headed out to Mawnan Woods for a midnight encounter with the creature. Richard, in the guise of Muzzlehutch the magician, was to summon up the Owlman. In his notes written up later, Richard recalled what happened next.

The elements were called on once more. Their visual embodiments are different according to what is being summoned. Instead of the four dragons of the four quarters I called upon winged humanoids from differing cultures. The north was the *Skovman*, a form of Scandinavian elf that could take the form of a giant owl. The east was the *Tengu* of Japan, grotesque bird demons. The south was *Popobwa*, a bat-winged baboon that anally rapes sleeping men in the folklore of Zanzibar. The west was *Mothman*, the red-eyed, winged horror that terrorized Point Pleasant, Virginia in the 1960s. Into a silver brazier of hot coals I poured a mixture of certain herbs and oils. An ugly red cloud of foul-smelling gas billowed up like an Arabian genie. I snorted in its noxious vapor and began to rant like a madman speaking in tongues. Jester capered about the circle as I brayed my incantations. His presence had twin purpose: As a jester, he was the embodiment of chaos, without which order is totally impotent. He also reflected the essentially absurd nature of the ritual, the phenomenon, and the universe in general. I bid the beating of wings to come galumphing from the inky branches. Yet even as the verbal deluge poured from my lips like tallow from a candle, I knew the most important component of the spell was missing—there were no young women present.

As we drove along the winding roads of Devon, Jon continued the story: "After Richard had finished his ritual, we left Jester there for the night and when he returned to us in Exeter a few days later he told us how his dreams had been bedeviled with strange winged entities and how at one point during the long, cold night he had felt something strange and heavy clinging onto his back.

"During the next few months we received more reports of sightings from the Cornish woods—they were mostly inconclusive, but three or four groups of young women reported seeing strange, gray feathered objects fluttering around through the upper branches of the trees above them.

"But I should have known better," said Jon with more than a tinge of sadness and regret in his voice as he recalled the phenomenal run of bad luck, death, and personal tragedy that bedeviled him in the summer of 2000 and that was only broken following a nine-hour ritual that Jon and Richard (together with two very powerful witches from Yorkshire) took part in on New Year's Day 2001. As a result, said Jon, he was willing to investigate the many and varied beasts of the U.K. during the course of our six-week expedition, but the Owlman, he said, was strictly out of bounds.

"I cannot go down that path again," he said firmly. "If there is even the slightest inkling that this thing at Glastonbury and the Owlman are related, then we leave it well alone." And so it was that we made our tentative way in search of the Glastonbury gargoyle.

10

THE SKY BEAST

Now, I got glowing eyes.

"PSYCHO THERAPY," THE RAMONES

Glastonbury is a strange town, one that you either love or hate. Personally, I love it. The area is steeped in ancient tradition, myths, and legends, and appears curiously out of time with the rest of England. Walking along the old streets of Glastonbury is a notable experience, too. Strung-out hippies with thin dogs tied to pieces of string adorn the area and colorful stores, selling all manner of things magickal and mysterious, dominate the High Street. Centuries-old buildings rise up from every corner of the town, old taverns stand relatively unchanged for hundreds of years and the surrounding rich and green countryside creates a feeling of familiar—yet ancient and equally unfamiliar—well-being.

A phenomenon that cannot fail to mesmerize one and all on their first sighting of it is Glastonbury's 500-foot-high Tor, which dates back 5,000 years. Was it a center for fertility rites based on legends of the great Mother Earth Goddess, as some believe? Or was it the site of King Arthur's fabled Avalon?

According to ancient myth, Avalon, named after the demigod Avalloc or Avallach, who ruled the Underworld, was the meeting place of the dead and the location where they would pass from one realm of existence to another. Notably the Tor was also the alleged abode of Gwyn ap Nudd, the Lord of the Underworld, and a place where the little folk, such as the fairies of old, lived.

It is widely believed that locating the legendary Holy Grail that Joseph of Arimathea is said to have hidden in Glastonbury, was the driving force that lay behind the famous quests of King Arthur and the Knights of the Round Table. Indeed, Glastonbury has been linked with Arthur, the legendary English king who was reputedly raised by the wizard Merlin, on numerous occasions. As a boy, and after many had tried and failed, Arthur succeeded to the throne by withdrawing the magical sword Excalibur from a stone. Moreover, according to legend, it was in the graveyard of Glastonbury Abbey, and south of the Lady Chapel beneath two huge pillars, that Arthur was laid to rest after his death.

Legend further asserts that following the death of the mighty Arthur, a powerful spirit haunted the ruins of the Abbey, appearing to one and all as a black-armored knight with glowing red eyes, who was possessed of an overwhelming wish to destroy any and all records of the ancient legends of Arthur. That, so the story goes, is why those seeking to discover the truth find their quest fruitless.[1] And it was against this backdrop of mythology, folklore, legend, and history, which, to this day, continues to dominate the town of Glastonbury, that the next leg of our quest began.

I had been to Glastonbury on numerous occasions and for the best part of a decade, sometimes for a well-earned break and to escape from the madness of the real world, and sometimes to hang out at the offices of the now sadly defunct magazine, *UFO Reality*. But this occasion was quite different. The three of us were due to meet a man who had told Jon quite a strange story in a brief telephone conversation two weeks previously. The man claimed to have been digging deeply into aspects of the Arthurian legends and had, as a result, awakened from its slumber a horrific and menacing gargoyle-like creature with glowing red eyes that he was sure was somehow linked with his research. So the stories of the ghostly, red-eyed, armored knight might just have a basis in fact, I thought.

We had arrived two days early for our appointment with Colin

Perks (that, in one of those synchronicities that seemed to forever plague us, was also the name of a police constable who was involved in a famous UFO incident in 1966 that was investigated by the British Ministry of Defense) and so had forty-eight hours to ourselves. Jon spent the days chilling out in Glastonbury's Chalice Well Gardens and recovering his composure after the tumultuous events at the home of Mother Sarah Graymalkin. Meanwhile, Richard and I scoured the stores for all manner of weird and wonderful artifacts that had more than a passing link with the dark side. We arranged to meet together again at 7:00 on the second night at the Who'd a Thought It Inn on Northload Street, that was barely a two-minute walk from the Abbey. At seven precisely we strolled through the door of the Inn's lounge bar and there was Jon, comfortably seated and surrounded by three little old ladies, who he was taking much delight in scaring half to death with tales of his monster-hunting activities.

"My boys," cried Jon as he put his Popeye-like arms around the shoulders of his new octogenarian friends. Richard and I smiled at each other: Jon had his trusty monocle firmly wedged in his left eye. He duly motioned us over. Pleasantries exchanged and explanations given as to why Jon insisted on referring to us at every opportunity as his boys ("Well, that's what they are," he cheerfully said), we all sat and drank for thirty minutes and discussed the Loch Ness Monster. After having downed a couple of whiskies and two pints of powerful lager in that time, however, Richard and I began a dark and disturbing conversation that centered upon the contents of another of his much-loved magazines, *Fighting Girls Monthly*, and one that was not really appropriate for churchgoing ladies of any age.

To our surprise, however, they found Richard's love for, and admiration of, the world of the dominatrix to be most amusing and enthralling. For the next forty-five minutes we were in a truly surreal situation where Richard held court and reeled off, with much fondness, tale after tale (increasingly exaggerated as time passed and more alcohol was consumed) about his sexual adventures while hunting for giant snakes in Thailand in 2000. Accompanying him was a team from the Discovery Channel and "a gorgeous bird who gave me the beating of my life." By 9:15 P.M., the little old ladies had departed, chuckling and whispering to themselves as they went. "This is only adieu," I cried as they exited the door and we all laughed loudly.

By this time, the alcohol intake had reached ridiculous proportions—even for us—and we decided that there was no point in trying to plan a course of action for the following day. It was all we could do to plan a course of action to the bar. And so as the bell rang for final orders we ordered a round of double whiskies and lager, chugged them down, headed into the cool and calm evening, and began our fifteen-minute walk to the Mystery Machine. "Hooray for the three chums!" shouted Jon as he whirled around drunkenly in the middle of Glastonbury High Street, before toppling to the ground in an alcohol-soaked haze and an almighty crash. The remainder of the night was a blur but, thankfully, the next day we awoke to find that we had successfully negotiated our way back to the camper. "Will someone please get me some aspirin?" wailed Jon as he poked his head out of his blanket at 6:00 the following morning.

⁛ ⁛ ⁛

Colin Perks was a frightened man. Of that much we were certain. We had arranged to meet with Perks at the Who'd a Thought It Inn at midday. He had told Jon what he looked like and locating him in the lounge bar proved to be a simple task. With a mane of long red hair pulled back tightly into a ponytail, ragged beard, thick glasses and dressed in a simple suit and tie, he reminded me of one of my old college professors. "Hippie," I said quietly and with venom and scorn in my voice as we spied Perks from across the room and walked over to him.

We approached the table and Perks ushered us to sit. With introductions out of the way and four pints of lager ordered, Perks told us his remarkable tale. Even before he began, it was clear to us that he was greatly troubled. His right leg shook nervously the entire time we were there; he constantly fidgeted with his hair, with his fingers, with everything. He chain-smoked for the duration, looked distinctly haggard in appearance and had a continuous quiver in his voice.

"You have to help me," Perks said quietly and almost pleadingly after nervously scanning the room.

"Then you'd better tell us what this is all about, hadn't you?" I replied, putting the ball back firmly in his court.

For a moment, Perks stared at us and then continued. "I've been interested in the Arthurian legends for years." He proceeded to tell us how for more than two decades he had been both carefully and quietly keeping out of the limelight and away from the more well-known members of the Arthurian research community as he spent all of his free time researching the old legends. What had begun as a quest to locate the remains of the fabled Arthur, however, had mutated into something very different.

Perks brought out from underneath the table a large and worn leather briefcase that, as he opened it, we could see contained a huge amount of papers and notes that he duly positioned in front of us on the table. He picked up various thin piles that were held together with paper clips and let us briefly peruse them. There was no doubting the scope of his work. Perks had journeyed throughout the country chasing down every possible lead in his quest to locate the remains of King Arthur.

As he explained, and as all three of us already knew, the theories concerning the alleged burial site of Arthur were as numerous and as varied as the theories concerning the final resting place of Noah's Ark and the location of the legendary island of Atlantis. Perks also showed us countless photographs that he had taken of old burial sites, stone circles, and ancient mounds around England that he believed were in fact subtle clues or signposts that pointed in the direction of King Arthur's remains. At that point Perks became extremely paranoid. He said that while he would not reveal to us where he believed Arthur was buried (which was fine with us, as we had more than enough on our plate already), he wanted our help in bringing to an end a dark and disturbing series of events that had begun some months previously.

During his investigations in October of 2000, he had received a bizarre and cryptic telephone call from a woman who wanted to meet with him to discuss his investigations of the Arthurian legends. This perturbed him, Perks said, because he had no family and aside from several close friends, very few people (if, indeed, *anyone*) knew of his passion. But as this woman evidently *did* know, he agreed to speak with her. A meeting was duly arranged for the following evening. At 7:00 P.M. sharp, there was a loud knock at his door.

On opening it, Perks was confronted by what he said was certainly the most beautiful woman he had ever met in his life. She was around six feet tall, with long and luxuriant flowing black hair, porcelain skin, and dressed in an expensive black suit. The woman, who was about forty, identified herself as Miss Sarah Key. Perks ushered her into his living room.

"Mr. Perks," she began, "I and several of my colleagues have followed your research closely these last few years."

"That's rubbish," he replied quickly. "I've published nothing and spoken to virtually no one. If you know anything about me, you'll know that I keep myself to myself and that's how I like it."

"Nevertheless," she said, smiling, "I *do* know all about you." Perks told us that she then astonished him by reeling off detail after detail about his quest and displayed intimate knowledge of where he was on particular dates, which stone circles and burial mounds he had visited and when, and left him in no doubt that, while he knew nothing about Sarah Key, she knew a great deal about him. Perks demanded to know what all of this cloak-and-dagger nonsense was about.

"Quite simply, Mr. Perks, you have all the clues that you need in your quest. In fact, you are so close yet so glaringly unaware of it that in some ways it amuses us," she added.

"Us?" he replied nervously.

"Yes. Us."

Key continued that she represented the interests of a number of people within the British government and the ruling establishment who had an interest in certain aspects of Perks's research. Her tone, which had previously been that of detached amusement, suddenly changed. "I am here to give you a friendly warning," she said. "No one on the outside has come as close as you have to finding the answers," she explained. "We already have those answers and we know that we cannot act upon our knowledge."

"What do you mean?" asked Perks, genuinely puzzled by the cryptic words of the mysterious Miss Key.

"At the height of the Second World War," Key said, "there were those within certain corridors of power in the British establishment who were looking for an antidote to Adolf Hitler's proposed use of the occult. Make no mistake, British Intelligence *has* undertaken exhaustive studies of the occult. Not necessarily because the people doing the studies are believers but because, simply, if the enemy is looking into something, then so must we.

"But to their surprise," Key continued, "they found that among the nonsense and the lies there existed a very real and very frightening power that, if it fell into the wrong hands, could wreak havoc across the planet and even lead to Armageddon and Judgment Day. The key to this power was found in a complex series of codes and ciphers that are hidden among numerous ancient sites and locations across the country. In some cases the clues are in the positioning of the stones, in others they can be found in ancient artifacts buried beneath them, and other answers can be found in the names of the places themselves. Put the clues together and you possess all that you need to summon up undreamed of power that in the right hands could work wonders and in the wrong hands could kill us all. You, Mr. Perks, have identified all of the relevant clues. British Intelligence realized half a century ago, and has hidden the facts ever since, what you are now on the verge of discovering. The answers elude you and we like that. That is how it has to be. But mark my words: If you persist and continue we will come down hard on you."

Perks stared at Key in silence as she drew the conversation to a close: "Again, Mr. Perks, you cannot begin to understand the enormity of what stands before you. That is why I am visiting you and not . . . someone else. If you continue and don't let this matter drop, that someone *will* come calling—believe me. And *that* you will *not* want."

Key stood up and headed for the door. "That's about it, Mr. Perks. You've done well, but don't go snooping anymore. What you are on the verge of uncovering is the gateway to another world. And you do not want to know what is there, believe me. And we do not want you to open that gateway. Go out and enjoy yourself and put all of this behind you. If you persist, though, you *will* receive another visitor and things will then be out of our control." Miss Key turned and vanished into the night as mysteriously as she had arrived.

And as Perks continued with his story we finally realized why he had sought us out. He had snubbed the wishes of Sarah Key and pressed on with his research. And then, as Miss Key had warned, a visitor *did* arrive. But it was not some dark-suited entity from the government. It was at around 9:00 P.M. in early November 2000 when Perks was driving home from the city of Bath along a moonlit stretch of road. His was the only vehicle on the road, he said. Suddenly he saw standing in the middle of the road and at a distance of about two hundred feet what looked like a tall man. He slowed his car and to his horror saw that it was no man. Rather, it was a hideous creature that Perks could only describe as a gargoyle.

Around seven feet in height and pale-skinned, it had thin and almost emaciated limbs. Attached to its arms and upper body were two large and leathery wings that reminded Perks of a giant bat. As his headlights struck the creature, he could see that its bones shone through its legs and appeared almost hollow. But most horrific of all was the creature's head: bald and with two large and pointed ears, its glowing, red eyes stared at him. An evil grin crossed its hook-nosed face and appeared to mock him, while two large fangs extended down from a wide and black-tongued mouth.

He was not, said Perks, about to stop, and drove straight at the creature. Like a true specter, it vanished into thin air at the moment of impact. He raced home and to the safety of his bed. For a week all was normal. Then during the early-morning hours of November 14, 2000, he suddenly awoke from his sleep and looming over his bed was the same hellish beast. The creature bent close and he could feel its foul breath on his face. He gagged and tried to move but was utterly paralyzed. Its arms suddenly grabbed his wrists and the creature straddled him, pinning him tightly to the bed.

"You were told that I would come," it rumbled in a deep voice. Perks informed us that he felt that he was on the verge of having a heart attack; and as well as being unable to move his vocal cords had also completely seized up. At that point the glow that extended from the beast's eyes grew ever brighter and it brought its face even closer to Perks. Suddenly Perks understood the scheme of things.

In what he could only describe in layman's terms as telepathy, Perks was told that he was in danger of compromising the gateway, the entrance point to a nightmarish world full of all manner of unnatural creatures, which, once opened, could not be closed again. If Perks continued with his work and succeeded (albeit inadvertently, since his intent was not to open doorways of any kind but to simply uncover the true resting place of King Arthur), a host of unparalleled catastrophes would befall England and the world, the like of which had never been seen before. He was further informed that the gateway and the resting place of Arthur were one and the same. The spirit of Arthur and those of his mighty warriors, Perks was told, acted as guardians between our world and this hellish location and prevented the nightmarish creatures from breaking free. However, in the physical plane, this gargoyle-like creature alone had the power to act. It was a disciple of the ancient kings of England and its sole function was to prevent anyone from upsetting the delicate balance that existed by inadvertently opening the gate if they had sufficient knowledge of how to do so—as Perks was coming dangerously close to possessing.

"Go no further," the gargoyle whispered in his ear before vanishing in a flash and amid an overwhelming stench of brimstone.

Needless to say, after hearing that story we were ready for another round of beer. Or two. We related to Perks our experience with Mother Sarah and the tale of the Cormons. Jon suggested that while there was good evidence to suggest that the witch's account of how the Cormons could be summoned up and let loose in the form of spectral big cats, man-beasts, ghostly black dogs, and lake monsters was genuine, Perks's tale offered another component to the story.

"This suggests to me," Jon said, "that while the Cormons have to be summoned to give them a semblance of reality in our environment, the existence of this doorway might mean that, if opened, there would be no need for the initial summoning to occur, as happened with the Nine and elsewhere on the planet. Now, we know from Mother Sarah that these creatures could come and go from our world to theirs after being summoned, but imagine if, when this doorway was opened, it allowed all the other beasts, or God knows what they are, to come through without an invite, so to speak. Can you imagine a planet that is home to not just a few hundred spectral creatures such as those seen occasionally today but one teeming with these things and all feeding on us as their prey?" We silently digested the horrific imagery that this dark theory conjured up.

Jon then went on to describe to Perks his own experiences with the very similar Owlman of Mawnan Woods and how calamity after calamity had fallen upon Jon when he delved deeper and deeper into the story. "But it's good that you've learned your lesson," said Jon to Perks. "Leaving all this gateway nonsense alone is the best thing you can do, believe me."

Perks looked at all three of us and fear spread across his face: "But that's it: I haven't left it alone."

"What?" Jon said as a sudden look of concern appeared upon his face.

"I haven't left it alone," Perks replied quietly.

"You bloody idiot," I said.

"I know," he said, holding his head in his hands. "I kept on and on and I know now what the gateway is and how to open it and—"

"Stop right there! Stop now!" shouted Jon. "I do not want to know and neither do Richard and Nick. If you tell us, you will condemn us to a visit from this gargoyle thing." Jon added firmly, "I am telling you: Stop this madness now."

Perks told us that he wanted to stop but feared that he had gone too far. Now, he added, he was seeing the gargoyle all the time. He would walk along the streets of Glastonbury at night and see the elongated shadows of the creature's form as it leapt silently across the rooftops, forever pursuing him. Out of the corner of his eye he would spy its evil face and glowing eyes peering menacingly at him from behind old doorways and amid the shadows of the town's darkened alleyways. He would hear the padding of its feet in his home during the night and the heavy beat of its leathery wings would ring in his ears as it soared overhead. Perks also told us that he knew the location of the beast's lair.

"Help me stop it, please. Make it stop," he whispered, almost crying.

"What do we do?" asked Richard.

"We can go to the lair or we can leave him here right now," I replied.

"No!" shouted Perks, genuinely alarmed.

"No, we can't do that," added Jon. "This half-wit has done damage that must be brought to a halt." He looked at Perks. "This lair: Where is it?"

Perks had business to attend to for the remainder of the day and evening—at least he *said* that he had business to attend to. So for us it was another night of merriment in the Who'd a Thought It and a day spent perusing the stores, the Chalice Well Gardens, and the ancient Tor. But at 11:30 the following night, the four of us were crammed into the front of the Mystery Machine as we headed for our next port of call: a small piece of woodland, perhaps a half-mile square, some twenty miles from Glastonbury.

"So, how do you know that this is where it lives?" I asked.

"I can't explain it, but it was as if I were being drawn there by the thing and I would see this place in my dreams and was even told the location," Perks replied.

"And why does it want you there?" inquired Richard.

"It wants to slaughter me," Perks replied in a voice filled with pure dread and fear.

"*What?*" screamed Jon. "You're taking us on a journey where we might find ourselves ripped to pieces by this thing in the middle of the night? You cannot be serious!"

Perks looked at Jon in a fashion that, we all knew, meant he was very serious. Fifteen minutes later we arrived. The woods were approximately half a mile away and on the other side of a farmer's field.

"God almighty, this is all taking me back to that bloody werewolf hunt thirty years ago," said a worried Jon, as we exited the vehicle and proceeded carefully across the field. The woods on the other side were extremely dense; even the bright moon seemed to be blotted out by its thick foliage and massive trees. The ground crunched under our feet and woodland animals could be heard scurrying—at least, we thought that they were woodland animals.

"Have you been here before?" asked Richard.

"Only to the edge of the road," replied Perks. "This is the first time that I've actually come into the woods. But I know it's in here somewhere."

"How reassuring," Jon said in sarcastic tones. "Help!" he shouted suddenly. I spun wildly and fully expected to be confronted by the closest thing to a demon you could possibly imagine. Instead, I found myself looking down at Jon as he rolled on the floor like a beached Moby Dick after tripping over a fallen branch. "Mother of God, get me up," he said. Jon may have had the misfortune to find himself flat on his back, but for Richard and me it was a moment of light relief.

"Now, will you take that monocle out of your eye?" I said, after Richard and I struggled to bring Jon to an upright position. "No one can see it out here, no one's impressed by it, and you'll only end up blinding yourself."

"Very well," he grumbled.

"Now what?" Richard asked.

"I guess we wait for it to come out of its lair," I suggested.

We sat on a fallen tree trunk in a clearing and the bright moon illuminated us. Jon said, "You know, I really don't like the use of that word."

"What word?" I asked.

"Lair," he said. "It conjures up precisely the image I'm trying to get out of my mind. Couldn't we talk about it having a pleasant little shelter instead of a lair?"

"Look—" said Richard, before being interrupted by a large shadow that suddenly covered the moon.

"No!" cried Perks, who jumped to his feet and began blindly running ever farther into the dense woods.

"For God's sake! It's just a cloud!" shouted Richard. We all looked up and sure enough, a cloud is all it was.

"Now, where's that stupid bastard gone?" I added. Perks was nowhere to be seen or heard. "Come on. We'd better go and find him." Despite the fact that the woods were relatively small, it was easy to become lost within their depths at the witching hour as the only light source available to us was coming from the moon.

"Where's the night-scope?" asked Richard.

"In the back of the camper," said Jon sheepishly.

"And what about the flashlight?" I asked.

"That's there, too," Jon replied.

"Great," Richard shot back. "Just great."

Ten minutes later, after trying to find our way through the tangled trees, we heard a disturbance ahead of us and there was Perks, running in our direction. "Go, go, go!" he screamed as he sailed past us at full speed, his arms swinging wildly in the air.

"What?" Jon shouted behind him.

"The gargoyle!" Perks was lost to sight in an instant and was racing back across the field. We looked at each other and even without words passing our lips we knew what the other was thinking. We pressed on with pounding hearts and went ever deeper into the woods. If there was a living, breathing gargoyle in there, we were going to find it. At a distance of about thirty feet, something seemed to flash through the trees as a break in the clouds cast the moon down on the scene before us.

"That way!" shouted Richard and the two of us hurtled onward as Jon's bulky frame wheezed and groaned behind us like an aging and arthritic bull elephant. But after about three hundred feet of running through dense foliage and trees, we suddenly found ourselves on the other side of the woods and facing a wide expanse of fields.

"It must have doubled back," I said to Richard as we caught our breath. Without a word we raced back the way we came and ran headlong into Jon, which sent the three of us sprawling to the ground.

"For God's sake! Not again!" Jon bellowed as for the second time in two minutes he was making friends with terra firma.

"Can you get back to the camper?" I asked Jon quickly, as Richard and I once again fought valiantly to raise his bulbous form from the ground. After he nodded in the affirmative, Richard and I were off again, running breathlessly through the trees and using every available bit of light to seek out our quarry. Thirty seconds or so later, we realized that we were looking for the beast in entirely the wrong place. This was not a man. It was a gargoyle—with wings. We turned our attention from the darkened scene in front of us and scanned the thirty-foot-high treetops. Only seventy-five feet or so away, the treetops were shaking vigorously. *Or were being shaken.* We plunged on through the trees, but as we arrived we were surrounded by nothing except for an eerie and all-dominating silence. The presence had gone.

Nevertheless, we continued to scour the woods for another hour or so, but by 1:30 A.M., having found nothing, we gave up and headed back to the Mystery Machine, where Jon and Perks—the wretched cause of all this bizarreness—sat drinking tea and whisky.

"Did you see it?" Jon pressed as Richard and I came running over.

"Well, we saw something in the trees, but . . ." Richard's words trailed off.

"Yeah," I added, filling my lungs with air, "I don't know what it was but *something* was in there."

"Bloody hell," said Jon quietly, realizing that perhaps we really *had* been in the presence of something truly monstrous. Or were we just spooked by an owl? Who knows? Perks sat silent, a look of shock on his pale and wide-eyed face. For two more nights we returned to the woods but neither saw nor heard anything unusual. But on the third night, Jon had an idea.

It was roughly the same time when we arrived—around 11:30 or 11:45 P.M. "Richard," said Jon, "what about trying to lay this madness to rest as we did last New Year with the Owlman? Can you do that?" Perks stared at Richard.

"I can do that." Richard replied calmly.

Ten minutes later he was heading into the woods on his own,

ready to face whatever was out there. Richard had insisted on going alone and said that the solitude would grant him a greater opportunity to commune with the beast and bring the accursed business to a close. It was not until 3:00 A.M. that Richard finally returned. We asked him what happened.

According to Richard, he lay down in the damp grass in the same clearing where we had been three nights previously, closed his eyes and began to recite over and again a series of words that had been passed on to him by a powerful witch friend, words that were designed for summoning up supernatural forces. For more than an hour nothing happened. However, at approximately 1:15 A.M. Richard felt the presence of something large and terrifying and visualized a large pair of glowing red eyes snaking through the trees. He did not dare open his own eyes, he said, for fear of breaking the vision.

An impression formed in Richard's mind of the creature and he knew that it was casting judgment upon Perks but sensed that the gargoyle was not hostile to the three of us. Richard projected a question: If Perks could be convinced to cease his work and destroy his notes, would the monstrous apparitions cease and could Perks be allowed to return to the normal world? A sense of calm overcame Richard and he took this as a sign that the answer was yes. He opened his eyes and was confronted by only trees. For another ninety minutes or so Richard stayed deep within the woods, winding down after his intense concentration and communion.

"You're very, very lucky," Richard said to Perks as he returned. "Destroy your notes. Destroy everything. And leave all this alone. Now." Perks nodded without a word.

"Okay, let's get back," said Jon and we headed back for the town of Glastonbury. We dropped Perks off at his home and he promised that he would do as Richard had suggested. We said our good-byes and drove out of darkened Glastonbury at 4:15 A.M., leaving behind its myriad secrets and legends.

Two weeks later, however, Jon would receive a call on his mobile telephone from a mutual friend in the UFO research community who was investigating the sighting of a "black hang glider" seen near

Glastonbury Tor late the previous evening. But we knew better. That was no hang glider. It was our winged friend faithfully and forever scouring the landscape and ensuring that the doorway to the unknown remained firmly closed.

Intriguingly, Colin Perks was not the only person fascinated with the Arthurian legends of Glastonbury and to whom strange and diabolical creatures had manifested. Dion Fortune, whose real name was Violet Mary Firth, was born in Bryn-y-Bia near Llandudno, Wales, on December 6, 1890. To this day, many students of the dark side consider her to be the leading occultist of her era. Although much of her early life is still steeped in mystery, at the age of twenty she is known to have worked closely with a woman who had traveled extensively to India and who had studied occult techniques that Fortune claimed the woman had used against her in the form of psychic attacks. Fortune reputedly fought off these attacks, suffering a nervous breakdown in the process. As the First World War drew to a close, she met and worked with the Irish occultist and freemason Theodore Moriarty, which led her to write her well-known book *Psychic Self-Defense*.

During the winter of 1923 Fortune spent time in Glastonbury, a place she would retreat to regularly and where she would develop her thoughts on Celtic history and the secrets of Glastonbury Tor. Indeed, she would claim that at this time she had been in spiritual contact with the renowned magician of Arthurian times, Merlin, and many of her claimed experiences would appear later in her book *Glastonbury: Avalon of the Heart*.

Notably, in *Psychic Self-Defense*, Fortune described how on one occasion she unintentionally created—or summoned up—a wolf. Fortune had been lying in bed half asleep and brooding resentfully against someone who had caused her trouble and with whom she had a grievance. Thoughts of revenge flooded her mind and she suddenly conjured up an image of Fenris, the huge malevolent wolf of Norse mythology.

"Immediately I felt a curious drawing-out sensation from my solar plexus," Fortune wrote, "and there materialized beside me on the bed a large wolf." As she tried to move the creature growled ominously at her, but she finally summoned up the courage to push it off the edge of the bed. The wolf suddenly vanished through the wall of the room, but the next morning another occupant of the house told of dreaming about wolves, and of waking in the night to see the glowing eyes of an animal in the darkness. Fortune died of leukemia in 1946.[2]

Was it only a coincidence that someone else fascinated by Glastonbury and the legends of King Arthur had also received a threatening nighttime visit from a spectral-like beast with glowing eyes? Or was this further evidence that there are forces at work attempting to silence anyone seeking to uncover the truth about those same legends? It is a possibility that we all considered carefully and seriously.

But as we departed from Glastonbury we knew that we had yet another task at hand. We were due to meet a man from Royal Air Force Intelligence who had his own remarkable story to tell about the beasts of Britain.

11

BLOWING THE WHISTLE

Couldn't keep a secret, got a concrete skull.

"MAMA'S BOY," THE RAMONES

Following the publication in 1997 of my first book, *A Covert Agenda,* which related the history of the British government's involvement in the UFO subject, I was approached by a number of military and government insiders with their own, previously unknown, stories to tell. One letter came from a man named Malcolm Lees.[1] Lees was particularly interested in what I had to say about a Royal Air Force establishment named RAF Rudloe Manor that was home to a branch of the RAF known as the Provost and Security Services.

Situated within the green and pleasant countryside of Wiltshire, Rudloe Manor has for decades been the subject of numerous stories concerning clandestine UFO studies undertaken by British authorities. The powers that be assert that the stories are nonsense and little more than modern-day folklore. Meanwhile, others maintain that several crashed UFOs and an untold number of alien bodies are stored deep below Rudloe and within the mass of tunnels and caverns that undoubtedly existed under the base and throughout the surrounding area. Determining where the tales end and the truth begins is somewhat problematic. But one thing can be said with certainty. This area of Wiltshire is the source of what is known as Bath stone, which has been quarried for centuries—hence the existence of the huge underground openings where the stone was extracted.

Until 1998, the duties of Rudloe Manor's Provost and Security Services (P&SS) included the investigation of crime and disciplinary matters involving RAF personnel, security vetting of personnel, and the issuing of identity cards, passes, and permits. Far more significant, investigators attached to the P&SS are also trained in the field of counterintelligence (C/I). Such training is undertaken at the RAF Police School. Prospective candidates for counterintelligence work are required to take specialized courses in subjects such as computer security and surveillance. Before being considered for C/I work, personnel have to attain the rank of corporal within the RAF Police. C/I investigators are responsible for issues affecting the security of the RAF, which includes the loss and theft of classified documents, matters pertaining to espionage cases, and the protection of royalty and VIPs when visiting RAF stations.[2]

Also situated with the headquarters of the P&SS is a division known as the Flying Complaints Flight, which primarily investigates complaints of low-flying military aircraft in Britain. In his book, *Alien Liaison,* Timothy Good related the account of a former special investigator with the P&SS who claimed specific knowledge of its involvement in the UFO subject. "I am sure beyond any reasonable shadow of doubt," Good's source told him, "that all initial investigations into UFOs are carried out by investigators of the P&SS who are serving in a small secret unit with the Flying Complaints Flight based at HQ, P&SS, Rudloe Manor."

Further corroboration came from a former counterintelligence investigator, who informed Good's source that, "I had access to every Top Secret file there was, except Low Flying, because I understand they dealt with UFOs. We could get in anywhere, but not in that department. I remember they used to have an Air Ministry guard in the passage—you couldn't get past them. We could see the Provost Marshal's top secret files but yet I couldn't get into the place dealing with UFOs."[3]

Despite the fact that Good's sources wished to remain anonymous, mine was quite open with his identity. Jonathan Turner served with the Royal Air Force for ten years as a medic and retired in 1993. While stationed at RAF Lyneham, Turner learned that reports of UFO sightings by military pilots were never recorded in the flight logs. Instead, details would first be channeled through to the Squadron Commander, who would then advise the Station Commander of the situation. From there, all relevant information would be forwarded to the P&SS for examination.[4]

Similarly, Neil Rusling, no less a source than the treasurer of the Royal Air Force Police Association, told me an illuminating story. In December 1996 I learned directly from Rusling that he had served with the RAF's counterintelligence section. "I go no further, because I can't," he told me when I asked him for details of the sort of work undertaken by counterintelligence personnel. Nevertheless, he was willing to assist me on the UFO angle.

Some six months previously, Neil had made a visit to RAF Halton. "Being the Association Treasurer," he explained to me, "I still have a lot of contacts with those still serving and I was able to confirm with those that any UFO interest the RAF would have would be done by the Flying Complaints unit."

"Flying Complaints involvement—is that as of today?" I asked Rusling.

"As of today," he replied firmly.

"That would be from Rudloe Manor?"

"That would be from Rudloe Manor, yeah."[5]

But it was not just UFO researchers who were picking up on tales of clandestine activities being undertaken at Rudloe Manor. On October 17, 1996, the late member of Parliament, Martin Redmond, asked a number of UFO-related questions in Parliament and touched upon the stories relating to Rudloe. Eleven days later he was informed, in part, that there existed at Rudloe several departments with intriguing backgrounds and duties, including the Detachment of 1001 Signals Unit, which operated the British military communications satellite system; No. 1 Signals Unit, which provided voice and data communications for the RAF, Royal Navy, Army, and Ministry of

Defense; and the Controller Defense Communications Network, a tri-service unit controlling worldwide communications for the military. Not only that but the DCN was situated 120 feet underground and was capable of housing no fewer than 55,000 people in the event of a national emergency.[6]

Flight Lieutenant Jeremy Wright of Rudloe Manor then revealed some extraordinary data: "The underground complex has forty miles of tunnel at various depths, of differing widths and heights, from tiny potholes to enormous caverns with floor spaces equivalent to twelve full-size football fields."

The real coup, however, came when I located a file at the Public Record Office at Kew that conclusively proved that the stories of clandestine UFO investigations undertaken by the P&SS were true and dated back to at least 1962. And one file in particular, which Andy Roberts and I discussed in our book, *Strange Secrets,* suggested that some of the so-called Men in Black reports in the U.K. could be traced back directly to the activities of the P&SS's Special Investigation Section.[7] In other words, something secret of a UFO nature was going on at Rudloe—and perhaps deep below it, too.

And so when I received a lengthy letter from Malcolm Lees and read the first paragraph that talked about Rudloe Manor, I naturally assumed that he wanted to supply more testimony to add to my ever-growing file. But on reading Lees's letter I discovered that, while his story touched upon UFOs initially, he wanted to discuss something else entirely. I confess that, at the time, I considered Lees' letter to be an outright hoax or the product of a deranged mind. Given that his tale focused upon the supposed existence of a monstrous wormlike creature inhabiting the lower levels of the Rudloe Manor tunnel complex, you can perhaps see why. However, after the bizarre escapades that Richard, Jon, and myself had found ourselves immersed in during the last two weeks, and which in that brief time had ranged from encounters involving wild men, werewolves, witches, and gargoyles, I now did not really know what to think—indeed, about anything at all.

Lees lived in the Wiltshire town of Devizes and, after stopping on the journey to catch up on our sleep, we arrived in the nearby town of Marlborough around lunchtime. I telephoned Lees and explained who I was and asked if he remembered writing to me. He did and was more than happy to meet with us. And so at twelve-thirty we found ourselves sitting in the middle of the bar of the Merlin Hotel on Marlborough High Street discussing monsters, quaffing copious amounts of old English ale, and tucking into a hearty lunch that was more like a king's banquet.

Lees was a heavyset man of about seventy-five years with a florid complexion, firm jaw, barrel-like chest and closely cropped silver hair. In fact, he reminded us all of an older version of General Norman Schwarzkopf of Gulf War fame—that is, until he opened his mouth and out came a broad and familiar Wiltshire accent. The story that he was about to tell us, he explained, was secondhand, and there was no point in us asking for the name of his informant since under no circumstances would he ever reveal it. Lees told us that he joined the Royal Air Force in the early 1950s and retired in the late 1960s. In 1962 he received a posting to an RAF station in Wiltshire, which he declined to name, and worked in the prestigious and secretive world of intelligence gathering. Most of the work, Lees explained, was routine and even mundane and he laughed heartily at the idea, spouted by many, that intelligence work was a glamorous one full of James Bond–style escapades. Nevertheless, Lees said, there was one aspect of his career that really was stranger than fiction.

Early one September morning in 1962, a call had come into the base from someone who had seen a UFO hovering in the vicinity of the ancient standing stones at Avebury. UFO reports would reach the base from time to time, said Lees. They were always handled by the RAF's Provost and Security Services and were for the most part mind-numbingly mundane and related to little more than sightings of unidentified lights in the sky that could in reality have been anything or nothing. Invariably, he said, the reports were a week old by the time they were received and so were simply filed and passed up the chain of command—that was then at Government Buildings, Acton, and relocated to Rudloe Manor in 1977. But this one case was a little different, said Lees.

The witness was a middle-aged lady who had lived in Avebury all of her adult life and who was fascinated by archaeological history. A spinster, she would often stroll among the stones at night, marveling at their creation and musing upon their history. It was on the night in question that she had been out walking at around 10:30, when she was both startled and amazed to see a small ball of light, perhaps two feet in diameter, come gliding slowly through the stones. Transfixed and rooted to the spot, she watched as it closed in on her at a height of about twelve feet. The ball then stopped fifteen feet from her and small amounts of what looked like liquid metal slowly and silently dripped from it to the ground. Then, in an instant, the ball exploded in a bright, white flash. For a moment she was blinded by its intensity and instinctively fell to her knees. When her eyes cleared, however, she was faced with a horrific sight. The ball of light had gone, but on the ground in front of her was what she could only describe as a monstrous, writhing worm. The creature, she said, was about five feet long, perhaps eight or nine inches thick and its skin was milk-white. As she slowly rose to her feet, the creature's head turned suddenly in her direction and two bulging eyes opened. When it began to move unsteadily toward her in a caterpillar-like fashion, she emitted a hysterical scream and fled the scene.

Rushing back home, she slammed the door shut and frantically called the airbase, after having been directed to them by the less-than-impressed local police. The Provost and Security Services were used to dealing with UFO reports, said Lees, and a friend of his in the P&SS was dispatched early the next day to interview the woman—amid much hilarity on the part of his colleagues, all of whom thought that the case was a practical joke. On returning, however, Lees's friend and colleague had a very serious and grim look on his face, and informed him guardedly that what had taken place was no hoax.

The woman, he said, had practically barricaded herself in her home, was almost incoherent with fear, and agreed to return to the scene only after lengthy coaxing. Lees's colleague said that he found no evidence of the UFO, and the worm, or whatever it was, had gone. On the ground near the standing stone, however, was a three-foot long trail of a slime-like substance, not unlike that left by a snail. Lees's colleague quickly improvised and, after racing back to the woman's house, scooped some of the material onto a spoon and into a drinking glass.

After assuring the woman that her case would be taken very seriously and requesting that she discuss the events with no one, he headed back to the base, the slimy substance in hand. A report was duly prepared and dispatched up the chain of command—along with the unidentified slime. For more than a week, said Lees, plainclothes military personnel would wander casually among the stones seeking out evidence of anything unusual. Nothing else was found.

Lees said that he was fascinated by this incident because it was one of the few UFO-related cases he had heard about that was taken very seriously at an official level and that had some form of material evidence in support of it. He did not know the outcome of the investigation but was told in confidence by another colleague two years later of a similar story that involved Rudloe Manor.

According to Lees's friend, a bizarre tale was circulating among informed personnel at Rudloe. Supposedly, one of the tunnels had been the subject of additional digging—with a view to creating a shaft that, in turn, would extend to a very deep level and would be completely hollowed out. This self-contained area of about seventy feet by fifty feet would act as an emergency command post for the intelligence service MI5. But after the digging was complete, said Lees, structural problems developed; the whole project was deemed unsafe and was subsequently abandoned. The digging had apparently disturbed something, however.

The area of the underground complex where the digging had taken place was out of bounds to most employees, asserted Lees, but several of those who did have access to the area reported hearing strange echoes throughout the tunnels and what sounded like something large and heavy dragging itself along the ground. No one could determine exactly where the sounds were coming from until late one night when two guards witnessed what they too described as a large worm, perhaps twelve feet long and thicker than a man's arm, moving with astonishing speed down one of the tunnels and vanishing into the darkness.

Despite their best efforts to keep the story under wraps, it inevitably began to circulate among the base employees. Whether it was simply a modern-day fairy tale, or if something really had been seen, Lees did not know. But from his friend, he did hear of others who had seen the mighty worm. Sporadic sightings occurred until the late 1960s, said Lees. Oddly, he had also heard tales of a seven-foot-long creature that resembled a giant lizard seen in the tunnels and caverns and of identical giant worms seen on two occasions at Stonehenge nearby.

The details of the lizard sighting were scant but the Stonehenge accounts were more substantial. On both occasions, Lees said, the incidents occurred late at night in June 1966, one having been reported by a husband and wife, the other by an off-duty policeman. In both cases, the witnesses had seen from a distance a giant worm some ten feet long and nearly a foot thick moving clumsily across the road and toward the ancient structure. No one stopped to take a closer look.

Lees told us that he was aware of other UFO encounters investigated by the P&SS that also involved sightings of strange-looking beasts such as apelike creatures and animals that appeared to be a curious blend of giant cat and dog. We smiled knowingly. Lees stressed that, as far as he was aware, no official "project" existed to investigate these events, but stated that the P&SS would look at each case on its own merit and would carry out an investigation if it were deemed necessary.

"I've always thought it strange," he concluded, "that the P&SS should have investigated this giant worm seen at Avebury in 1962; then there should have been the worm sightings under Rudloe; and then where does the P&SS move to in 1977? Rudloe."

As Lees continued to talk, his tone changed slightly and he admitted that he had misled us. The tunnel in question where the worm had allegedly been seen was in reality a short distance from Rudloe and was *not* directly below the base itself, as he had previously told us. We wondered if this was really true. Was Malcolm Lees now regretting speaking with us and trying to put us off the scent of our quarry, or was the change in his story an indicator of his dishonesty? Was he perhaps concerned that we would travel to the base and demand the answers for ourselves? And, if so, was this his way of steering us away from Rudloe Manor? It was difficult to know the answers to any of those questions. As far as he was concerned, the deception was for our own good and was, as he put it, "necessary before I decided whether or not I should reveal the real location to you."

We spoke with Lees for another hour or so and by 2:30 P.M. we had said our good-byes. And he steadfastly refused to reveal the incident's real location. His story was certainly bizarre. But was it *too* bizarre? Maybe not. In our book, *Strange Secrets*, Andy Roberts and I had shown that sightings of, and encounters with, unknown beasts were not unknown in the official world. For example, we had found nineteenth-century naval files at the Public Record Office on sea serpent encounters. The Ministry of Agriculture, Food and Fisheries took very seriously sightings of big cats around the U.K. and an elite branch of the Royal Air Force known as the Joint Air Reconnaissance Intelligence Center had in the 1960s studied film footage that purported to show the Loch Ness Monster. And on the other side of the Atlantic, in the 1970s U.S. intelligence agencies had displayed more than a passing interest in Soviet research into ESP in the animal kingdom.

But what of this bizarre and unholy beast seen burrowing deep below RAF Rudloe Manor? What on earth was it? And how, if at all, did it fit into the 1962 sighting of a similar creature at Avebury and others seen at Stonehenge four years later? And what of the UFO connection? We had the questions. We decided to find the answers. Our first stop: Avebury itself and then on to Stonehenge.

Avebury is perhaps the most significant and impressive remaining prehistoric earthwork in Europe. The initial phase of the construction involved the excavation of the ditches, or the Henge, as it is known. Estimates suggest that there were originally no less than 400 standing stones within the Henge and that formed Avebury's huge avenues, with the heaviest, the Swindon Stone, weighing an astonishing 65 tons.

Having been transported to the area (by rollers, some suggest), the stones were positioned into specific locations marked by chalk and the process of erecting them using stakes began. The original layout was of an outer circle that encompassed the inside of the Henge and consisted of 98 stones; while within this circle was constructed two more circles, both with the same diameter, but used for ritualistic purposes. Avebury is known to have been in regular use as a temple for at least 700 years; and it was around this time, 2000 B.C., that the immense task of constructing Wiltshire's famous Stonehenge began in earnest.

The original Stonehenge comprised of a ditch, a bank, and what are known as the Aubrey holes. The Aubrey holes are round pits in the chalk that form a 284-foot diameter circle; excavations at the site have uncovered the remains of cremated human bones in some of the chalk filling. The holes themselves, however, were probably built not as graves but as part of a religious ceremony.

Certainly the most significant stage in the development of Stonehenge began in approximately 2150 B.C. No less than 82 of Stonehenge's so-called bluestones, some weighing 4 tons, were transported from the Preseli Mountains in southwest Wales to the site, while the giant Sarsen stones that make up Stonehenge were brought from the Marlborough Downs near Avebury.[8]

Of the wealth of claims and counterclaims that surround the construction of the Avebury stones, Stonehenge, the Pyramids of Egypt, and many of the other ancient sites that pepper our planet, none creates controversy and whips up a veritable storm of support, criticism, comment, and hoots of derision the way that the so-called Ancient Astronaut scenario does. The idea that some of humankind's most impressive constructions were built with the assistance of advanced extraterrestrial beings is not a new one. The works of Morris Jessup, Robert Charoux, and Erich Von Daniken make that abundantly clear—as do the findings of those in the skeptical camp, such as Ronald Story, who has convincingly argued that much of the evidence in favor of an Ancient Astronaut scenario is highly dubious, to say the least.

It seems unlikely, however, that this particular controversy will ever be laid to rest convincingly and to everyone's satisfaction. The believers will continue to believe and the skeptics will continue to assert—not without some strong justification, it must be said—that we should not underestimate the technical capabilities of our ancestors.

As someone with more than a passing interest of the mysteries of our world, and official secrecy in particular, I have long been fascinated by the fact that government and intelligence agencies throughout the planet have taken a keen interest in the writings of some of those who have championed the Ancient Astronaut scenario—including a New Zealand-based airline pilot, Captain Bruce Cathie. Cathie put forward an intriguing theory that there exists around the Earth a form of power grid that UFOs use as a source of energy while soaring through our skies—try to imagine a cosmic version of the New York subway system—and that a technology fitting this description was also employed in the movement of the enormous stones that led to the construction of Stonehenge and the Pyramids.[9]

Like Richard, Jon was not a big fan of UFOs and guffawed at the idea that aliens from some far-flung corner of the galaxy had played a role in the construction of Stonehenge and the Avebury circle. "Nonsense and balderdash," he cried loudly as we drove toward Avebury. But there was no doubting the fact that the stones provoked furious debate and controversy and were still in many ways steeped in mystery. And our giant worm hunt was only adding to that mystery.

"Turn that bloody noise down," Jon shouted to Richard as Blink 182's "What's My Age Again?" echoed loudly throughout the cab as we arrived in town.

"So now what do we do?" asked Richard as I brought the Mystery Machine to a stop. "Knock on everyone's door and ask if they've seen a bloody big worm anywhere?" It was a fair question. Nevertheless, we did indeed knock on some twenty doors in the vicinity, and visited stores, pubs, and tourist outlets in the area. Again the response ranged from amusement to outright hostility. The reaction at Stonehenge was even less helpful, and when we telephoned RAF Rudloe Manor to ask if they knew anything about a giant worm roaming the deeper levels of the base, the initial reaction was one of stunned silence followed swiftly by the click of the receiver. They had hung up on us. This aspect of the investigation was not going well.

Nevertheless, as Jon pointed out, even if there was a remote chance that the construction of Stonehenge and the Avebury stones had paranormal or ufological links, the fact that monstrous wormlike animals had been seen at both locations suggested, again, a link between UFOs and unknown animals. And it also suggested a link with ancient sites and strange beasts—as Mother Sarah had said was the case with the Nine and the Cormons on Dartmoor. "And that link, my friend, is further evidence that we are dealing with more than just nuts-and-bolts UFOs and unidentified species of animal," Jon added. I was in full agreement. We could, of course, have simply dismissed this whole affair as the result of nothing more than rumor and a friend of a friend tale. Yet there was one aspect of this story that led us to consider the possibility that it did have a basis in reality.

Richard may insist in dressing in pirate fashion for every waking moment of the day and he may be a firm devotee of all things Gothic, but, by God, he knows his stuff. Several years previously he had spent an inordinate amount of time traveling around England and immersing himself in legends and tales from centuries past about sightings of huge worms and giant dragonlike lizards that would roam the countryside and terrify the populace—very much like those allegedly seen at Avebury and Stonehenge and deep below RAF Rudloe Manor in recent times. And so, having spent the evening devouring dinner and drinks at a hostelry in nearby Beckhampton, we decided to return to Marlborough and parked the Mystery Machine on the outskirts of town in the pleasant Wiltshire countryside.

We, like most folk, have found that the best time to tell a good story that is full of adventure and intrigue is around a big, glowing campfire after sunset. Since we didn't have a campfire, we had to settle on the interior lights of the vehicle. Armed with several bottles of powerful homemade cider that we had purchased along the way and two large boxes of chocolates, Jon and I crashed out on our respective beds and listened as Richard told us of his dragon- and worm-hunting adventures.

Of all the legendary monsters, said Richard, the dragon is both the most widespread and the most ancient. The Heraldic, or "true" dragon, also known as the "Fire Drake," was the most powerful of all dragons, he added. A giant quadruped, it had huge, batlike wings, savage teeth and claws and a mighty tail. Its most formidable weapon, however, was undoubtedly the white-hot flame that emanated from its massive jaws.

"Heraldic dragons were the most magical of all the beasts," Richard went on, "since they had the power of not only invisibility, self-healing, and mind-reading but also that of shape-shifting."

"You see?" said Jon. "Shape-shifting is one of the attributes of the werewolf; and this talk about dragons being able to render themselves invisible is probably a legend based on these beasts being Tulpa- or Cormon-like also."

Richard looked at Jon with a stern face: "Can I continue?"

"You may, dear boy," Jon replied good-naturedly as he leaned back on his pillow and proceeded to throw chocolates into the air that he would catch in his mouth like a monstrous and hideously bloated old walrus performing stunts at the local zoo.

"According to legend, it's also very difficult to kill these things, and that too might be an indication that some of them are Tulpas that have resisted destruction," Richard explained. "Now, in England the Guivre Worm is the commonest form of Celtic dragon. This worm was described as being a vast limbless serpent and it inhabited the lakes, marshes, and rivers of the country five, six, seven hundred years ago—maybe even earlier.

"These worms reputedly killed by crushing their victims in their coils, rather like a constricting snake, and with their poisonous breath, which they used in much the same way as the other species supposedly used their breath of fire. This poison allegedly had the ability to shrivel crops and to choke anyone and everything that got in its way."

"I once went out with a girl with breath like that," I said, reflecting on the hot summer of 1984 and the holiday town of Brixham where our two-week-long romance began, blossomed, and spectacularly imploded after I took a particular liking to her buxom sister.

"The world's largest known lizard is the Komodo dragon or *Varanus komodoensis*," said Richard. "It was discovered in 1912 on a handful of tiny Indonesian islands and can reach ten feet in length. However, in Australia, an even bigger monitor lizard existed until the end of the Pleistocene epoch. *Megalania prisca* grew to over thirty feet in length and was the continent's supreme terrestrial predator. And reports suggest that this creature might still stalk the wilder parts of the continent. Since the 1830s people have been reporting what the native Australians have also been seeing for centuries.

"The most important sighting, at least as far as I'm concerned, was made in 1979 by a professional herpetologist named Frank Gordon. Gordon had been conducting fieldwork, and when he returned to his Land Rover and started the engine he was astonished to see a nearby 'log' rear up and lumber away. The 'log' was a thirty-foot-long lizard! The problem is that these things live only in the tropics; yet dragon legends are universal and thousands of them come from temperate or even subarctic areas, including England."

Richard then went on to describe a unique theory to explain dragon sightings that had been postulated in 1979 by author Peter Dickinson in his book *The Flight of Dragons*. "Dickinson's idea," said Richard, "was that dragons evolved from large carnivorous dinosaurs like *Tyrannosaurus rex*. They developed large, expanded stomachs filled with hydrogen gas. The hydrogen evolved from a mixture of hydrochloric acid in the digestive juices mixed with the calcium found in the bones of their prey. This lighter-than-air gas then allowed them to fly and they controlled their flight by burning off excess gas as flames."[10]

Jon interrupted again: "Richard, this is all well and good but what about sightings of these things in England? If there is anything even remotely real with the story Lees told us, then it should have historical precedents, even if these things are Tulpas or Cormons."

Richard nodded: "Okay, well, for a start we have to go back several hundred years and to Yorkshire." Richard smiled at the ceiling and let out a long sigh. "Do you know how superior Yorkshire and the North are, Jon, compared to this southern hellhole that you live in?"

"Just get on with it!" Jon shouted, and all three of us laughed.

"Well, one of the most famous cases was that of the Dragon of Wantley. This was, for all intents and purposes, a true-winged, fire-breathing dragon. It supposedly terrorized the country surrounding Wantley, killing livestock and people, and burning crops and buildings. The populace then enlisted the help of a huge knight known as More of More Hall. For payment More insisted that prior to the battle he be anointed by a fair-skinned, black-haired girl of sixteen."

"Bloody hell!" Jon exclaimed. "We're in the wrong line of business."

Richard continued. "More had fashioned himself a suit of armor that was studded with spikes about six inches long. He then hid in a well to ambush the dragon when it came down to drink. According to the legend, the fight lasted for two days and a night, with neither opponent being able to pierce the others armor. The dragon seized More, intent on hurling him into the air like a rag doll. But when More saw the beast's vulnerable spot and delivered a fatal kick with a spiked boot, it turned out that the spot was its arse."

At that point Jon and I erupted into fits of laughter and there then followed five minutes of nonsensical tomfoolery before the story was resumed.

"The legend was recorded in a lighthearted ballad in 1699," Richard explained. "But some say that the whole tale is just a satire based on a lawsuit over tithes during the reign of James 1; the dragon, being Sir Francis Wortley, who held the disputed tithes, and More, being the attorney who set a lawsuit against him on behalf of the local gentry. The spiked armor was a document full of names and seals of men pledged to oppose Wortley. However, several motifs in the tale, such as the spiked armor, the well, and the almost invulnerable dragon argue, as far as I am concerned, that the 1699 poem was adapted from a far more ancient legend. Wantley, it seems, may once have had a very real dragon.

"Now there's another one: The Dragon of Filey. The hero of this tale is not a knight, a wizard, or a lord, but a meek little tailor named Billy Biter. He was walking along the cliffs one misty morning when he tumbled into a ravine that again turned out to be the lair of a true Heraldic-type dragon. The dragon was about to devour him when Billy offered it a Yorkshire delicacy known as a parkin. So the legend goes, the dragon enjoyed this piece of gooey confectionary so much that he demanded more and turned Billy loose. Running home, Billy told his wife, who insisted on making more parkin for the dragon.

"But," added Richard as an aside, "you remember the woman you picked up at the LAPIS conference in 1999 that we had to get the police to deal with when you brought her back to Exeter? Well, just like her, Billy's wife was domineering and a dreadful cook."

"I remember," said Jon icily, as he recalled one occasion when the woman had cooked for him and almost succeeded in turning his kitchen into a towering inferno.

"Well, legend has it that Billy's wife produced the biggest and stickiest parkin in the history of Yorkshire. Billy rolled the parkin into the dragon's lair, and when the beast began to eat it, its jaws became stuck fast. The dragon then flew into the sea to wash the parkin away but was overcome by the icy waves. Its bones turned to stone and became Filey Brigg, a mile-long projection of rocks that juts out to sea.

"There are also three other tales of Yorkshire dragons and worms. In fact, they may all be distorted versions of the same story. One puts the action at Loschy Mill, one at Slingsby, and one at Kellington. A confusing one, this."

Loschy Mill, Richard elaborated, was in the parish of Stonegrave and was the lair of a great worm that was possessed of truly poisonous breath. Not only that, but the serpent's body had the power to recombine after being severed and was reputed to have venomous blood. Sir Peter Loschy, a local knight, fought the worm while wearing razor-studded armor and brandishing a huge sword. He was aided by his faithful dog, whose name history does not recall, and the hound would grab segments of the worm whenever his master sliced into the beast, whereupon the dog would race to the neighboring village of Nunnington with the body parts to ensure that the worm was unable to rejoin with its severed sections. However, when the knight congratulated his hound, it licked his hand and both master and hound died from the worm's deadly blood.

"But in the Slingsby version," said Richard, "it's Sir William Wyville and his dog who kill the worm and succumb to its blood. At Kellington, however, it's a shepherd and sheepdog who perform the deed and pay for it with their lives. And the stories don't end there. On a hill in the village of Sexhow, a giant worm took up residence and demanded the milk of nine cows each and every day. Its venomous breath killed all those who opposed it until an anonymous knight rode into Sexhow. After a savage fight, he slew the worm and went on his way asking for no reward. The villagers skinned the giant snake and displayed the hide at nearby Stokesley church where it remained for many years.

"Now, there was a creature known in legend as the Handale Worm," Richard told Jon and me. "This beast is a bit of a hybrid. It was said to have a crested head and to breathe fire like a dragon, to have a sting like a wyvern, but to be a serpent and like a worm, presumably. It haunted the woods near to Handale priory, devouring young women. But eventually a brave peasant named Scaw fought the worm, armed only with a sword. After a savage struggle he slew the serpent and found an earl's daughter in its cave. Scaw married her and acquired vast estates. The wood where the worm once lurked is now called Scaw Wood, and a stone coffin in the ruins of the priory is said to be Scaw's."

The county of Yorkshire was also home to fabulous sea-beasts, as Richard's studies had shown. "The most dramatic encounter took place on February 28, 1934, on Filey Brigg," Richard revealed. "Fishermen had been reporting seeing a strange creature out at sea off the Yorkshire coast between Scarborough and Flamborough Head from a distance of about three miles. On the dark and moonless night of the twenty-eighth, the coastguardsman, Wilkinson Herbert, was wandering along the Brigg."

Richard would later send me his notes on this case that included the following firsthand testimony from Herbert: "Suddenly I heard a growling like a dozen dogs ahead. Walking nearer I switched on my torch, and was confronted by a huge neck, six yards ahead of me, rearing up eight feet high! The head was a startling sight—huge tortoise eyes glaring at me like saucers. The creature's mouth would be a foot wide and the creature's neck would be a yard around. The monster was as startled as I was. Shining my torch along the ground I saw a body about thirty feet long. I thought, this is no place for me, and from a distance I threw stones at the creature. It moved away growling fiercely, and I saw that the huge black body had two humps on it, and four short legs with huge flippers on them. It was the most gruesome and thrilling experience. I have seen big animals abroad but nothing like this!"

And Richard was by no means finished. "In 1938, Mrs. Joan Borgeest saw a sea dragon off Eastington in North Yorkshire. She had been looking out to sea from the beach when she suddenly saw a huge creature rise; it was a green color, with a flat head, protruding eyes, and a long, flat mouth, which opened and shut as it breathed. It was a great length and moved along with what she described as being a humped glide. The beast was about three hundred feet away and dived when she called to some other people. Mrs. Borgeest was teased by friends and kept quiet about her story until 1961, when the BBC broadcast a radio program about sea monsters. In August 1945, Mr. B. M. Baylis of Spilsby, and some friends of his, saw a monster."

Again, Richard would send me a copy of Baylis's personal testimony: "We were sitting on the edge of low mud cliffs at Hilston between Hornsea and Withernsea. There we saw a creature with a head and four or five rounded humps each leaving a wake. It was moving rapidly, but quite silently along the shore, northwestwards in the face of a northerly wind. Nobody at the time believed our report, but we are convinced that we saw something."

But by far the most intriguing case, said Richard, was that of the Lambton worm. "This all took place at the River Wear near to the manor house of the Lambton family just north of Lunley. It's known that the family was a very old one and may date back a thousand years or more. There was a castle at the site for many years and this was destroyed just before the turn of the nineteenth century to make way for the present manor.

"So the tales goes, at some point in the fourteenth century, the then heir to the estate of Lambton, John Lambton, led a fairly wild life and instead of going to church on a Sunday would spend his time fishing in the Wear. On one particular Sunday, he felt something pulling on his line. He naturally thought that this was a fish, and the force with which it was pulling made him believe it was a big one. Well, he finally reeled it in and found that it wasn't a fish. It was a large and strange-looking worm that he proceeded to throw into a nearby well.

"As time passed the worm grew and grew and finally the well was too small to support it any longer and it emerged from its lair and slithered down to the river. It would coil itself around a large rock in the river during the day and at night would wrap itself around a local hill in the vicinity. To this day that hill is called Worm Hill and is about half a mile from Lambton Hall.

"The legend says that the worm fed on the milk of cows, ate lambs and sheep, and terrorized everyone who came across its path. It had reportedly destroyed the land on the far side of the river and then set its sights on Lambton Hall. The son, who had caught the thing, had left by now to fight in the Crusades. Well, the household was petrified when it saw this huge, lumbering worm approaching the house, but they had a plan. They filled a large trough with milk and when the creature came close, it noticed the milk, drank it and, apparently satisfied, left the scene. The worm then returned to the hill, which it coiled itself around for the night. The same thing happened the next day and the villagers realized that they had a big problem on their hands. To keep the thing at bay they had to keep feeding it milk. Now, as with many of the similar tales from Yorkshire, there were various knights and heroes who tried to kill it. But no one succeeded, as this worm, too, could reconnect its body parts after they were severed.

"For seven years the worm ruled the area, but then the heir to Lambton returned from the Crusades and was shocked to see how the worm had decimated the place and had led his father to ruin. The heir met with someone who was described in the legend as the wise woman of the village and she advised him to put on his suit of armor and do battle with the creature. But there was a price to pay. If he was successful in killing the worm, he would then have to slay the next living creature that he saw. If he didn't, then for nine generations the successive lords of Lambton would all meet a grisly fate. The heir made the vow in Brugeford Chapel, donned his armor, and prepared to do battle. Now, unlike many of the others who had tried to kill the creature, the knight attached to his armor vicious spikes so that when the worm tried to constrict him like a huge snake, the spikes would pierce its skin and kill it. The plan apparently worked and the River Wear ran red with the beast's blood after its death.

"Well, as the battle was taking place the Lambton family barricaded themselves in the house; and, as a result, John Lambton said that if he was successful in killing the creature he would give a long blast on his bugle to let them know that all was well. This was to be a sign for his father that he should let loose the family's pet hound, which they had decided had to be the sacrifice that the old, wise woman had told them they should make. But, in his excitement, the father completely forgot about the plan and ran outside to meet his son. Well, John Lambton was, of course, unable to kill his father and so the hound was slain in the hope that it would fulfill the promise, or curse, depending on how you look at it. But it didn't and the family curse laid waste to succeeding generations of Lambtons, just as the old woman had said it would."

Richard's tale was at an end. However, the story of the Lambton worm lives on in the world of literature, as the following, from a local and long-deceased poet makes abundantly clear:

The worm shot down the middle stream
Like a flash of living light,
And the waters kindled round his path
In rainbow colours bright.
But when he saw the armed knight

He gathered all his pride,
And, coiled in many a radiant spire,
Rode buoyant o'er the tide.
When he darted at length his dragon strength
An earthquake shook the rock,
And the fireflakes bright fell round the knight
As unmoved he met the shock.
Though his heart was stout it quailed no doubt,
His very life-blood ran cold,
As round and round the wild Worm wound
In many a grappling fold.

"Now, I'm not saying that these legends are true in the literal sense of the word," said Richard. "But, I think that like the Ghost Ape of Marwood, Martyn's Ape, and the Shug Monkey, these legends were created by superstitious villagers to account for sightings of large wormlike animals that roamed Britain centuries ago. Maybe they were real flesh-and-blood creatures or maybe they were paranormal, like the gargoyles and the werewolves and the Cormons that that bloody witch kept going on about."

Perhaps, said Richard in conclusion, a few of these things still lived deep below England in some of the more remote and complex caves and caverns that existed, having been driven there as the human population increased and spread both far and wide. All three of us instinctively looked at the floor of the Mystery Machine. Perhaps there really were vile wormlike beasts slithering throughout the rocky underworld of Britain, I offered. But how would that explain the bizarre events at Avebury in 1962 and later at Stonehenge that seemed distinctly paranormal in nature? We could only conclude that, if we were not the victims of a hoax, then this was further evidence of yet another breed of Tulpa or Cormon in our midst.

Then there was the issue of the Provost and Security Services and their investigations of strange creatures seen in conjunction with UFOs at the ancient sites of both Stonehenge and Avebury. In some ways this tied in with Colin Perks's account about a powerful and hidden group of people within the British government having knowledge of the truth concerning the Arthurian legends and the diabolical beasts of another realm. The cosmic zoo was perilously close to overflowing, said Jon. Richard and I agreed. We said our good-nights and before we knew it, another day was dawning.

⁘ ⁘ ⁘

RAF Rudloe Manor may have given us short shrift but we weren't about to be put off that easily and so, after breakfast, we made a determined decision to visit the Wiltshire town of Corsham and take a closer look at that most mysterious of Royal Air Force establishments. Before leaving Marlborough we telephoned Malcolm Lees and told him of our plans. On learning that we intended pulling up outside of RAF Rudloe Manor and engaging the staff in an earnest conversation about giant worms—and perhaps even attempting a stealthy penetration of the old tunnels—Lees became distinctly uneasy and made every attempt to dissuade us from proceeding with our plans. Was this an indication that his story was a hoax, or was he concerned that, as a whistleblower, he would find himself in deep trouble if the story were traced back to him? We didn't know. We *did* know, however, that if we failed to take a close look at the tunnels for ourselves we would always regret it.

"Look," Lees said, as he spoke with me on Jon's cell phone, "I told you that where all this happened wasn't actually directly under the base itself."

I replied: "I know. But how about you take us to the real place so we can see for ourselves?"

Lees was silent for a moment and then replied, "Okay. There's no harm to be done. I told you it's all shut down now, anyway." Lees's only demand, when he was informed that I was writing this book, was that I should deliberately obfuscate the exact location of the tunnel in question. Lees agreed to meet us in town at 1:00 P.M. and we followed his vehicle on the short journey from RAF Rudloe Manor to a house-sized and anonymous-looking red-brick building that was positioned on an industrial estate. As bizarre as it may sound, if you ask the staff at Rudloe in a pleasant tone for a tour of some of the less sensitive tunnels (and particularly those that have now been abandoned), they can be quite receptive. And, indeed, a number of the local caving groups in the area have formed good relationships with the Royal Air Force—to the extent that access to some of the caves and tunnels that ten or twenty years ago would have been undreamed of is now relatively routine.

And so when we arrived at our location and jumped out of the Mystery Machine, we were not entirely surprised to see two burly Royal Air Force dog-handlers leaning casually against the wall of the building and smoking cigarettes. Malcolm exited his vehicle and motioned us over to the two men, both of whom were in uniform and appeared to be in their mid-forties.

"Hello, Malcolm," said one genially, while simultaneously nodding his head. Malcolm Lees might have retired from RAF Intelligence decades ago but he seemed to have an ongoing and friendly relationship with the staff from Rudloe. Perhaps, I thought, his retirement wasn't quite as permanent as we had been led to believe. Lees warmly shook hands with the men and all three looked in our direction and laughed. What was being said? Although we were barely twenty feet away, the incessant growling and barking of the German shepherds tugging on their leashes drowned out the voices of the three men.

"These are the guys I was telling you about," Lees said to his two friends when the dogs finally calmed down, which, curiously, coincided with Jon removing his trusty monocle.

"Come to do a spot of monster hunting, have you?" asked one in slightly mocking tones. His colleague laughed aloud.

"Yes, we have," I replied. "Malcolm told us everything." The two men eyed us warily and looked at Lees for a moment before returning their gaze to us. "So, can we go down and have a look?" I asked.

Jon, who stood slightly behind me, whispered in my ear, "Don't piss them off, for God's sake. We survived a gargoyle and a bloody wild man. I do *not* now want to risk becoming dinner for a dog, as well." Neither did I, but I didn't like being mocked, either.

"Okay, come on," said one of the men. He unlocked the door to the building and on entering it we could see that it was totally empty. Indeed, all that could be seen was a metal hatch positioned in the dusty concrete floor that resembled a large sewer cover.

"This is the entrance to the tunnel," said Lees quietly. Richard and I looked at it with relish. Jon was appalled. Everyone knew what he was thinking.

"You'll be okay, sir," said one of the two RAF men. "It's plenty wide enough. Even for you." Again they laughed heartily and Jon glared. As the man pulled the thick metal cover off and let it drop to the floor, a powerful echo enveloped the empty building, before a deadly silence fell upon us.

"You know this story, do you?" asked Richard. "The worm, I mean?"

"Oh, yeah. We know it. I don't believe it, but everyone here has heard it," the man replied. "We hear all sorts, don't we?" he said to the other man with a knowing grin.

"Yeah, we hear all sorts," his colleague added sternly.

"And we can go down there?" Richard pressed.

"Yeah. Public Relations said that it's okay. This was all deactivated years ago. Take a flashlight and you'll be okay; it goes for maybe a mile in each direction. If you see anything long and slimy just give us a shout." Once again there was laughter on the part of the two men. Lees remained silent and kept to the edge of the room. In fact, when the cover was lifted, a frightened look came across his face. Perhaps he thought that the mighty worm was about to come flying out of its darkened tomb after decades of imprisonment.

"Stay on the pathway, lads," one of the men said, as we began our approximately twenty-foot descent into the depths of the tunnel. Stay on the pathway, lads. That sounded very much like a certain quote from *An American Werewolf in London.* Someone was having a laugh at our expense. Thankfully, the concrete steps were easy to negotiate—even for Jon, and there was none of his flamboyant drama and nonsense that accompanied our descent into the cellar at Alfred's home. Having reached the floor we looked up, and I half expected to see the two RAF men wearing malicious grins as they replaced the lid and encased us forever in this icy-cold tomb. Instead they waved genially and suggested that we head left. We decided to go right.

The flashlight illuminated the tunnel for us and we could see that it was about fifteen feet wide and perhaps ten feet high. Every twenty feet or thereabouts, we would see air ducts and occasionally we would come across large and rusted iron doors that were clearly entrance points to other parts of the tunnel complex.

"Everything okay?" a voice shouted in the distance and from the upper level.

"Yeah!" Richard replied with full voice. As we reached a point approximately one hundred yards into the tunnel we came across another door. But this one was ajar.

Jon looked at it and then looked at Richard and me, resigning himself to his inevitable fate. "You just can't resist it, can you?" Jon said. "You know that some mate of those guys upstairs is going to come jumping out of that door and have an uproariously big laugh at our expense, don't you?" Richard and I waved him aside and forced the door open. It didn't seem that it had been touched in decades and it took us two or three minutes to force it open to a point where all three of us could enter into the next tunnel. Curiously, this tunnel, unlike the main one, displayed neither a concrete floor nor air vents. As we entered and scanned the tunnel with the flashlight, we were surprised to see that after fifty feet or so it opened into a wider tunnel that looked more like a natural cave and that was about twenty feet high and at least twenty feet wide. The cave descended at a slight angle and it was clear to us again that this area had been out of use for years. Piled against the walls were old chairs, desks, and cupboards that had no doubt been dumped here as RAF Rudloe Manor had been updated years before. A few pieces of broken cups and saucers were scattered around the floor.

"Come on, then," Richard said to Jon impatiently, as Jon wavered and complained about the dirt, the dust, and the fact that after getting lost in Alfred's passageways we were now about to get lost in the Royal Air Force's tunnels. Nevertheless, after grousing and grumbling for a few seconds, Jon followed behind as Richard and I eagerly scanned the cave for any sign of life—human, giant worm, or otherwise. On three occasions we came across large iron doors that had been built into the cave walls; these, however, were firmly locked and no amount of force on our part would prize them open.

"You know," said Richard in a frustrated tone, "if this *is* where it all happened, the worm might have actually been behind one of those doors. And maybe it still is."

"And you actually want to come face-to-face with a giant worm, do you?" asked Jon, with astonishment in his voice. "And what about that seven-foot-long reptile thing? That doesn't perturb you slightly?"

"No!" Richard and I shouted.

"I've got an idea," said Richard. He ran back toward the entrance to the cave and came back with two wooden legs he had broken off one of the old, abandoned chairs that we had seen stacked against the walls.

"What are they for?" I asked.

"Watch," Richard replied, with a grin. He proceeded to march up to each of the three doors and pounded on them heavily with the chair legs. The sound of wood upon metal echoed loudly around the cave.

"What in God's name are you doing, boy?" asked Jon, as he came breathlessly running over to Richard and grabbed the legs from him. "You'll have the army, navy, and air force down here if you keep that up!"

"I'm trying to attract its attention," said Richard matter-of-factly.

"Yes, and what happens when we are surrounded by giant worms and reptiles, Richard? You're going to presumably fight them off with those sticks, are you?" asked Jon in worried tones. I wasn't at all worried, and neither was Richard, but I did find the whole situation surreal. Fifty feet above us people were going about their everyday tasks, oblivious to the secret world that existed below their feet. And here we were, chasing giant worms in an abandoned, government-controlled cave.

Despite Richard's incessant banging, neither worm nor reptile surfaced from the darkness. But at a distance of about two hundred feet into the tunnel, we *did* find an area of the soil that had been disturbed and that looked like something had been dragged across the ground for approximately thirty feet. Richard examined and measured the disturbance and was convinced that the drag marks were indicative of the presence of a huge snake- or wormlike beast. Richard shone the flashlight on the disturbance, whirled around wildly, and looked Jon in the face. "It's near," he said quietly and ominously.

"Nonsense! Absolute nonsense!" Jon bellowed. "I am forty-one years old and I am a respected writer and cryptozoologist. I am *not* some twelve-year-old on a *Hardy Boys* adventure!" But then something rumbled in the darkness. The three of us froze and listened intently. Where was it coming from? And more importantly, what was it? Richard waved the flashlight around but nothing untoward could be seen. And then the rumbling came again.

"It's coming from behind there," said Jon in quiet and deliberate tones, as he pointed warily at one of the old, rusted doors. Richard charged the door with one of the chair legs and hammered on it for thirty seconds. We could then hear shouting getting closer.

"What the hell are you doing?" came a voice from the darkness. It was one of the two dog-handlers. "We can hear you banging all the way along the tunnel."

"What's behind there?" I asked, pointing at the door.

"That's still in use," he said icily.

"By whom?" I continued.

"By whoever it is that works there," the man replied. "And before you ask, no, you can't go in there. As a courtesy, we allow people with a genuine interest to come into some of the closed-down tunnels but that doesn't include beating the shit out of our doors with wooden sticks."

"Actually, they're old chair legs," said Richard, in friendly tones. "I found them over there."

"That's government property," said the man. Jon nervously rubbed his hands together.

"Well, it's all been dumped, hasn't it?" I asked. The man glared at me.

"Alright, back to the surface," he barked. "Now!" And so we trudged off, leaving the secrets of this subterranean abode behind us.

"It was probably a piece of machinery we heard, you know. Like a digger or maybe a small train line for transporting things," said Jon, as we walked the short journey back to the surface. And he was probably right. But to this day, Richard and I are still not entirely convinced. Nevertheless, to actually have had the opportunity—albeit briefly—to spend time in the tunnels of one of Britain's most secretive establishments was a rare and memorable experience for all three of us. Malcolm Lees and his colleagues seemed less impressed by our brief excursion, however, and on reaching the surface we were sent on our way with instructions to exercise great care when walking around military establishments in the future. We left behind RAF Rudloe Manor and its secret world of tunnels, UFOs, and giant worms.

12

DOGGONE ANIMALS

**I saw her walking in the woods last night,
and I knew something wasn't right.**

"SLUG," THE RAMONES

A t 7:45 A.M. the next day I awoke and looked out of the steamy windows of the Mystery Machine. It was raining and raining hard. Dark clouds filled the sky and the joys of summer had gone. Oh well, I thought, we've had good weather so far, and after all we *are* in England. What else can be expected?

"It's raining," said Richard blankly, as he, too, peered out of the window.

"Is it?" asked Jon as his blubbery face emerged from beneath the blankets like H. P. Lovecraft's Great C'thulu rising from the depths of the ocean.

"It is," I said.

"No," Jon replied.

"Yeah," I said mutedly. It's strange how the weather, and particularly bad weather, can be a source for such fascinating and in-depth conversation on the part of the British. But the three of us resolved not to become embroiled in an endless debate about such mundane matters and instead concentrated on the task ahead. After breakfast we faced a journey to the east coast of England and the county of Suffolk, where we were going to meet a woman who had carried out research into the phantom black dog legends of British folklore.

Diane Facer had been Jon's good friend ever since he first met her at the 1995 Fortean Times Unconvention. Diane lived in the Suffolk town of Woodbridge, Jon explained, and in 1987 she had become interested in the notorious UFO landing incident at the nearby Rendlesham Forest that involved numerous U.S. Air Force personnel from the (also nearby) Royal Air Force facility at Bentwaters. Diane had soon discovered, however, that the location of the "landing" was saturated with other mysteries and anomalies. As a result, she soon found herself rejecting the "alien" solution to the UFO incident and concluded that it was part of a much wider phenomenon that encompassed both cryptozoology and the occult.

As was often the case, our meeting with Facer could not be scheduled for several days and so, having spent the next few hours driving to Suffolk, we decided to head farther up the coast to the ancient city of Norwich, where we spent the following seventy-two hours sightseeing, checking out a local band at one of the numerous taverns that peppered the city, and generally loafing around doing not much at all beyond having a good time. But with our brief excursion out of the way, it was time to head back down the coast to Woodbridge.

Like so many of the locations in the course of our quest, the history of Woodbridge stretches back millennia. There is evidence in the form of archaeological relics that Neolithic man lived in the area as far back as 2500 B.C. Similarly, the region was occupied by the Roman Empire for three hundred years following the failed rebellion of Queen Boadicca in A.D. 59. After the Romans departed in the year 410, a strong Anglo-Saxon settlement flourished and among its most powerful rulers was Redwald of Rendlesham who, on his death in 625, was interred along with a mountain of treasure in an eighty-foot-long burial boat that would be discovered in its watery grave in 1939. Today, Redwald's treasured possessions can be viewed at the British Museum in London. But we had other topics on our minds.[1]

By the time we arrived in Woodbridge, it was already 11:00 P.M., and so we left a message on Diane's answer phone and asked her to call us the next day. At exactly nine o'clock the following morning Jon's cell phone rang. It was Diane and arrangements were made to meet her at 1.30 P.M. at the (relatively) close-by town of Orford at the Old Warehouse restaurant on Quay Street for that most British of lunches: fish and chips.

A thousand years ago Orford was a very small town; by the twelfth century, however, King Henry II had transformed it into a bustling coastal port. Work began in 1165 on the town's castle and was completed in 1173. It provided the perfect defense from anyone trying to invade England, but today, sadly, only its ninety-foot-high tower remains. As we had time on our hands, we went sightseeing and ended up down at the riverside, across from which is Orford Ness, a site steeped in intrigue and mystery that was the focal point of much secret government work undertaken in both the pre- and postwar eras in the fields of weapons development, radar, and much more.[2]

As we entered the Old Warehouse, a waving hand from across the room signaled to us where Diane was sitting and we walked over. Diane was in her late thirties, slim and attractive, and she wore her dark hair in bangs. She had spent the best part of a decade working in London and was a wizard with stocks and bonds. As a result, Diane had done very well for herself financially and the world of nine-to-five was one that she had left behind—with much relief, she added. Indeed, as far as we could tell, she was living very well and very happily on the handsome profits that she had made from those same stocks and bonds. Diane also had a fine sense of humor and shared endless tales of merriment with us in the following two hours.

"You look a bit like Daphne from *Scooby-Doo*," said Richard at one point. Diane laughed hysterically and replied: "Well, at least you didn't say I looked like Shaggy!" In fact, we were all having such a good time talking about anything and everything *but* the unexplained, that we decided to continue our two-day break and rescheduled our business to later that evening at the Jolly Sailor Inn, also on Quay Street.

"The Rendlesham Forest incident was really interesting to me," Diane began as we all drank ale and ate snacks at the Jolly Sailor, "because my dad worked in the RAF and he had got interested in it and told me about it when I was about twenty-two or -three. I bought the book on the case that was published by then and living right in town before I went to London meant that I could track down some of the people involved—the witnesses, I mean. After doing that I realized that things weren't quite as straightforward as they seemed.

"It was kind of strange. I think with me being local and not wanting to publish anything that people were a bit more open with me. I'd spoken with various people who had had some sort of involvement in the UFO thing or had seen something weird, had a friend who had, things like that. But I also got a lot of leads from people who had seen other things in Rendlesham."

"Other things?" said Richard, trying to sound as mysterious as possible and rolling his eyes wildly in the process.

"Isn't he adorable?" Diane laughed and gave Richard's goatee a playful tug. He blushed a deep red and found himself the butt of many jokes for the next five minutes. "What I mean," Diane continued, "is that I got a couple of reports from people who had seen strange animals in the exact same place the UFOs had been seen in 1980. But these reports were from 1956 and 1983. We can go and meet the witnesses tomorrow," she said casually, while sipping on her cider. When she told us that one of the people had seen a large and spectral black dog and the other had seen something that had to have been the Shug Monkey, we could only accept her kind offer. And so with the work out of the way, monsters and mysteries were once again relegated to the farthest corners of our minds. Shortly before closing time and after what had been a surprisingly sober night for us, we said our good-byes—at least for the next twelve hours.

As we opened the door to the Mystery Machine the next morning, the three of us smiled widely. Summer had returned and the hot sun was bearing down upon the landscape. At 10:00 A.M. Diane pulled up alongside the camper in her Volvo amid a screech of brakes, and after sharing a pot of tea we all drove off in her car for our first port of call.

Sam Holland lived in a nearby town and greeted us warmly as we entered his bright and pleasant home. Aged seventy-three, he was now retired after a career as a carpenter and spent his time caring for a beautiful garden packed with all manner of plants, flowers, and trees.

We sat down over coffee and cake in his lounge, where Holland would tell us his remarkable tale. He began by congratulating Jon on his 1998 television appearance on *To the Ends of the Earth*. He had enjoyed the program immensely. Jon winced slightly. Ostensibly this was a one-hour documentary based on an expedition that Jon and Graham had made with a Channel 4 television crew to Puerto Rico in search of the island's vampirelike Chupacabras or Goat Sucker—so named after its alleged fondness for goats' blood. Even Jon would admit on seeing the finished, screened version, however, that the monster-hunting aspect of the story was secondary. As Jon stated: "The production team made it obvious that they were not interested in filming an investigation into the Chupacabras but were more interested in making a film about a fat bloke getting in and out of small cars and sweating like a pig under the blazing-hot tropical sun." Nevertheless Sam Holland had enjoyed the program and seemed to hold Jon in a high degree of awe, much to our amusement.[3]

Diane related to Holland the purpose of our six-week-long quest and he was happy to speak with us, provided that we would all agree to head out to the forest with him to the location in question. We unanimously agreed to do so and off we went. It was two or three days after New Year's Day in 1956, he explained, and he had been walking his spaniel dog, Harry, in Rendlesham Forest on what was a cold and icy morning. He strolled casually along and threw sticks for Harry to fetch—when he wasn't on the trail of the scent of a fox, said Holland, fondly recalling his faithful and long-departed old friend.

All was normal until they reached an area of the forest that, we were able to determine as we walked the same route as Holland had all those years before, was only fifty feet or so away from the location of at least one of the alleged UFO landing sites of December 1980. Both Sam Holland and Harry froze. Around forty feet in front of them was a diabolical creature striding purposefully along a rough pathway. It walked on four well-proportioned and incredibly muscular legs and its fur coat was black and glossy. Large claws curled out of its paws and a long, powerful tail flicked in the air. The creature was easily ten feet in length, said Holland, and so could not have been anything as mundane as a wildcat.

As he stood rooted to the spot, Holland said, he watched in horror as the animal suddenly stopped, seemingly aware that it was being watched, and turned its head in his direction. It was then that Holland got a good look at the creature's head and face. The best description he could give was to say that its head looked very much like that of a large male silverback gorilla, with a huge neck, wide nostrils, and immense jaws. But this was no normal ape. In fact, said Holland, it reminded him of a combination of ape, dog, lion, and rhinoceros! If it had wanted to, the creature could easily have killed him and his dog, Holland added. Instead, it seemed unconcerned by their presence. After gazing casually at them for what was no more than ten seconds, the creature continued on its way and disappeared into the undergrowth, making a crashing noise as it did so. Both man and dog fled the forest and raced back home.

Holland's wife, who had passed away in 1997, had been at home and was shocked by the sight of her husband as he ran breathlessly into the house and slammed the door behind him. Harry the spaniel ran shaking to the safety of his basket and Holland slumped into a chair. He and his wife talked at length about what dog and master had seen and debated endlessly over the course of the next few hours about whether or not they should inform anyone in a position of authority—such as the army, perhaps. Ultimately, they decided to remain silent.

"I'm no zoologist, that's for sure," Holland told us. "But I know in my heart that there is nothing on this planet that looks like that thing did. And I also knew in my heart that it wouldn't be found if anyone went looking for it. I don't know why I thought that, but I knew it wasn't something of this world. So what could I do? I said nothing."

That is, until just before his retirement, when Holland had fitted a new front door to the home of Diane's father and the two men got talking about the UFO landing in the forest. Holland finally decided to reveal the facts and agreed to speak with Diane.

"And that's really the story," said Holland. "I wish I could tell you more but it was all so brief that it was over after it had barely begun. But I know what I saw and won't ever forget it. Never." With that Jon crashed to the ground, having tripped over a fallen and decayed old tree trunk, and echoed his two near-calamitous falls in the woods during our gargoyle hunt. It was left up to Richard and me to try to raise Jon's gargantuan bulk to a standing position again. In a series of swift moves that reminded me of the way in which the mighty pillars of Stonehenge could have been erected, we had Jon back on his feet amid a hearty round of applause from Sam Holland and Diane.

Until he spoke with Diane, Holland had never heard of the legends of the Shug Monkey; however, the description of the beast as part mastiff and part ape seemed to suggest that Holland had indeed undergone a rare encounter with one of the elusive beasts. And at the site of Britain's most famous UFO encounter, no less. We stayed with Sam Holland for another two hours and toured his large and impressive garden. We asked him endless questions and asked him to repeat his story—which he did, without hesitation. He never elaborated or speculated and would, to his credit, only relate the facts as he recalled them. We were left with no doubt that the Shug Monkey was a very real phenomenon and we felt privileged to have met someone of such credibility who was willing to risk ridicule and speak out.

The second interview Diane had secured for us was with a couple: Paul and Jayne Jennings of Woodbridge. They, too, told us that they had seen a strange, four-legged beast deep within Rendlesham Forest on a winter afternoon in 1983. Both in their early twenties at the time and engaged to be married, they were walking very close to where Sam Holland's encounter had occurred twenty-five years previously when they saw what Jayne Jennings described as "a big black dog that kept appearing and disappearing." When I asked her to elaborate, she explained that they had been walking along a pathway and on rounding a bend in the path came face-to-face with the dog.

It was a huge creature and, strangely, she said that while the head was unmistakably that of a large hound, the body was more feline in nature. For a moment the Jenningses and the dog stared at each other. The dog was not aggressive, Jayne Jennings said. In fact, it had a mournful expression on its face. But they were shocked when it vanished in the blink of an eye. They were even more shocked, however, when a moment later it reappeared and proceeded to "flicker on and off" four or five times before vanishing permanently. Paul Jennings told us that after the dog's final disappearance, the air was filled with a strange smell that resembled "burning metal." Like Sam Holland, the Jenningses did not wish to speculate upon their strange experience and instead said that the facts they had related told the whole story. We thanked the couple and said our good-byes.

Later that evening Diane joined us for a Chinese take-out meal and bottled beer in the Mystery Machine (no one can say that we don't know how to treat a lady) and we discussed the events and Diane's additional research. She told us that Sam Holland's case was the only one that she had been able to uncover that involved the Shug Monkey. However, in her files were seven or eight additional reports from people who had seen spectral dogs and cats within Rendlesham Forest; these were not flesh-and-blood beasts—at least not in the way that we understand them, she added. Most of the additional witnesses, Diane said, didn't want to comment publicly, but she had no doubt that they were being genuine.

Diane's research had also led her to investigate what was probably Britain's most famous phantom canine story, the Black Dog of Bungay, Suffolk, which paralleled the tale of the lightning strike at the church of Widecombe-in-the-Moor in 1638. It was August 4, 1577, when a terrifying event occurred at the village church in Bungay. An account written shortly afterward, which can be found at the Parish Church of St. Mary in Bungay, tells the story of what took place. Although written in old English, its contents are decipherable. Diane passed us a copy of the document, titled "A Straunge and Terrible Wunder wrought very late in the parish Church of Bungay":

Immediately hereupon, there appeared in a most horrible similitude and likeness to the congregation then and there present a dog as they might discerne it, of a black colour; at the site whereof, together with the fearful flashes of fire which they were then seene, moved such admiration in the minds of the assemblie, that they thought doomsday was already come. This black dog, or the divil in such a likenesse (God hee knoweth all who worketh all) running all along down the body of the church with great swiftnesse and incredible haste, among the people, in a visible forum and shape, passed betweene two persons, as they were kneeling upon their knees, and occupied in prayer as it seemed, wrung the necks of them bothe at one instant clene backward, in so much that even at a moment where they kneeled, they strangely died. There was at ye same time another wunder wrought; for the same black dog, still continuing and remaining in one and the self same shape, passing by another man of the congregation in the church, gave him such a gripe on the back, that therewith all he was presently drawen together and shrunk up, as it were a peece of lether scorched in a hit fire; or as the mouth of a purse or bag, drawen together with string. The man albeit hee was in so strange a taking, dyed not, but as it is thought is yet alive; whiche thing is marvelous in the eyes of men, and offereth much matter of amasing the minde.

It was only shortly afterward that the beast appeared at the church at nearby Blythburgh:

Placing himself upon a maine balke or beam, whereon some ye Rood did stand, sodainly he gave a swinge downe through ye church, and there also, as before, slew two men and a lad, and burned the hand of another person that was there among the rest of the company, of whom divers were blasted.

Diane related that she had dug deeply into the legends of the Bungay black dog and the similar events from Rendlesham Forest and told us of her findings. We all made ourselves comfortable and opened four more chilled bottles of beer. There were, she had learned, dozens of legends of such beasts all across the land. Throughout Suffolk and Norfolk there were references to Black Shuck and Old Shuck. "And it's almost certain that the Shug Monkey of Rendlesham is a derivation of the word Shuck, which comes from the old English word of scucca."

"What does that mean?" I asked.

"Demon," said Diane cheerfully. And around Britain there were numerous tales of similar beasts that were deeply rooted in British folklore, including Padfoot, Black Shag, the Gurt Dog, the Wisht Hound, and Skriker. She also provided for us a copy of an extract from a manuscript housed at Nottingham County Library. Dating from 1952, it told the story of a Mrs. Smalley:

> Her grandfather, who was born in 1804 and died in 1888, used to have occasion to drive from Southwell to Bathley in a pony and trap. This involved going along Crow Lane, which leaves South Muskham opposite the school and goes to Bathley. Frequently, along that lane he saw a black dog trotting alongside his trap. Round about 1915 his great-grandson, Mrs. Smalley's son Sydney, used to ride out from Newark on a motorcycle to their home at Bathley. He went into Newark to dances and frequently returned at about 11 o'clock at night. He too often saw a black dog in Crow Lane; he sometimes tried to run over it but was never able to. One night Sydney took his father on the back of the motorcycle especially to see the dog, and both of them saw it.[4]

Diane's files also contained accounts of spectral black dogs that possessed the familiar glowing red eyes, a characteristic of the Glastonbury gargoyle and of several of the man-beast incidents that Jon had investigated. For example, she was aware of a ghostly hound with huge red eyes that haunted an old well near Baildon and the nearby (and aptly named) Slaughter Lane.[5] And interestingly, her files contained one report that could conceivably have involved a much bigger and far more powerful Shug Monkey–type beast.

It was in 1613, said Diane, at the church of Great Chart, Kent, that a large animal materialized among the congregation and killed and seriously injured a number of people, destroyed a wall, and subsequently vanished into thin air. "The creature was as big as, and vaguely resembled, a bull," said Diane.[6] Could this be the same huge creature seen in Rendlesham Forest by Sam Holland more than four hundred and fifty years later?

We told Diane about our quest so far and she was highly excited by everything that we had to say and lamented the fact (as did we) that she didn't have the time to accompany us on the rest of our journey. But she was greatly intrigued by Mother Sarah Graymalkin's tale of the Cormons and conceded that it gelled perfectly with her own theories about why such creatures were seen in the same vicinity as UFOs and other creatures.

"Do you have any ideas why so many of these black dog sightings occurred in churches?" asked Richard.

She thought for a moment and shifted slightly uneasily in her seat. "Well, this realm that Mother Sarah said that the Cormons came from: What if it's hell?" For a moment we all sat in silence. "What if this realm is really hell and the sightings occurred in churches because holy places were seen as being the one place able to do very real harm to the Cormons? And was there an instinct on the part of the Cormons to kill anyone associated with churches?" Was it possible that the gateway Mother Sarah talked about was really an entrance point to the underworld? We all felt a chill go through our bodies at the possibility.

But Diane's research did not end with black dogs and Shug Monkeys. She gave us a word-for-word copy of the text of Ralph of Coggershall's account of 1200 that concerned a wild man captured in the area forty years previously. In *Chronicon Anglicanum,* he wrote:

In the time of King Henry II, when Bartholomew de Glanville was in charge of the castle at Orford, it happened that some fishermen fishing in the sae there caught in their nets a wildman. He was naked and was like a man in all his members, covered with hair and with a long shaggy beard. He eagerly ate whatever was brought to him, but if it was raw he pressed it between his hands until all the juice was expelled. He would not talk, even when tortured and hung up by his feet. Brought into church, he showed no signs of reverence or belief. He sought his bed at sunset and always remained there until sunrise. He was allowed to go into the sea, strongly guarded with three lines of nets, but he dived under the nets and came up again and again. Eventually he came back of his own free will. But later on he escaped and was never seen again.

Once again, here was evidence of yet further unusual activity of a cryptozoological nature at the site of a famous UFO incident. And with that fact firmly fixed in our minds, Diane said, regretfully, she had to leave as she had an early appointment the following day. We walked Diane to her car and waved her good-bye. "Keep me informed," she shouted as she vanished at speed, spinning wheels into the Woodbridge night.

The night might have just been coming to a close for Diane but for us it had barely begun. Two hours later we were deep within Rendlesham Forest looking for phantom black dogs and Shug Monkeys, this time armed with our trusty night-scope and flashlight as we prepared to seek out the beasts. The Shug Monkey remained elusive but after being in the forest for the best part of an hour, and even before we had tried to invoke the beast, we heard an eerie and drawn-out howl. It was not a fox—that was for sure. And were it not for the fact that they had died out in England centuries before, I would have sworn it was the howl of a wolf—or maybe that of a werewolf.

As we continued to scour the forest, a thought came to Richard. Perhaps, he mused, the reason why we were having so much apparent success in our quest for wild men, gargoyles, and other beasts was because now that we had uncovered their secret, the Cormons were keeping a watchful and careful eye on us. It was true that our quarry always seemed to remain just outside of our grasp; but it also seemed to be forever toying with us and teasing us—and from a close range, too.

On leaving the forest, we made our way to the old (and now decommissioned) Royal Air Force base that had played such a central role in the infamous UFO incident twenty-one years previously. Again a loud and ominous howling could be heard in the distance and for a moment Jon thought that he had seen something running low and fast across the old and long-deserted runway. We checked it out, but found nothing. But Rendlesham Forest was a strange and magickal place. Of that much we could be certain.

13

CANNIBALS AND CATS

**Like a cat caught up a tree,
this could only happen to me.**

"CRUMMY STUFF," THE RAMONES

The next major stop on what was rapidly turning into a tour of the entire country was the Lincolnshire town of Skegness, also on the east coast of England. Jon was unsure how productive our excursion to the town was going to be, but he told Richard and me that a man named Morris Allen had written to him in 2000 expressing a strange theory. According to Allen, he had in his possession solid evidence that there were small pockets of cannibals living in the wilds of Britain and that the authorities, knowing this, were too afraid to inform the public. As a result, a huge cover-up had been put into place that he, Allen, had succeeded in penetrating.

Since this sounded very similar to the theories postulated by our doctor friend, Alfred, as they related to tales of wild men running rampant around the U.K., we decided that no harm would be done by at least looking into the claims of Morris Allen. Indeed, a day spent with him might open yet more doors for us, we concluded.

A minor scuffle over music broke out on our way to Skegness. "Please," said Jon, "can we have a break from all this punk music? I am not feeling at all sane today and this is not helping me." He chugged down a couple of diazepam pills with his glass of Diet Coke and Jack Daniel's as the Anti-Nowhere League's classic song "I Hate People" boomed out of the speakers.

"How about we listen to some George Harrison?" asked Jon. Richard and I looked at each other with appalled expressions on our faces. However, considering that we *had* subjected Jon to a steady stream of all things punk ever since we had left Exeter, we agreed that he deserved a break. And it *was* his CD player, after all. We were in no real rush to get to Skegness and so we took a long and leisurely drive, stopping at a pleasant little coastal village for lunch, and spent the afternoon strolling along the nearby sands with a flask of hot tea. Allen had told us that we could meet him at any time as he and his mother kept a bed-and-breakfast outlet in town and he was there at all times.

"How old is this guy?" asked Richard.

"Well, I spoke to him on the phone once and I'd say he sounded about mid-fifties," Jon replied.

"And he lives with his mom?" Richard said.

Jon looked at Richard with a slightly apologetic expression on his face. "I know. But let's hear him out." We arrived at Skegness around 6:30 that evening and decided that, once again, merriment would have to come before work and we spent the next eight hours checking out the town's nightlife and lowlife. We would meet Morris Allen the following morning at 9:30 sharp.

We found the Allen's bed-and-breakfast establishment with relative ease; and after finally locating a suitable parking place for the Mystery Machine, we hired a taxicab to take us on the five-minute journey across town. We proceeded up the steps and knocked on the front door. In a few seconds the door was opened by a large lady of about seventy-five years. "Hi, is Morris in?" I asked.

Given that Morris was in his fifties and still lived with his mom, I thought for a moment that the lady was going to tell us that he couldn't come out to play today and that we should go back home. But instead she invited us in and shouted in the direction of the staircase at the top of her voice: "Morris, there's people to see you."

Thirty seconds later, Morris Allen came running down the stairs, exuding boundless enthusiasm. Yes, Morris *was* in his fifties. And he lived with his mom. He also wore a ridiculously bad black wig that stuck out at an alarming angle at the base of his neck. I rolled my eyes at Richard.

"Come on up," said Morris eagerly after the introductions and we all followed him upstairs. "Mom," he shouted, "can we have some tea and biscuits, please?"

"Yes, I'll bring them up. And don't forget to wash your hands," she added.

"Mother of God," groaned Jon, as Morris quickly headed for the bathroom to fulfill his mom's request and we stood outside of his bedroom.

"This is gonna be a good laugh," said Richard, nudging me.

"Jon, you certainly can pick 'em!" I added. In a moment Morris returned, wiping his hands on his trousers.

"In we go, then," he said, ushering us into his bedroom. For a moment we all stood in awe at the spectacle before us. One of the walls was adorned with posters of Sylvester Stallone from his Rambo years, and another was packed with all manner of images and pictures, pulled from various magazines and newspapers, of the American actress Morgan Fairchild.

"Do you like her?" Morris asked me eagerly.

"Er, I guess so," I replied, wondering how long it would be before we could leave.

"She's great. Sly is too," he said to himself more than to anyone else. Morris had already brought chairs into the room for us all and so we sat down and, after Morris had finished relating to us, in mind-numbing detail, the history of the glamorous Morgan's television and film career, we got down to the matter at hand: the cannibals. Morris pulled out from under his bed four large cardboard boxes. They contained, literally, about two or three thousand clippings culled from both regional and national newspapers.

"Read a few," he said, prompting us to dig deep into the boxes. We each pulled out a handful of reports, some new and some yellowed by age. The first one I looked at concerned the crash of a truck on a Suffolk road in 1985 that had been carrying dangerous chemicals. I read on and saw that the police and the fire service had been forced to block off the road.

"And this means what?" I asked, dumbfounded.

"Well, don't you see?" No. I didn't. Morris elaborated: "I suspect that this was one of the cannibal attacks and the police created this cover story with the chemicals to keep people out of the area while they removed whatever was left of the bodies of the victims."

Morris was a lunatic. "Your turn, Jon," I said. Jon dug into his pile and pulled out a small cutting from a local paper that was more than twenty years old and concerned an old wartime German mine that had been washed up on a beach on the east coast. Once again, the authorities had sealed off the area to ensure that no one ended up blown to pieces.

"Another cover?" asked Jon, with a weary look on his face.

Morris nodded. "Of course! Some of them live near the beaches in caves, so that's where they will attack you."

"I see," Jon said diplomatically. Richard proceeded to scan a few of the clippings and found many in the pile that referred to incidents in which sheep had been killed under mysterious circumstances in the north of England. Speculation was rife in the media that these killings were the work of big cats, such as panthers and pumas that were on the loose. But Morris knew better. When the cannibals couldn't get their hands on people, they would resort to killing animals for food.

"And where did you come up with this theory?" asked Richard. Despite the fact that Morris was undoubtedly as mad as a hatter, we listened with great interest as he told his tale. In 1968 Morris had been walking with the family's pet dog along the coast near, of all places, the town of Orford. He said that in the distance he had seen someone squatting on the sand and leaning over something. As he got closer, Morris said, he could see that the man was dressed in what looked like an animal skin and was tearing into the flesh of a dead rabbit. The man was dirt-encrusted, with long, tangled hair and had wild, staring eyes. Morris held the dog tightly and could only watch with a mixture of fascination and horror. Suddenly the man held his head aloft and quickly looked in Morris's direction, as if he had picked up his scent. The man quickly scooped up the rabbit, bounded off into the grass and was lost to sight. And it was that encounter, thirty-three years previously, that had led Morris to devote his life to resolving the mystery of the wild man.

I am no psychiatrist but Jon would later tell us that based on his experience as a mental health nurse in the 1980s, Morris probably *had* undergone a genuine encounter all those years ago. However, the event had so severely traumatized him that it had now become an obsession; and anything that, in Morris's eyes, seemed remotely out of the ordinary (such as the recovery of an old wartime mine or the crash of a truck laden with chemicals) was incorporated into his bizarre theories.

Morris told us that he had never seen the wild man again and had never actually met anyone else who had seen him, either. But he knew that the wild man was still out there—as were more of his kind, all living off the bodies of the many people around the country that go missing each and every year. We stayed with Morris for several hours that day and it was a truly unique and weird experience. Despite the fact that, yes, he was a somewhat eccentric character, we all wondered how different his life would have been had he not had that chance encounter back in 1968. Would he still be living with his mother and in a bedroom filled with thousands of old newspaper clippings and dozens of pictures and posters of Hollywood stars who he would probably never meet? Almost certainly not.

But for all the general weirdness that accompanied Morris's story, we were still greatly intrigued by his 1968 encounter, which tied in with Alfred's tale of cannibals roaming the countryside. It also tallied very closely with the story told by Ralph of Coggershall about a similar wild man seen in the same vicinity centuries before.

Morris could remember nothing else of any significance and he asked us if we could make our own way downstairs and out of the house. We left him to his lonely existence, his precious newspaper clippings, and his pictures of Morgan and Sylvester and continued on our quest.

But there was another reason why we wanted to come to Skegness, too. Back in 1986, Andy Roberts had written a small, privately published booklet titled *Cat Flaps!* that chronicled numerous reports of Alien Big Cats (or ABC's, as they are known) in the north of England. The booklet was a minor classic among the Fortean research community but after going out of print it, like the ABC's were prone to, vanished without a trace. More than a decade later, however, we published, with Andy's approval, a new edition of his seminal work.[1] What was most interesting to me in light of our current expedition was that *Cat Flaps!* contained a number of cases that seemed distinctly relevant to our quest for the truth about British monsters and the Cormons, including one case from Skegness in 1976 that allegedly involved the sighting of a cougar. So here we were again, chasing wild men in a town with a history of big cat encounters.

The alleged cougar was seen roaming around the grounds of Seely House, a Skegness seafront convalescent home, late in the afternoon of September 20, 1976, by Alec Jamieson of the Skegness police force. Jamieson was quoted in the local papers as saying, "It was a large cat about five feet long and sandy-colored; definitely a cougar." The police were subsequently called in and Police Constable Jock Gartshore shortly thereafter saw the creature, which he described as "a large cat about the size of a Labrador." Police searching the grounds of the convalescent home came up with evidence in the shape of several large paw prints measuring two-and-a-half inches by three inches; but unfortunately, local newspaper accounts of the time did not report whether these prints were of a cougar or something more mundane. But the story was far from over.

Members of the staff at Seely House also reported having seen the animal on many occasions over the preceding weeks and they thought that it was a large dog. Baffled, the police brought in an inspector from the RSPCA (Royal Society for the Prevention of Cruelty to Animals), and he, together with local naturalist John Yeadon, hid themselves in the house grounds in the hope of seeing and photographing the beast. They had no success.

A senior police officer at the time said, "We are keeping an open mind. Obviously we must take precautions, but from all we have heard, it seems that whatever it is, it is not dangerous."

The Skegness sightings had, true to form, followed the classic mystery cat pattern. Several people, some of them reliable witnesses such as policemen, had seen the creature. Unsubstantiated evidence in the shape of the paw prints was found, but a search had proved fruitless. In other words, like so many other monsters that we encountered on our journey, and in the fashion of the Cormons, too, the Skegness Cougar had vanished back to the unknown plane from which it had so mysteriously arrived.[2] Perhaps not surprisingly after a passage of twenty-five years, no one in the area recalled the sighting, but it was a case that intrigued us all and that made us mindful of the fact that like so many other places that we traveled to on our journey of discovery, Skegness was a strange one—a very strange one.

⊞ ⊞ ⊞

Having departed from Skegness later that day, our next port of call was over the border in Scotland, where we were going to confront what is arguably the world's most famous monster: Nessie, the dark and mysterious denizen of Loch Ness. But on the way, we decided, we would do a sightseeing tour of the north of England where there had occurred a number of big cat encounters that Andy Roberts had chronicled in *Cat Flaps!*

Our first visit was to the small North Yorkshire hamlet of Lower Marshes, near Malton. In early September 1985 an encounter had taken place here involving five young farmers who had seen a "black panther with orange eyes and a long black tail disappearing into a cornfield." As was the case at Skegness, the trail here had long gone cold, but the reference to an out-of-place animal with brightly colored eyes suggested to us something far more unusual than a mere wildcat.

One month later, Andy's research showed, a similar beast was seen by Richard Clifford of Starbeck, Harrogate. Eighty years of age at the time and a retired farmer, he kept a small farm just off the A59 Harrogate-to-Knaresborough road, and had informed Andy that he had seen the mysterious animal on at least six occasions in October 1985. All of the sightings were in clear weather conditions and from a distance of about forty yards, he said. Clifford had described the animal as being the size of a small German shepherd, with a long tail and a low-slung belly. The creature was jet black with a shorthaired, shiny coat. The mysterious animal was seen in the fields adjoining Clifford's small farm, running across the fields and jumping into and sitting among the branches of an old oak tree.

Despite having observed the mystery animal on many occasions for periods of up to several minutes and being certain that it was a big cat of some description, Richard Clifford remained puzzled about some aspects of the animal's behavior, Andy had noted. For instance, he was fully aware that if an animal of this type *was* living in the vicinity, then there should have been evidence of its eating habits, such as rabbit carcasses. Clifford had looked for such signs in the fields in which the animal was seen but found none. Nor were any paw prints ever discovered that could have been attributed to an unknown animal. Like so many of the other creatures encountered on our search, this one, too, seemed to possess phantomlike qualities. But Richard Clifford was not the only witness to the beast.

Brian Cooper of Forrest Lane Head, Harrogate, was the next person to catch sight of the animal in early October 1985—and at the same location as Richard Clifford. It was a clear and sunny afternoon at three o'clock when Cooper viewed the animal from a distance of about 250 yards for a period of about ten minutes. He described what he saw as a "big black cat on the ground . . . my Jack Russell chased it into a tree, barking furiously." He thought that what he had seen was a puma with "a low-slung belly and a very long tail." As for its size, Cooper estimated it to be "three times the size of a domestic cat." And then another witness came forward: Mr. C. T. Matthews, also of Forrest Lane Head, Harrogate.

At lunchtime on a warm and cloudy Sunday afternoon in October 1985, Matthews saw the mystery animal in the same fields as in the previous sightings and watched it for five minutes from a distance of about one hundred and twenty yards as it entered the field and skirted the perimeter before exiting near its point of entry. The animal passed close to a diseased rabbit but appeared uninterested in it. Matthews described the animal as being black and the size of a large cat and considered it to be a "young puma."

Perhaps the most significant case investigated by Andy, however, was that of the Rossendale Lion. Rossendale is a collection of valleys on the fringes of the Pennines hill chain about fourteen miles northeast of the city of Manchester. The valley bottoms are heavily populated, but in a matter of minutes, you can be on the high moorland that surrounds the area. It was on farmland bordering this moorland that the Rossendale Lion had its brief moment of glory.

As with the Harrogate Panther sightings, the first report of the Rossendale Lion only came to light in retrospect. Fourteen-year-old Bury schoolboy Owen Jepson was the first, and one of the very few people to see the beast. "I just saw its back legs and tail as it jumped over some rushes. The tracks were cat prints. I got books out of the library and decided that it only matched up with a mountain lion," said Owen. No one, however, took his sighting seriously, until a number of mysterious sheep killings occurred in the area. The killings took place on the fifty-acre Hawthorn Farm at Whitewell Bottom. The sheep had had the flesh completely stripped from their carcasses and there was evidence that a cow had been mauled, too.

With the animal killings demonstrating a sudden and serious development, the police became involved. Aided by local farmers armed with sticks, they searched the Whitewell Bottom and the Scoutbottom Moor areas, both on foot and on horseback. The acting police chief of Rossendale, David Nutter, advised people to stay away from the moors saying, "We have had reports that would suggest there is a possibility that it is some kind of large cat. If it is, we have no idea where it can have come from. Until we establish what it is, I would advise people to stay away from the area. At this moment we do not know what it is." Elsewhere, an unnamed police spokesman was more definite as to the existence of the creature: "People are advised to keep away from the area while this wild animal is at large."

Tracks, purportedly left by the mystery creature, were soon found on St. Naze Hill and the mammal curator of Chester Zoo, Peter Wait, was called in to inspect them. After seeing the prints, which were somewhat dried out in a patch of mud, Wait pronounced his verdict: "Definitely dog prints. These were not made by a big cat." The prints may have only been those of a dog, but Wait did not rule out the possibility that an animal of more exotic origins was roaming the moor, too. "If there is a puma up here, I'm afraid they'll have to shoot him. After a while living wild they become very cunning and almost impossible to trap alive. Nowadays all dangerous cats must be licensed and none has been reported missing."

Despite all-night vigils by armed farmers and the setting of traps baited with dead sheep, the farmers caught nothing and nothing more was ever seen or heard of the Rossendale Lion. But the most bizarre aspect of the case was still to come and involved a woman named Barbara Brandolini. A witch who headed a coven in Manchester at the time and who went under the name of Margansa, was attempting with her coven to buy an old Baptist chapel at Slack, next to Hepstonstall, high on the moors above Hebden Bridge in West Yorkshire and only ten miles or so away from the scene of the Rossendale events. Margansa and her friends wanted to buy the old chapel with a view to turning it into an occult temple and were at the time receiving stiff opposition from local vicars who had visions of hordes of naked pagans having wild orgies and sacrifices in a house of God. Seizing the chance for a bit of free publicity, Margansa, in a radio interview on August 15, claimed that *she* was responsible for the sheep killings in Rossendale. But how was she responsible? Was she the owner of an errant mountain lion, perhaps? Nothing so simple. Margansa claimed that she had actually *become* the panther and had done the dirty deed herself. Threatening to do the same again, she said, "I will appear as a big cat in Hepstonstall. People tend to think it all belongs in books and so on but it does not. It is very real."

The following evening's *Halifax Evening Courier* reported that no panthers, black or otherwise, had been seen in Hepstonstall on the previous night; although, interestingly, strange animal noises *had* been heard. But Brandolini's publicity stunt backfired on her and due to the hue and cry she created, the chapel was sold to God-fearing Christians instead. The witch faded from prominence, although she was still claiming as late as August 1986 that she *had* shape-shifted into the Rossendale beast.

The local folk of Rossendale held many and varied opinions as to what the mystery creature actually was. Some thought it was just a dog, most likely a Great Dane, while others held more exotic theories. Among them was the widespread belief that the killings were the work of a population of wild lynx that had been roaming the moors above the Rossendale Valley for the past five years, living in caves in one of the quarries on the edge of the moor. But the story now becomes even stranger still.

The quarries in question are all located above the Rossendale village of Stacksteads, which is approximately five miles from the Whitewell Bottom area. This connection with the creatures allegedly living in quarries is intriguing, since Rossendale was, in the late 1970s, host to another visitation from unexplained phenomena, this time in the shape of a wave of UFO encounters. These events were heavily featured in Jenny Randles's book *The Pennine UFO Mystery*.[3] Briefly, hundreds of UFOs were seen in the Rossendale area with more than a few being seen flying over—and appearing to land in—the very quarries where the locals thought the mystery lynx could be living. A Rossendale tailor, Mike Sacks, saw such a UFO apparently land in one of the quarries. When he drove up to take a better look, he saw something in the quarry that definitely could not have been of earthly manufacture. The UFO flap lasted considerably longer than the mystery animal sightings, and needless to say, no UFO was ever actually found that might have accounted for the wealth of sightings.

Although these various encounters occurred almost two decades ago, they were highly instructive and demonstrated to us that, as in the south of England, the north of the country, too, was a prime location for mystery animals, UFOs, and witchcraft. And in the same way that many of the strange creatures that we had investigated had reportedly been seen for hundreds of years, the same was true of the alien big cats. One case that Andy had investigated, and that we paid a visit to the location of, concerned the Barnborough Wood Cat.

According to legend, a local man, one Percival Cresacre, died at the claws of a "wood cat" in 1475. Riding out from Barnborough through the South Yorkshire countryside in the depths of winter, Percival was accosted by the cat, which jumped onto his horse's saddle. The horse broke into a gallop and unseated Percy, who then realized the cause of the horse's sudden actions. The cat flew at him, fastened itself at the back of his shoulders and wounded him terribly. The fight between the two raged as Percival tried to return to Barnborough. Several times he almost overcame the cat but was weakened tremendously in the struggle. Upon reaching the church porch, the cat was still clinging to him. Utterly exhausted, and in a last attempt to kill the creature, Cresacre fell across the cat and crushed the life from it. This final act was to be Percival's last, too, and he died shortly after being discovered by the church acolyte the following morning. The story of this battle went down in Cresacre family history and is embodied in their crest—still to be seen on the tower of the church at Barnborough.[4]

It should be noted, too, that the action of the mystery cat jumping onto Percival Cresacre's horse and scaring the life out of both parallels very closely the tale of the Man Monkey of Ranton and the ensuing struggle that occurred atop a horse and cart. Were these many and varied cases that Andy Roberts had investigated evidence of the presence of the spectral Cormons, we wondered? There was one way to find out. It was time to attempt an invocation, to invoke the monsters ourselves!

Although we are certain that it would not have gone down at all well with the local populace had they known of it at the time, we decided to proceed with our invocation within the grounds of the churchyard itself: at night under a starry sky. We could in reality have conducted the invocation at any time, but it would have been very difficult to explain our presence to people who saw us sitting cross-legged in the church grounds while trying to summon up demons. And doubtless we would have been ceremoniously slung out, or, worse still, arrested. So by night it had to be. We parked the Mystery Machine nearby and took with us a supply of cola and cookies and a large blanket to sit on.

"So, Richard, now what?" said Jon in hushed tones, as we sat near the doorway of the church. "You are the invocator extraordinaire. Do some invocating."

Richard glared at him. "You can't just do it like that. We have to concentrate."

"Right now, dear boy, I am just concentrating on explaining to the local police what we are doing here if we get arrested. Saying that we are looking for a ghostly cat isn't going to be much of an alibi, I fear," Jon—always anxious—shot back.

"Look, the police aren't here now. So are we going to do this or not?" I said. Richard nodded and Jon agreed. It was now or never. Richard jumped to his feet.

"Mighty cat of the moors; might—" Jon stood up with a speed that surprised me, considering his Jabba the Hut-like frame, and threw a hand across Richard's mouth as Richard screamed his invocation at full blast.

"*What are you doing?*" hissed Jon. "That is the one way that will guarantee that we *do* get locked away for the night. Can't you do this with a bit more decorum?" Richard agreed to turn down the volume.

"Think of a cat's face," Richard said, as we sat in a circle and lit a small candle. Eerily, his voice seemed to change and became much deeper and practically unrecognizable. Somewhere nearby the sound of a glass bottle shattering could be heard as a powerful wind began to blow. "Think of a black cat; think of those eyes, those diabolical, red eyes. Think of the creature walking the moors by night." We concentrated hard and seriously for twenty minutes, as a veritable typhoon seemed to batter the church doors. Richard then forgot his promise to Jon and shouted loudly, "We summon ye! We summon ye!" Jon jumped alarmingly and we all looked around the grounds. Nothing was happening. No red eyes anywhere. No darkened forms darted among the shadows. Nothing. For ten minutes we continued to sit there, wondering if we had succeeded in our quest. But still the creature did not come. Or at least, not right away.

A week later while staying with friends on the English-Scottish border, Jon plugged in his laptop to download his emails and was amazed to find one from a colleague in the big cat-hunting community who had forwarded two reports of big cat sightings, which had occurred two nights previously and only a quarter of a mile from where we had attempted our invocation. Both animals were black in color, around four feet in length, and disappeared as mysteriously as they had arrived. This was surely no coincidence. *We had invoked a Cormon.* But something far stranger was to come.

I had parked the Mystery Machine on the ample driveway of the house of our friends, Paul and Sheila Mottram, and in the morning was startled to find that something had been digging furiously where the driver's-side wheel of the vehicle touched the lawn. Clumps of dirt and grass were everywhere; the Mystery Machine was covered in the stuff; and in one case, dirt had been thrown a distance of about fifteen feet onto the middle of the lawn. Having examined the scene and been unable to ascertain anything conclusive, we said good-bye to Paul and Sheila and continued on our way. We had barely driven for five miles, however, when there was a loud bang, followed by a lurch. I knew immediately what had happened. The driver's-side front tire had blown. This was the same tire that had been covered in grass and dirt by the mysterious animal that had paid a visit to Paul and Sheila's house during the night. After fighting with the steering wheel for about five or ten seconds, I managed to successfully bring the camper to a halt. Changing a wheel on a vehicle like this was an arduous task but having completed it, we continued on our way.

"You know," said Jon, "a less competent driver might have been in real trouble there. Or imagine if it had blown when we were on the motorway doing seventy." It was a sobering thought.

"You know what I think?" said Richard.

"What?" I asked, as Jon looked at him with a puzzled expression.

"I think our invocation worked," Richard replied. "I think we were responsible for those two cat sightings. I think it then paid a visit to the house last night and left a warning mark and then, when we drove off, I think that was an attempt to kill us. It was deliberate sabotage." We had awoken a slumbering beast and it wanted our blood, added Richard.

Fortunately as we headed even farther north and to the great glens and lochs of darkest Scotland, the journey remained incident-free. But I made sure from that moment on that those tires were always full of air. There was no way we were going to fall foul of the Cormons' assassination plot. Or maybe it had all been the work of the witch, Mother Sarah, suggested Richard. Perhaps, he elaborated, this was her way of using the Cormons to take revenge on us for having departed from her house under a dark cloud. Perhaps it was. But the hag was not going to get the best of us. We had lived to fight another day.

14

GREAT BEASTS

Touring, touring, it's never boring.

"TOURING," THE RAMONES

It had been a long time since I had last visited Loch Ness; too long, in fact. I had first gone to the loch at the age of three and a half with my parents in 1968. I have vague memories of playing by the shore and listening to my dad discuss the monster with an elderly couple that had driven there in a camper-style vehicle to investigate sightings of the monster. Now, thirty-three years later, I was about to do the same thing. I had seen nothing unusual in 1968 and neither had my parents, which isn't surprising, and the same could be said for the two subsequent times that I had journeyed to the loch—in the latter part of 1988 and early in 1991.

The journey to the loch was a smooth one and, again, we took our time and spent three pleasant and relaxing days traveling there, making overnight stops at the homes of friends and acquaintances, enjoying banquetlike feasts and partaking in much other merriment. Our quest was proceeding in fine fashion. When we reached the town of Inverness, our journey was almost over.

No less than two hundred and fifty million years ago, movements in the Earth's crust led to the creation of a huge rift across Scotland that, today, is known as the Great Glen. As the centuries passed, the deeper parts of the glen filled with water and it now exists in the form of three main lakes, or lochs, to give them their correct title: Loch Oich, Loch Lochy, and Loch Ness. For more than a century and a half they have been connected by the sixty-mile-long Caledonian Canal that provides passage for small marine vehicles from the North Sea to the Atlantic Ocean.[1]

By far the largest of the three lochs is Loch Ness. Twenty-four miles in length and almost a mile wide, it contains more water than any other British lake; and at its deepest point the loch extends to a mind-boggling depth of almost one thousand feet. Surrounded by trees, mountains and with water as black as ink, it is little wonder that Loch Ness is viewed by many as both a magical and a sinister location.

As we drove past Lochend, we marveled at the majestic scene and pondered on what really resided within the loch's murky waters. As the road began to curve we knew that a good opportunity was coming up to park the Mystery Machine and take in the breathtaking spectacle of Loch Ness's Urquhart Bay and its splendid castle.

Situated at Strone Point, Castle Urquhart could once boast of being one of the largest castles in Scotland, but has stood in ruins for more than two centuries.[2] Nevertheless, there is something about an old, ruined castle that creates an air of mystery and intrigue, and the fact that it overlooks a huge expanse of water that might be home to a true leviathan of the deep, makes Castle Urquhart an even more impressive spectacle to the naked eye. But before we began our hunt for Nessie, we had our sights set on another great beast: Aleister Crowley.

Born on October 12, 1875, in Leamington, England, Crowley was the son of a rich brewer and was raised in a strict Christian household. Indeed, Crowley's father, Edward, was a preacher in a sect known as the Plymouth Brethren. In 1881 the Crowley family moved to Redhill, Surrey, and the young Aleister was sent to an evangelist school. Although it was his original intention to become a chemist, Crowley soon became interested in religious studies and developed a passion for alchemy and magick. In 1898, that interest led him to the Hermetic Order of the Golden Dawn.

He moved in with Allan Bennett, a member of the Golden Dawn, and under the guidance of Bennett began to experiment with ritual magick. Inheriting a considerable fortune from his father, Crowley lived life to its fullest in London, Paris, and in Mexico, where he quickly became a 33rd-degree Mason, and then in 1900, returned to England and at the age of twenty-five headed to Scotland and purchased a house on the shores of Loch Ness.

Originally a hunting lodge for noblemen, Boleskine House was constructed more than two centuries ago on the southern side of Loch Ness. During his time at Boleskine, Crowley was engaged in a magical sequence that was designed to create a "knowledge and conversation with the holy guardian angel." The ritual was an elaborate one, consisting of several weeks of purification and ritual work for Crowley.

Interestingly, at the site of what is probably the world's most famous monster, Crowley's actions (including black masses and wild orgies) led to some disturbing phenomena. In his autobiography, Crowley described how the spirits he had succeeded in summoning got perilously out of hand, causing one housemaid to leave, and a workman to go mad. He also insinuated that he was indirectly responsible for a local butcher accidentally severing an artery and bleeding to death. Crowley had allegedly written the names of demons on a bill from the butcher's shop.

Across from Boleskine House is a graveyard with a reputation for high strangeness, which was established long before Crowley set foot on the scene. One legend suggests that a tunnel exists that links Boleskine and the graveyard, and is said to be the haunt of a band of unholy witches.[3] If you thought that lake monsters were the strangest things in residence at Loch Ness, think again!

After dinner in Inverness that evening we returned to the loch and parked the Mystery Machine as close as we could to its shores and, at around 8:00 P.M., walked down to the water's edge. The dark and steep hills that surrounded the loch made for an imposing sight and the peat-sodden and icy-cold waters of its twenty-four-mile length lapped at our feet. Jon had brought with him his notes on Crowley, and as Richard and I skimmed stones and pebbles across the surface of the loch's mysterious depths, Jon read from a diary that he had kept of his spring 1991 visit to Loch Ness.

Driving past the gates of Boleskine House, Jon had felt a chill run down his spine. He realized that he was within "figurative spitting distance" of one of the most notorious buildings in the British Isles. But the one thing that surprised Jon more than anything else was that even in the early spring, every parking space on the shores of the great peat-soaked loch was crammed with carloads of tourists and monster hunters, all desperate to catch a glimpse of the beast that many had already concluded was some form of ancient dinosaur. It was then that Jon realized there would probably be "a better chance of seeing a bona fide prehistoric survivor behind the bacon counter of your local store." Nevertheless, Jon did not doubt for a moment that something unusual lurked within the loch and referred to the published work of Ted Holliday, a renowned monster hunter and the author of the celebrated book, *The Dragon and the Disc,* and who had also concluded that the monsters of our world were not all that they appeared to be. Commenting on his monster-hunting activities at Loch Ness and elsewhere, Holliday stated:

> Either a camera was not available to record what was observed or, if it was available, circumstances frustrated the photographer. Almost everyone rejected such a notion because it introduced an element of irrationality. It also raised doubts about the true nature of dragons, which those who were anxious to press the claim for an unknown animal chose not to encourage. Normal animals do not behave in such an inexplicable way because they cannot; therefore you had to conclude that the peculiarities were due to chance. This was the prevailing attitude amongst the investigators. An explanation based on chance seemed to me most unsatisfactory. Chance is a random effect; it is just as likely to work in favour of the investigator as against him. If the ten years of intensive effort at Loch Ness which resulted in failure to get a detailed film was the result of chance then it was not a random effect and the expression became meaningless. In that event, the explanation lay elsewhere.[4]

"Holliday was right," said Jon, as we laid blankets out by the shore and opened three cans of lager. "He knew that the sightings of the monster couldn't be explained in rational terms, as if he were just chasing an unknown species of animal. He had experienced the weird synchronicities and the jamming cameras. That's the problem with so many monster hunters and particularly Nessie hunters. In the one camp you have the believers, who suggest that maybe a surviving creature from the time of the dinosaurs lives in the loch, such as a plesiosaur. And in the other camp you have the debunkers who say that it's all nonsense, hoaxes, and misidentifications."

"The plesiosaur theory is bull," said Richard, and Jon and I both agreed. The loch simply didn't have an adequate supply of fish to sustain a thriving colony of such creatures. "If there's anything physical in there, it's a giant eel," said Richard.

"Or maybe a sturgeon, as sturgeons up to twelve feet long have been caught here in the past," said Jon. "But in all probability, something supernatural is going on here not unlike the Cormons. And I don't think it is a coincidence at all that sightings of the monster happen to occur at the exact location where Aleister Crowley, the Great Beast himself, was trying to summon up demons; and where, by Crowley's own admission, some of these same demons got wildly out of control."

And there was another problem, too, with the conventional theories that had been postulated to explain the monster sightings in the loch. It is a little-known fact (and one often overlooked or even ignored by even the most respected of monster hunters) that not everyone who has seen unusual creatures in Loch Ness has described them as having the now-familiar long neck and hump. For example, in 1932 a Miss K. MacDonald saw a creature in the River Ness that closely resembled a crocodile in shape and that had a short neck, long snout, and even tusks, according to some newspaper reports.[5]

As we opened three more cans of lager and a large bag of potato chips, Jon continued: "Now, it's just about remotely possible that the loch could be home to one unidentified species of creature, such as the long-necked variety. But it's stretching credibility just too far to think that there is another type of beast in there, too, or maybe three or even four, and yet people report them. Let me give you another example."

Jon went on to tell us that several years previously he had received a letter from a woman who had seen one of his many and varied monster-hunting exploits advertised on television. She duly tracked him down via the TV station and sent him a remarkable letter. It was the summer of 1938 and then-fourteen-year-old Alice Davenhill was holidaying in Inverness with her family. On the third day of their excursion, the family decided to pay a visit to the loch.

Davenhill told Jon that she was unsure of the exact location where the encounter took place, but she recalled that it was in the vicinity of Castle Urquhart. The family had been driving adjacent to the loch, she said, when they noticed something lying in the middle of the road about three hundred feet away. At first it just looked like a shapeless mass, but as the Davenhills closed in, they saw with horror that the mass was in fact a strange-looking creature that seemed to be basking on the road under the warm sun. As the car came within about one hundred feet of it, the beast began to move and it was then, said Alice, that she and her parents could see its form perfectly. The animal was the color of an elephant, about twelve feet in length, had four stubby legs "like a tortoise's," and two large and rounded eyes protruding from its wide head that was attached to a barrel-like body by a short neck.

Her father brought the car to a rapid halt and the family watched awestruck as the animal, seemingly concerned for its safety, waddled in comic fashion to the side of the road and, in seconds, had disappeared into the undergrowth. The incident had lasted less then a minute, Jon was told, and had remained a family secret right up until the day that Davenhill confided in Jon.

"Now, this was no plesiosaur and it was no eel," said Jon. "But this is the problem: Alice Davenhill's case was no less credible—or incredible—than the body of evidence in support of the existence of a long-necked beast in the loch. But so many researchers just aren't willing to look at these more problematic cases that don't fit nicely into their framework."

I asked Jon, "So what do you think she saw?"

He responded quickly. "I think she, and many of the others, saw a Kelpie."

According to Scottish legend, the Kelpie—or water-horse—is a supernatural entity that haunts the rivers and lochs of Scotland and that has the ability to shape-shift. The most common form that the Kelpie takes is that of a horse. It stands by the water's edge, tempting any passing and weary traveler that might consider continuing his or her journey on four legs rather than two, to mount it. That, however, is the downfall of the traveler, as invariably the beast is then said to rear violently and charge headlong into the depths of the river or loch, drowning its terrified rider.

Interestingly, the Kelpie was also said to appear during thunderstorms and its cries and wailing would be heard as a storm approached. But most intriguing of all was the startling fact that the male Kelpie could transform itself into a large and hair-covered man that would hide in the vegetation of Scottish waterways and leap out to attack the unwary. The females, when in human form, were always spectacularly beautiful.[6]

"So," Jon continued, "there is a Scottish tradition of a lake monster that can alter its form, which may suggest a Cormon-type phenomenon; that was linked with thunderstorms, as was the Black Dog of Bungay and the beast at the church at Widecombe-in-the-Moor; and that was also associated with sightings of big hairy men."

The picture was coming together. Here was further evidence, in the form of the legends and tales of old, of a link between the many and varied creatures that we were pursuing and their paranormal powers and origins, as Mother Sarah had offered was the case. As evidence to support the notion that in Scottish folklore the monster of the lochs were considered to be supernatural in nature, rather than flesh-and-blood creatures, take note of the following from a pamphlet published in 1823:

In the former and darker ages of the world, when people had not half the wit and sagacity they now possess, and when, consequently, they were much more easily duped by such designing agents, the "Ech Uisque," or water-horse, as the Kelpie is commonly called, was a well-known character in these countries. The Kelpie was an infernal agent, retained in the service and pay of Satan, who granted him a commission to execute such services as appeared profitable to his interest. He was an amphibious character, and generally took up residence in lochs and pools, bordering on public roads and other situations most convenient for his professional calling. His commission consisted of the destruction of human beings, without affording them the time to prepare for their immortal interests, and thus endeavored to send their souls to his master, while he, the Kelpie, enjoyed the body. However, he had no authority to touch a human being of his own free accord, unless the latter was the aggressor. In order, therefore, to delude public travelers and others to their destruction, it was the common practice of the Kelpie to assume the most fascinating form, and assimilate himself to that likeness, which he supposed most congenial to the inclinations of his intended victim. The likeness of a fine riding steed was his favorite disguise. Decked out in the most splendid riding accoutrements, the perfidious Kelpie would place himself in the weary traveler's way, and graze by the road-side with all the seeming innocence and simplicity in the world. But this horse knew better what he was about; he was as calm and peaceable as a lamb, until his victim was once fairly mounted on his back; with a fiend-like yell he would then announce his triumph, and plunge headlong with his woe-struck rider into an adjacent pool, [and] enjoy him for his repast.

But the Kelpie could be defeated. Supposedly, the Kelpie's power to shape-shift rested in its bridle. Anyone who could wrestle the bridle from the Kelpie would find the creature at his or her mercy. Indeed, there is a legend among the MacGregor clan of just such a bridle taken from a Kelpie by one of the clan's ancestors centuries ago at Loch Slochd.[7] Notably, Loch Ness, too, has a rich history of Kelpie encounters that precede the modern-day fascination with plesiosaurs and giant eels.

The earliest such account dates to A.D. 565, when St. Columba was traveling in the Loch Ness area converting the then-heathen Picts. According to biographer St. Adamnan, St. Columba, while on the banks of Loch Ness, had stumbled upon a group of Picts burying a man who had been ravaged by, as they described it, a "monster of the water." St. Columba, however, miraculously restored the man to life by laying his staff across the man's chest.

Another version of the story says that one of the Picts, uninterested in the sermon of the saint, decided to try to swim the width of the loch. On sensing a disturbance, the monster arose from the water and rushed toward the terrified swimmer with a huge roar and gaping jaws. On seeing this, St. Columba raised his hand, gave the sign of the cross, invoked the name of the Lord, and commanded the monster, saying: "Thou shalt go no further nor touch the man—return with all speed." With that the beast was gone.[8] Even until relatively recently, the creatures of the loch were viewed as having sinister and unnatural origins.

For example, Jon had spent considerable time researching old copies of the *Inverness Courier* for any potential leads on sightings of the creatures of Loch Ness in centuries past. Two reports in particular stood out. The first concerned a story published in the *Courier* in October 1833. In a small article titled "Death of a Warlock," it was reported that a local resident, one Gregor MacGregor, alias "Willox the Warlock," had passed away. Found among his possessions was "a piece of yellow metal resembling a horse's bridle, which in the days of yore was sported by a mischievous water Kelpie, who haunted the banks of Loch Ness and Loch Spynie." In other words, in the early part of the nineteenth century, local lore suggested that a Kelpie resided in the loch.[9] Twenty years later the situation was no different.

On July 1, 1852, the *Inverness Courier* published a feature titled "A Scene from Lochend" in which two unusual animals were seen swimming across Loch Ness. Some witnesses, said the newspaper, "thought it was the sea serpent coiling along the surface, and others a couple of whales or large seals." The inhabitants made ready to defend themselves with everything from battle-axes to pitchforks. "At last, a venerable patriarch came to the conclusion that they were a pair of deer." He duly ran for his gun and was on the verge of firing when he threw it down and shouted in Gaelic: "God protect us, they are the water-horses," thinking that they were a pair of Kelpies. In the end, the beasts *did* turn out to be horses: two ponies from the Aldourie estate that was situated no less than a mile away. But, again, this is prime evidence of a local tradition that accepted that the much-feared Kelpies inhabited the loch. More importantly, Jon pointed out, these cases reinforced the belief on the part of the locals that the beasts were supernatural in origin rather than flesh-and-blood animals.[10]

There was a way for us to resolve this mystery, however. It was possible, said Jon, that we could induce the presence of one of the Kelpies of Loch Ness by way of a powerful invocation. "Richard is the man for that, I would suggest," he added. And it would not be the first time either. In addition to trying to commune with the Glaston-bury gargoyle and an alien big cat in Yorkshire in early 1998, Richard had tried to invoke the presence of a legendary British sea serpent known as Morgawr.

Jon passed me his diary to read his notes on this now-legendary endeavor. By this time the light was fading and so I turned on the flashlight and began to read.

It was only about ten days after Graham's and my return from Mexico in pursuit of the Chupacabras and it was a typically cold and gray morning in early March. Graham and I were shivering as we daydreamed wistfully about cold beers under the desert sun and did our best to keep out of the sleety wind which cut through us like a knife. Toby, by then quite a venerable old dog at the age of thirteen, was still fairly spry and he wandered happily about the beach, trying to eat seaweed and cocking his leg against the jagged rocks oblivious to all that was happening around him. Apart from Toby, everybody else was staring awestruck at Richard who stood, legs akimbo, impressive in a long black robe and brandishing a fierce-looking sword toward the sea. He was chanting an ancient invocation in a mixture of Gaelic and Olde English in an attempt to summon the ancient sea beast from its lair.

Around him on the shell-strewn sand were four candles marking the cardinal points of the sacred circle that he had cast. They spluttered bravely against all odds, and I am sure that everyone present was amazed that they had not been extinguished by the sleet and the wind. Each of the candles was a different color: green for the north, signifying the element of Earth, red for Fire marked the southernmost point of the circle, a yellow candle signifying the element of Air stood in the east, and the western point was marked by a blue candle representing the element of Water. As his invocation reached its peak, Richard screamed the ancient Gaelic incantation at the unyielding sea and threw a bunch of elderberries wrapped in gray cloth into the waiting sea as a gift to the cailleach. Suddenly he started to scream, in English: "Come ye out Morgawr, come ye out ancient sea dragon, come ye out great old one," and as he screamed his face began to change shape, and the friendly happy bloke that I have known for years and who currently resides in my spare room imperceptibly seemed to change into something darker, stranger, and as old as the Cornish landscape itself.

Without even realizing it, all the people present turned as if synchronized toward the sea, all of us expecting to see the dark head and long neck of an ancient sea dragon rise from beneath the slate gray waters. . . .

The TV crew, Graham, and I stared at the sea for several minutes, but absolutely nothing happened at all! Toby cocked his leg and peed all over one of the ritual candles and Graham, mistaking one of the other candles for a piece of flotsam washed up on the beach, drop-kicked it into the sea. "You've broken the bloody circle!" shouted Richard. "The invocation will never work now!" Everybody laughed (except Richard, who was mildly put out as he had hoped that the ritual would be a success) and we all adjoined to the boozer in Mawnan Smith for lunch.

And so a drunken decision was made. Richard would attempt to re-peat this feat and invoke the presence of Nessie. It must be said that the atmosphere in which this action was taken was in stark contrast to the oppressive air that dominated our gargoyle and big cat invocations. First, we all went back to the Mystery Machine and picked up some more beer and made beef sandwiches, which Jon and I took down to the edge of the loch along with two deck chairs. Meanwhile, a less-than-sober Richard was grandly preparing for his activities. Thirty minutes later he appeared, wearing his long black cape and a black skull-like mask, which altogether made him look like Batman's younger and slightly overweight brother.

Jon and I sat happily munching on our sandwiches and quaffing the ale as Richard threw himself into the cold waters of the loch and walked out into its depths. Jon shone the powerful flashlight on him and I watched through the night-scope. When the water reached Richard's shoulders, Jon shouted: "Don't go too far, for God's sake, Richard; I'm far too drunk to swim out."

"Yeah," I chimed in, "and one monster in the loch is plenty." I felt Jon's palm hit me on the back of my head. Fortunately, Richard came to a halt and we could hear him muttering quietly to himself. We strained to listen for about thirty seconds. Suddenly, he flung his arms into the air and shouted, "Mighty beast of the loch, mighty Kelpie of old, we command you to show yourself, we . . ." At that point Richard disappeared into the water. I stood up quickly and scanned the area frantically with the night-scope. Jon panicked and fell out of his chair. Richard was gone. Really gone.

By now the comic atmosphere had vanished and we were very, very concerned. I leapt into the water and scoured the area where Richard had been. There was no sign of him. Jon was wailing on the shore and jumping around like a madman. I dived into the depths of the waters once more and came up with absolutely nothing, except for a mouthful of black water. I turned back to Jon, whose huge frame I could see on the shore and was about to shout to him when I saw a darkened form loom up from behind him and jump onto his back. Not quite believing what I was seeing, I dragged my water-sodden self back onto dry land as Jon whirled around wildly with the darkened form clinging to his buffalo-like back.

"Help!" he cried with sheer terror in his voice, which had reached an absurdly high-pitched level. "It's a Kelpie! Get it off me!" As I raced toward him I burst out laughing. It was no Kelpie. It was Richard. Realizing this, Jon shrugged him off and totally lost his balance. For a moment time seemed to stand still. Jon appeared to perform a bizarre and less-than-graceful pirouette that took him about eight feet into the loch, where he tumbled headfirst under the water. After rolling around for about five seconds, as he tried to get his balance, Jon surfaced and slowly crawled to the shore. He did not look happy, not at all.

"It worked! It worked!" shouted Richard, as he pointed to a soaking-wet Jon. "I invoked the beast of the loch. Look upon its vile form as it does rise from the water!" he cried to me in a manner that only Richard can. At that point, Richard and I collapsed on the floor with laughter as the huge leviathan emerged onto dry land and proceeded to give Richard a lengthy and expletive-laden warning never to attempt anything like that again. Finally, after Jon had calmed down we headed back to the Mystery Machine to dry off. But one question remained. How had Richard managed to disappear into the waters of the loch and get back to shore undetected?

"Easy," he said, and held up a snorkel.

Jon looked at him, puzzled. "Forgive me, dear boy, but why on earth did you bring a snorkel with you for this trip?"

"Well," he replied matter-of-factly, "you never know when you might need one." Jon shook his head and retired to his bed and his nightly ritual of carefully placing slices of cucumber over his eyes. I congratulated Richard on a job well done and we drank a toast to the successful invocation of our very own monster of the deep.

The next day Jon was still complaining about the activities of the previous night. However, we had other priorities. After making a brief detour to look at the now privately owned Boleskine House, we departed from Loch Ness and made our way toward the Cairngorm Mountains and one mountain in particular: Ben Macdhui, the rumored home of "the Big Gray Man."

Although Richard's attempt to invoke the Kelpies of Loch Ness had failed, we all agreed on one crucial point. The whole history of monster sightings at Loch Ness was linked with paranormal forces and the occult, as evidenced by the nature of the Kelpies, the variety of creatures seen there, the experiences of monster hunter Ted Holliday, and the activities of Aleister Crowley. Again, the probability that the beasts were some form of Cormon loomed large in our minds, as did the possibility that perhaps Crowley's activities had succeeded in reinforcing the presence of such beasts at the loch, hence the huge wave of sightings of strange animals that would begin there in the twentieth century.

15

THE MONSTER OF THE MOUNTAINS

I'm not a creature in the zoo;
don't tell me what to do.

"ANIMAL BOY," THE RAMONES

Ben Macdhui, at nearly 4,300 feet, is the second highest mountain in the U.K. and lies in the heart of the Scottish mountain range known as the Cairngorms. The mountain is comprised of a high plateau with a subarctic climate and is often covered in snow for months at a time. Weather conditions can be extreme and unpredictable. Sadly the Cairngorms have been defaced by ski lifts and restaurants but until recently remained remote, and require considerable physical effort and mountain craft to navigate successfully. The wild nature and relative inaccessibility of the area has contributed to their popularity and the Cairngorms have been a playground for hundreds of years for climbers, walkers, skiers, naturalists, and those who love the high and lonely places. Ben Macdhui has several spellings and its English translation is Gaelic for "hill of the son of Duff."

While on Ben Macdhui, witnesses to the phenomenon known as the Big Gray Man describe how they have variously encountered footsteps, a sensation of a "presence," sightings of a large hominid and an overpowering sense of panic. The experience is terrifying enough to compel witnesses to flee in blind terror, often for several miles. Given that this takes place on rocky, dangerous ground, and often in misty and snowy weather conditions, we should not underestimate the power of the experience. A solitary witness usually, but not exclusively, experiences the phenomenon.

We are not skilled or even semiskilled mountain climbers and to attempt to climb the peak would have been sheer lunacy, not to mention a waste of time and money for the emergency services that would almost certainly have had to come and rescue us. Instead, it was our intention to drive as close as we could to the Cairngorms and at least say that we had been there. In addition, Andy Roberts had been good enough to share with me his huge mass of data on the Big Gray Man that, in the surroundings of the mountain range, made for eerie and thought-provoking reading.

Although the first recorded Big Gray Man experience did not take place until 1891, and was not made public until 1925, according to Andy, there are antecedents to the matter that set the phenomenon in some geographic, folkloric, and historical context.

Hugh Welsh, camping with his brother by the summit cairn of Ben Macdhui in 1904, heard the type of footsteps that later became synonymous with the Big Gray Man. They heard the noise both at night and in daylight, describing it as being like "slurring footsteps as if someone was walking through water-saturated gravel." Welsh also recalled that they were, "frequently conscious of 'something' near us, an eerie sensation of apprehension, but not of fear as others seem to have experienced." They questioned the head stalker at Derry Lodge who told them, "That would have been the Fear Liath Mor you heard." Fear Liath Mor is Gaelic for Big Gray Man and, if this account is true, then it is the first known reference to the Big Gray Man by name. That it was proffered as an explanation by a local stalker may indicate a larger body of tradition regarding the Big Gray Man that has gone unrecorded. Since then, near-identical encounters with the Big Gray Man have proliferated on Ben Macdhui. However, as Andy learned, similar experiences had been recorded elsewhere, too.

During research for a book dealing with landscape mysteries one informant told Andy of a mountain experience from the early 1960s which tops even that of the "best" account from Ben Macdhui. The informant was a boy at the time, and out with a friend to investigate one of the many aircraft wrecks from the Second World War that still litter the 2,000 foot Bleaklow plateau in the Derbyshire Peak District today. After visiting the crash site he heard his friend shout.

"I looked and saw, all in one instant, grouse exploding out of the heather toward us, sheep and hares stampeding toward us and behind them, rolling at a rapid rate toward us from the direction of Hern Clough, a low bank of cloud or fog . . . but what was truly terrifying was that in the leading edge of the cloud bank—in it and striding purposefully toward us—was a huge shadow-figure, a manlike silhouette, but far bigger than a man, as high as the cloudbank, as high as a house. And the terror that hit me and was driving the birds and the animals and my friend was utterly overwhelming—like a physical blow—and I have never felt the like since!" Needless to say, both lads fled.

The two boys had never heard of the Big Gray Man and his friend attributed this terrifying incident to "Th'owd Lad," a Pennine appellation for the Devil. Had this incident happened within a twenty-mile radius of Ben Macdhui it would be the jewel in the legend's crown.

"We fled," the informant concluded the experience. "We plunged over the crags above Gathering Hill—and every time I go back and look at those crags, I wonder why we didn't break our necks. We fled in mindless terror down that mountainside toward the Shelf Brook and Doctors Gate—and all the sheep and wildlife that could run or fly went careering down with us in utter panic. And then, about halfway down, we seemed to run out into the sunlight—and it was all over! All of the panic was gone. The sheep stopped, put their heads down, and started to graze. Everything returned at once to normal. But back up there, on Higher Shelf Stones, wisps of mist were still coiling round."[1]

Precisely what the Big Gray Man of Ben Macdhui is remains a matter of conjecture. However, Jon, Richard and I did wonder, as we stared up at the mighty Cairngorms, if perhaps the intense fear and panic that the incidents generated in the minds of the witnesses and participants was indicative of the emotion-sucking activities of the Cormons. Perhaps, if a breed of Cormon *did* inhabit the wilder and darker corners of Ben Macdhui, this one had learned not just how to feed on emotion but how to amplify the emotions of the witness in the form of fear to ensure an even greater feeding. And there were other reports of "big men" from Scotland, too.

Mark Fraser is one of Scotland's most respected researchers of unknown animals and mysterious beasts and he very generously supplied me with copies of his reports when I told him of our quest. The area of Falkland in Fife, Scotland, was said to be the home of a family of Bigfoot type creatures, ranging from four feet in height upward, said Mark. Several residents had seen the creatures in the area, which was also rich in werewolf legends dating back several centuries. These creatures, Mark added, could apparently jump from a standing position into the branches of trees without bending their knees.

Mark was also able to supply a clipping from the *Daily Star* newspaper of August 27, 1997, that made for illuminating reading. It was "Girls Flee from the Holiday Phantom."

A mysterious beast—dubbed the Friskerton phantom—terrified four South Yorkshire girls enjoying a holiday walk near the Lincolnshire village. The friends say they were horrified when they came face-to-face with a four-foot-tall, jet-black, bearlike creature feeding on dead animals.

Sheffield girls Rachel Rowan, 12, Nicki Handley, 11, and Nicola Proctor, 9, were wandering about with Joanna Brogan, 10, from Rotherham, when they spotted something in the bushes.

"We saw something moving, so we went to take a look," said Nicola, who has now returned home after the caravan holiday. "When we saw what it was we just froze. It was very frightening. It looked like it was eating a pheasant. It had some very big teeth and great big claws. After a few seconds we ran off, but later when we went back to see if it was still there it had gone. It had left some big paw prints, though."

All four girls were staying at a caravan park next to the Tyrwhitt Arms pub at Short Ferry, near Friskerton. In their panic the girls ran into the pub for help. Pub manager Dave Brumhead said the sighting had left the girls badly shaken.

"There was no way this was a schoolgirls' prank—they were really shocked," he said. "We had another sighting that evening near to where the girls had been. A motorist stopped his car in the middle of the road after he thought he had seen something. It's all very strange."

Locals are puzzled by the latest in what has become a series of mystery creature sightings in the area. Earlier this year several reports of a pantherlike animal on the loose were recorded.

But perhaps the most important report that Mark Fraser was able to share was the full account relating to the events at Dundonald Hill in 1994 that Jon had briefly told me about before we had set off on our monster quest. Mark's comprehensive report showed that macabre things were afoot at Dundonald Castle.

Even hundreds of years ago Dundonald Hill was said to be the home of a "creature," and not many dared venture out onto the hill alone or without good reason. The dogs of Dundonald Castle were said to become very restless, agitated, and excited at times while looking out toward the hill, barking and yelping, never under any circumstances would they wander up it, or so I'm told. People have reported a strange creature or haunting, call it what you will, on the hill right up to the present time. Frightened folk have told of "shadows that haunt the trees." One badly shaken man related how, when walking on the hill, he heard whispering voices behind him; on turning around he saw nothing. This happened two or three times before he decided to take solace with a stiff drink in a local bar.

Another man reports of seeing two ghostly, squat-shaped,

featureless shadows trailing him from nearby trees; these shadows then merged together as one, growing to twice its size. He then also left the hill not waiting to see what happened next. This same "entity" has also been described as being able to jump straight into the branches of trees, as the creatures in Fife.

Dundonald Hill seems to figure heavy in the minds of locals as an area to be avoided, but nobody really seems to know why. Schoolchildren in Irvine have said that they dare not go up as it is haunted but when asked what by, they didn't know. I have been told that there is a high count of suicides in the area with several youths having been found hanged on the hill, although I have not checked these facts out. Scott Webb of Irvine said to me that the hill has a presence and "exudes an oppressiveness" and claims that many friends feel the same way about the place.

Josephine Aldridge from England says she will never go up the hill again as long as she lives. She had recently been spending a little time in Kilmarnock (summer 1994) and for a day out decided to visit Dundonald Castle. While walking on the hill her two Labradors suddenly went berserk, running around in circles, growling and snapping at the air before finally slinking to the ground as far as they could go with their tails tucked beneath them, crawling backward in obvious terror. Then Josephine saw "this huge creature" that appeared some distance to the side of her. She had not noticed it before and she assures us that if it had been there earlier she would most certainly have seen it. It did not seem to be solid, as Josephine could see the grass of the hill through its body, but it was covered in "longish, charcoal-colored hair. It made no indentations in the grass," and Josephine on reflection thought it ghostlike. "The thing that struck the most terror was its eyes, two long slits which glowed a bright red. It had two holes where the nose should have been, very thick lips. . . ." In fact it was not dissimilar to a gorilla in shape, although it stood well over ten feet tall on two legs. When confronted by the strange sight Josephine began to pray; the creature after a few moments slowly faded out of sight, but the dogs' attitude never changed and the Englishwoman felt sure that the "monster" was still around. Josephine left Dundonald Hill in a hurry, not too far behind her whimpering dogs.

George (pseudonym), who likes to spend a lot of time fishing, walking, and camping decided to spend a night on the hill during the summer of 1993. He took along his dog, Rover (also a pseudonym!), who had never left his side since it was a pup. He arrived just after the sun began to set, and erected his one-man tent. Deciding to settle down with a book, he lay atop his sleeping bag fully dressed.

After about an hour George saw a shadow pass by the side of his tent through the lamplight. He thought it strange that anybody would be in the area this time of night; again the shadow loomed over the tent, and at this point George swears he heard a kind of rasping or breathing sound. By this time he had come to the conclusion that some of his mates had come up after him and were now playing a joke. He said to himself that he would not rise to the bait and once again settled down with his book.

George's heart then leapt into his mouth as the whole tent shook violently as though somebody had tripped over a rope. At this George went outside to look, his nervousness turning to apprehension when he found the area outside totally deserted. He quickly went back inside the tent, securing the flaps as tight as he could. By this time Rover was whimpering and cowering in the corner; then the tent began to sway as if caught in strong winds. George sat on top of his sleeping bag, now too scared to even contemplate sleeping.

The secured flaps suddenly burst wide open; the dog who had never left George's side gave out an almighty yelp and ran off into the darkness. Someone or something then grabbed hold of George's ankle, and slowly but surely the man was pulled out of the tent. He could see no one and struggled desperately, but the grip did not loosen. When he had been pulled about ten feet clear of the tent's entrance, the invisible force lifted George clear off the floor, his head about two inches off the grass. The sky became black, a clap of thunder rang out, and a streak of lightning flashed across the sky. Then suddenly the grip let go of his ankle, and George fell limp onto the grass, petrified. George ran back into the tent, the sky clearing as he did so. He then spent a very tense night sitting at the entrance of the tent, being too scared to make his way home in the darkness, and jumping at every little noise that the night made, which seemed to surround him like some huge black blanket. He had called for Rover often, but each time the dog failed to answer. Morning eventually came and after packing away his belongings he headed down the hill. As he reached the bottom Rover came bounding out of the undergrowth toward him and they both went home together.

George has never been up the hill since and he has no intentions of ever doing so again; he can offer no explanation as to what had happened to him, only that it was a very real experience. He does express hurt at his dog leaving him, a thing it has never done before. Just as a footnote:

Dundonald Hill and the surrounding area have always been a source for mysterious phenomena. Big cats have been seen in the area for decades, and it has long been a UFO hot spot. The castle that sits atop the hill has its fair share of ghosts, too.

As Mark Fraser's report made clear, man-beast accounts in Scotland have proliferated to the present day. And yet, as Josephine Aldridge's encounter in 1994 at Dundonald Castle reinforced, these beasts, like so many others we had investigated, appeared spectral and Cormon-like in nature. And the fact that Dundonald Hill was also a hot spot for mysterious big cats and UFOs should not be dismissed. But Mark still had further reports in his files to relate, including his firsthand report on another case that Jon had briefly referred to: the July 1994 event at Torphins.

Local men Pete and George (pseudonyms) were walking through a forestry track in woods near their home of Torphins, which is situated twenty miles from the city of Aberdeen.

When nearing the end of the track Pete saw a dark figure run from the trees on the left, across the track, disappearing into the trees on the right. He at first thought it was a man but the figure left a strange foreboding in Pete. George did not see the figure and was busy telling Pete he was imagining things when a face appeared out of the trees behind Pete's back. George was chilled to the bone as the face he was looking at "looked human, but was not human." It darted away just as quickly when George threw a large stone in its direction. The two friends then left the area feeling somewhat unnerved.

A few weeks later the two friends, along with a third, were to have another encounter with the "creature" as they were driving along the road into Torphins, approximately two miles from their first meeting.

In the witnesses' own words: "Suddenly from the side of the road there came this great muscular, hairy figure bounding out, which started to run behind the car. At one point it caught up and ran alongside the vehicle, not seemingly out of breath as it approached speeds of up to thirty-five to forty miles per hour."

Pete describes the creature as ". . . strong and muscular . . . red, glowing eyes . . . body covered in hair . . . about six feet to six feet five inches . . . jet black . . ."

After several minutes the figure stopped abruptly in the middle of the road, leaving the terrified car occupants to carry on their journey into Torphins alone, as the "creature" faded slowly out of sight in the eerie glow of the car's red taillights.

The same or similar "creature" has also been reported by a lady who lives in an isolated cottage on the edge of the forest where Pete and George first saw the figure. She has seen it on two occasions watching her house; she too describes the red glowing eyes. The only other report that I am aware of is that of a man catching a fleeting glance through high-powered binoculars as it darted through a forest clearing.

In this case the animals witnessed did not appear phantomlike in nature; the reference to their glowing red eyes, however, was, by now, a familiar characteristic. Again, this reinforced our beliefs that we were dealing with something supernatural in origin. From the wilds of windswept Dartmoor to the jagged mountains and the flowing hills of Scotland, the Cormons, it seemed, had established firm footholds.

☷ ☷ ☷

The time was now upon us to leave Scotland. But before doing so we decided to visit that scene of much action of a cryptozoological nature, Dundonald Castle.

Set atop a hill that overlooks north Kilmarnock, the castle is visible for miles around and the hill was occupied as far back as 2000 B.C. In the twelfth century Walter, the High Steward of King David I, built an earthwork and timber fort. And the Stewart family constructed a more substantial Dundonald Castle in the thirteenth century. Although much of the castle was destroyed during the Wars of Independence with England early in the fourteenth century, it was rebuilt in the middle of the fourteenth century by King Robert II and remains standing to this day. In 1482 the castle was sold by King James III to the Cathcart family and was subsequently purchased by Sir William Cochrane in 1636. In recent years, however, the castle has been looked after by the Friends of Dundonald Castle and by Historic Scotland, who have a small visitor center on the site.[2]

Somewhat surprisingly, and in sharp contrast to the situation when we visited Lustleigh Cleave and Avebury, many people in the area had heard legends of dark activities in the vicinity of the castle and of strange creatures being seen there and on Dundonald Hill. However, a late-night invocation failed to summon up anything except a slight cold for Jon, despite the fact that we felt we had been successful at Glastonbury, Rendlesham, and Barnborough Church.

16

THE FINAL COUNTDOWN

This is insanity, this could be the end.

"GARDEN OF SERENITY," THE RAMONES

Having pursued wild men on Dartmoor, gargoyles at Glastonbury, cannibals at Skegness, black dogs in Rendlesham Forest, giant worms in the West Country, and lake monsters, big gray men, werewolves, alien big cats, and a host of other bizarre beasts at a whole range of locations, our six-week expedition was rapidly coming to a close. We had seven days remaining and it was time to uncover the truth about the one thing that, more than any other, had led us to embark on this truly surreal quest in the first place: the Man Monkey of Ranton, Staffordshire. *The History, Gazetteer and Directory of Staffordshire of 1851* states:

> Ranton, or Ronton, is a small scattered village, five miles W of Stafford, comprising within its parish the scattered hamlets of Extolls, Long Compton, Park Nook, and including 320 inhabitants, and about 2670 acres of land, belonging chiefly to the Earl of Lichfield, and Francis Eld, Esq., and the former is lord of the manor, which, at the time of the Norman Conquest, was held by Goderick, a Saxon nobleman, and afterwards by the Noels and Harcourts. Swynfen Jones, Esq, and a few smaller owners have estates in the parish.
>
> About a mile W of the village is Ranton Abbey, an extra

parochial liberty of 700 acres belonging to the Earl of Lichfield. The ancient abbey was founded by Robert Fitz-Noel, in the reign of Henry II, for regular canons of the order of St. Augustine. Considerable remains of the abbey are still standing, including a lofty well-built tower, and the outer walls of the church. The abbey liberty contains 28 inhabitants and the Abbey House which is the seat of ED Moore, Esq.

Twenty-eight years later, at the time of the Man Monkey encounter on January 21, 1879, the town had not changed. Indeed, even by 1991 the population of the village had only risen to 415. But for such a small hamlet, it had an extraordinary number of weird occurrences. For example, there was a celebrated UFO encounter at Ranton in October 1954, when villager Jessie Roestenberg and her children viewed a classic flying saucerlike object at very close quarters over a farmhouse. According to Roestenberg, the disclike craft had a large "observation window" that contained distinctly humanlike entities with long blond hair—and very much like the descriptions of the aliens reportedly seen during the same time frame by numerous so-called UFO contactees, such as George Adamski and George Van Tassel in the 1950s and 1960s.[1]

Similarly, after writing in the *Chase Post* about the exploits of the Man Monkey, I was contacted by an elderly resident of Ranton who claimed to have seen, as a child in the 1920s, a parade of ten-inch-tall pixies, adorned in green, dancing merrily around an oak tree at the foot of her parents' garden in the village. As she (a little girl of five) slowly approached them, the atmosphere changed and the friendly little creatures stopped dancing and turned their attention to her. Their faces took on disturbing and malevolent frowns and they slowly began walking toward her—or perhaps stalking her would be a better term, the woman informed me. For a five-year-old child this was a terrifying experience and she ran screaming to the house. When her concerned mother ran into the garden, the little people were gone. The woman seemed genuine enough, and said that if her name were omitted she would be happy to have her story published.

Likewise, another resident of the village wrote to me care of the newspaper and told me about what she had seen eight years previously. While returning home from a Friday night out, a large black cat ("like a panther with big red eyes") bounded across the road in front of her as she approached her house and disappeared into a neighbor's yard. Until now, she had discussed the incident with no one. Once again, the site of a famous UFO encounter was also a beacon for other unexplained phenomena.

But we had our sights set firmly on the Man Monkey. As I had told Richard and Jon before we set off on our adventure, after my article on the Man Monkey was published in the *Chase Post,* seven people who had similar tales to relate had contacted me. Two of the letter-writers had had firsthand encounters with very similar creatures on the Cannock Chase in the 1990s; one had seen such a beast in the area in the1980s; three had friend-of-a-friend-style accounts to relate of a similar nature and one—and perhaps the most crucial of all—came from an elderly woman who asserted that members of her family had passed down the generations a tale of a relative who had seen the Man Monkey itself.

"Well, we've got a week before you go gallivanting across the Atlantic, Nicky, so we'd better get a move on," said Jon as we crossed the border into Staffordshire after our excursions in Scotland. With time definitely no longer on our side, we decided to interview the elderly lady at the earliest opportunity. I pulled out my address book, looked up the woman's telephone number, and ninety minutes later we were sitting on a couch in the large house where she and her husband lived in the Staffordshire town of Armitage.

To our much welcome surprise, her long-departed relative who had seen the Man Monkey was not the same individual involved in the 1879 encounter. Rather, this report dated from 1848. The woman's relative was a servant girl who worked in a nearby village and who had been walking back to her home in Ranton on a cool autumn night that year. But as she approached her home something large and black standing in the shadows of the adjacent property's front door startled her. At first, she thought it was just the man of the house, until, that is, the creature came out of the shadows and loomed into view.

What she saw before her at a distance of about twelve feet was a manlike figure, some five feet tall, covered in dark black, matted hair, and with an equally hairy head that was dominated by a pair of glowing red eyes. Stricken with fear, the girl was too terrified to move or cry for help and for a good minute the two stood watching each other intently. She would later tell her family that the animal stunk of rotting meat and would make short grunting noises every ten seconds or so that sounded vaguely like a language that she couldn't understand. She could, however, make out some of the finer features of the animal's face and said that those parts not covered by hair, such as the nose, chin, and cheeks, were dark and leathery. Large canine teeth protruded from its mouth.

After a minute, the creature turned and began walking quickly down the deserted road, all the while looking over its shoulder at the girl. The girl duly summoned up the strength to follow. After five or ten minutes, she broke off her pursuit when the creature appeared intent on entering a nearby field. Before doing so, however, it turned toward her one more time, then vanished in a bright flash of light.

"And this story was passed down through your family? Is that correct?" asked Richard.

"That's right," she told us.

"I heard the story, too, just after we got married in 1946," her husband added.

The lady continued. "My brother and sister and I were all told this story as children and that if we were mischievous the Man Monkey would come for us. But I never really believed the story and thought it was just something to scare us into going to bed when we wanted to stay up late. But then I read your story in the newspaper and realized that what the man saw in 1879 sounded like the same thing." It did, indeed.

"And who told you the story?" asked Jon.

"Well," she replied after thinking for a few moments, "my mother and father, definitely. But I also remember my uncle teasing me about it and I seem to remember hearing about it at a party once from a cousin, but I'm not definite of that. But the story was well known in our family when I was a little girl."

"Madam," said Jon, "at the risk of offending you, may I ask how old you are now and how old you were when you first heard this tale?"

She laughed. "Yes, you may! I'm seventy-seven and I probably first heard this tale when I was about four, I would think."

"So that would make it around 1928 or 1929, then?" I added, after doing a minute of calculations. Math was never my strong point. She nodded. There was little more that she could tell us and both her brother and sister were now dead. But here was another example of what appeared to be a bona fide sighting of the Man Monkey. And the fact that the creature had vanished in a bright flash of light suggested that, like so many of the other beasts that we had investigated, this one, too, was not a normal flesh-and-blood entity.

Spurred on by this breakthrough, we called all the other people who had written me. Unfortunately, one had now decided against speaking out, one telephone number was nonexistent (and may, with hindsight, have been a hoax), and the remaining number had been disconnected. But we did have our three remaining firsthand witnesses to similar beasts on the vast forested expanse that was Cannock Chase. And so it was that we arranged to meet at ten o'clock the next morning, Pauline Charlesworth, who had a strange and remarkable tale to tell us about an encounter she had had deep within the woods.

"You know, Nicky," said Jon as we ate a breakfast of cereal the following morning, "it seems that we have spent more than enough time running around forests and woods and—"

I interrupted him. "Well, you think that because every time we're in one you end up flat on your back!" Richard laughed, as he munched on his cornflakes.

"Alright," Jon replied, "let's get on with it. Where does this woman live?"

"Actually, we don't need to go to her house; she's going to meet us on the Chase where she saw the thing."

"On the Chase?" asked Jon apprehensively.

"You mean I have to go trudging through another bloody wood?"

"It certainly looks like it, mate," I said cheerfully. Richard smiled to himself.

A high plateau bordered by the Trent Valley to the north and the West Midlands to the south, Cannock Chase has been an integral feature of the Staffordshire landscape for centuries. Following an initial invasion of Britain in A.D. 43, Roman forces advanced to the south of what is now the town of Cannock and along a route that would later become known as Watling Street, a major Roman road. The surrounding countryside was heavily wooded even then, as can be demonstrated by the Romans' name for the area: Letocetum, or the Gray Woods. But it was at an area of the Chase known as Castle Ring that we were due to meet Pauline Charlesworth.

Constructed between 500 B.C. and A.D. 40, Castle Ring is an Iron Age structure commonly known as a Hill Fort. The highest point on Cannock Chase is 801 feet above sea level, and its main ditch and bank enclosure is 14 feet high and, at its widest point, 853 feet across. Little is known about the people who built Castle Ring or its purpose, except to say that its creators were already in residence at the time of the Roman invasion and remained there until around A.D. 50.[2]

"I don't think I can walk any farther," groaned Jon as we began the walk up to Castle Ring on what was a blisteringly hot morning. Indeed, it was so hot that Jon had forsaken his monocle and his deer-stalker and, on a distinctly rare occasion for him, was dressed in jeans and a grubby Charlie's Angels T-shirt. But, we finally arrived and Jon slumped to the floor in a crumpled mass that reminded me of a giant and grossly mutated sack of potatoes. Thankfully, he had twenty minutes to recover before Pauline Charlesworth arrived. "I'm on the ground again and in a bloody forest again, you'll note," he wheezed as we took a walk around the ring. We laughed and waved to him from across the far side of Castle Ring. "You don't care, do you?" he wailed.

"No, we don't!" I shouted back. "Lie there and get your breath back."

"That, dear boy, is all I can do," he moaned.

Then out of the blue came another voice, shouting, "Hello? Are you Nick?" It was Pauline Charlesworth, waving to us from one hundred and fifty feet away. Richard and I made our way over to her as she headed along the pathway to Castle Ring. We exchanged greetings and explained that there was a third member of our party lying prone in the grass on the other side of the Ring.

"Is he alright?" asked a worried Pauline.

"Apart from being southern, mad, and fat, he is," said Richard. I laughed. Pauline looked confused and bewildered—curiously, that was the response that, collectively, we often provoked in people. Having returned to Jon and having successfully hauled his vast form up from the ground, we listened intently as Pauline told her story. It transpired that the creature that she had seen at Castle Ring did not really resemble the Man Monkey, but it was certainly a man-beast all the same.

Pauline explained that she would often come up to the Ring to sit and read during the summer and on her day off from work, on Thursdays. And it was on a particular Thursday morning in July 1986 that she had her fateful encounter. She had prepared herself a place to sit, stretched a blanket out on the ground and opened up her picnic basket that contained drinks, fruit, and sandwiches. For more than an hour she sat and read, but then something curious happened. It seemed, she told us, that she was sitting in a vacuum and all of the surrounding noises, such as those of the birds whistling and the branches of the trees gently swaying, stopped. She also said that somehow the area didn't seem "quite right." She elaborated: "The best way I can describe it is to say it was like I wasn't really on the Chase but it was as if I was in someone's dream of what the Chase should look like. As if it was all a mirage, but a good one."

Then out of the trees came a horrific form running toward her. It was, said Pauline, a man. The man, however, was unlike any that she had ever seen before. He had long filthy hair, a matted beard, and a face that was more prehistoric than modern. He was relatively short in height, perhaps no more than five feet two inches, and was clad in animal skins that extended from his waist to his knees and with a long piece of animal skin that was draped over his right shoulder. In his right hand he held what was undoubtedly the large antlers of a deer that had been fashioned into a daggerlike weapon.

It was hard to know who was more afraid, Pauline said. She stared in stark terror at the man. He, in turn, appeared perplexed and eyed her curiously. He would instinctively jump back at her slightest movement. He spoke to her, she said, in a language that seemed complex but that was unknown to her. It was evident, however, that he was asking her questions. But about what, she had no idea. Then things got even stranger. In the distance Pauline could hear other voices getting closer and closer and that, collectively, grew into a huge rumbling sound. And then she found the source of the noise. Through a break in the trees came perhaps thirty or forty more similarly clad people, some men and some women, and all chanting.

It was clear to Pauline that some sort of ceremony was about to take place inside Castle Ring and she was right in the heart of the action. The men and women all proceeded to sit down at the edges of the Ring. One man, much taller than the rest and whom she took to be their leader, marched over to her and said something unintelligible but that she understood by the wave of his arm meant that she should get out of the circle. This she did and retreated with shaking legs to the tree line. For more than fifteen minutes she sat, transfixed with terror by the sight, as this curious band of people continued to chant. Then out of the sky came the most horrific thing that Pauline had ever seen in her entire life.

It was, she said, a creature about four feet in height, human in shape with oily black skin, thin arms and legs and a pair of large, batlike wings. And it had two hideous, red, glowing eyes. It slowly dropped to the ground and prowled the Ring for a minute, staring at one and all and emitting hideous shrieks. Suddenly seven or eight of the men pounced on the creature, wrestled it to the ground, and tied it firmly with powerful ropes. It writhed and fought to get loose and tore into the flesh of the men with its claws but was finally subdued and dragged into the forest by the same group of men. The remainder of the party followed and Pauline said that the strange atmosphere began to lift and the area returned to normality. For several minutes she stood her ground, too afraid to move, but then finally returned on still-unsteady legs to her blanket and quickly scooped up both it and her picnic basket and ran to her car.

Without a doubt this was one of the strangest stories that we had come across. However, we reassured Pauline that we did not think that she was crazy and also advised her that this was not the first time that we had been told stories of this nature. We told her the tale of the Cormons as related to us by Mother Sarah and could only offer the possibility that Pauline had perhaps been afforded a glimpse into the past and a unique glimpse at an early (and apparently successful) attempt to invoke a Cormon.

She was fascinated by what we had to say and listened intently. Surprisingly, and unlike many witnesses to such events, Pauline had simply shrugged the incident off at the time that it had occurred and returned to her normal life without telling a soul, apart from her husband. "I just put it down to one of those things," she said matter-of-factly.

"What things?" Richard asked.

"Well, you know, ghosts, UFOs, all that funny stuff." All that funny stuff was an apt description, I thought. Like others we had spoken with, Pauline simply wanted to discuss what she had witnessed in the event that it might be helpful to us and that we might be able to provide her with some answers. We thought the interview had been successful on both counts. And so we began our descent of Castle Ring. Suddenly there was a mighty crash in the trees behind me, and something hit the ground hard and amid a loud cry. This time, I didn't even bother to turn around. I knew it wasn't the winged horror or the prehistoric man. It was only Jon again, on the floor again. And Richard and I were the poor souls who would have to try to get him on his feet. Again.

Having said good-bye to Pauline Charlesworth, we headed into the heart of the Chase and to the location of what was known as the Glacial Boulder. Made out of granite, the boulder is large and impressive. It is also made curious by the fact that there are no natural granite outcrops anywhere in the area. Indeed, the nearest rock of this type can be found in the Lake District, more than 120 miles to the north and on Dartmoor, Devonshire, no less than 165 miles to the southwest. The boulder, however, has been matched conclusively to a rocky outcrop at Cniffel in Dumfries & Galloway, which is over 170 miles away from the Chase in the Southern Uplands of Scotland. At some point during the last Ice Age the boulder was carried by the great glaciers down the country and to its present location on the Cannock Chase.[3]

After spending the evening at a local pub in the nearby town of Milford, where we obtained a plentiful supply of both liquid and solid refreshment, we returned to the Glacial Boulder and parked the Mystery Machine as close to it as we could. Tomorrow at 9:30 A.M. we were to meet a man named Gavin Addis, who had seen a strange apelike beast standing atop the boulder in 1997. Never could we say life was dull.

At 7:00 A.M. we were all awoken by a series of loud knocks on the door of the Mystery Machine.

"Who the hell's that?" I asked, wondering if Jon or Richard had gotten locked outside after an early-morning excursion. Jon wondered if it was the police, finally catching up with us after the events at Castle Alfred. He and Richard watched warily and wearily as I crawled out of bed and slowly opened the door.

"It's me. I'm Gavin," said a smiling man of about thirty.

"You probably are but you're also two and a half hours early," I said sharply.

"I know, but I couldn't wait."

"Well, we can," I said. "You are gonna have to come back in a while. At the right time."

"Okay," he replied all too cheerfully for that time in the morning and headed back to his car, where I watched him from the door turn on its ignition and radio. He began to tap his fingers on the steering wheel and I closed the door of the Mystery Machine.

"Some people don't seem to know that there's only one seven

o'clock in the day and it's still twelve hours away," I said. We all went back to bed for another hour. At nine-thirty, there was another knock at the door. Gavin had returned. Gavin Addis was an unusual-looking fellow. Although barely out of his twenties, his hair was already rapidly going silver—but then who was I to talk? I had been shaving my head to the bone every day since my own hair decided to head slowly south when I was about twenty-five. Plus he was easily as big as Jon, if not bigger, and had a curious twitch in his left eye that had truly hypnotic qualities. We were all glad that we had chosen to meet Gavin during daylight.

Gavin told us a rambling tale about how he and one of his many girlfriends had been parked by the Glacial Boulder on a winter's night in 1997 and were making out in the backseat when his girl-friend let out a loud scream. Standing atop the boulder was a large hairy man, waving his arms wildly at the sky. Gavin jumped into the front seat (although looking at his frame, I seriously doubt he was ca-pable of jumping anywhere) and floored the accelerator. Tires spun, dirt flew into the air, and the car shot away at high speed, but not be-fore the man-beast had succeeded in jumping onto the hood of the car. For five minutes the beast valiantly hung on, before being thrown to the ground. Gavin looked in his rearview mirror and could see the creature already back on its feet and running into the woods. Gavin and his girlfriend headed for home. "And that's it," he told us breathlessly.

We had heard some wild tales in our time but we were all very suspicious of this one. "Can we see the car?" asked Jon. "I could do some tests to see if there are any indications of the creature's hair on the front of it." Gavin had sold the car.

"Can we interview your girlfriend?" I asked. They had split up, said Gavin, nervously licking his lips. We concluded that there was no girlfriend and probably never had been. Ever.

"Can I come on your monster hunt?" he asked like a little boy ask-ing for candy. When we explained that it was almost over, a sad look came across Gavin's face. We genuinely felt sorry for him and wished him no ill will at all. It was obvious to us that his story was a concoction and that he had only invented it to get our attention and not for any malicious reason. Gavin was a lonely fellow and he quickly departed from the Mystery Machine after mumbling a brief and subdued good-bye. It wasn't even ten o'clock. Having dismissed Gavin's tale as that of a tragic and tortured soul, we had one final witness to see the following evening. We spent the rest of the morning and most of the afternoon cleaning and tidying the Mystery Machine.

By late afternoon, Jon, Richard, and I had packed away all of our belongings, apart from the necessities, and we all went out and had a mammoth dinner in Cannock. It looked like we were going to finish our quest two or three days earlier than expected and there seemed to be no point in wasting time at this stage of the game.

Even though things were almost at an end, we didn't want to dwell on the matter and instead focused on Jackie Houghton, who lived in Cannock and worked in nearby Stafford as a waitress in a restaurant. On February 18, 1995, she had been driving across the Cannock Chase and along the main road that links the towns of Rugeley and Cannock at one in the morning, after her shift at the restaurant was over. As she approached the village of Slittingmill, however, she was suddenly forced to swerve the car and narrowly avoided collision with a large shambling creature that stepped out into the road at a distance of about two hundred feet from her. Considering that she was traveling at high speed, said Jackie, it was a miracle that she didn't hit the thing.

The encounter lasted just seconds, but she had caught sight of the animal and was certain that it was manlike and tall, very hairy, with two glowing red eyes. It disappeared into the trees. Although in some ways this story was similar to Gavin's, Jackie Houghton's seemed much more believable. What it was, she had no idea. And neither did we. But it was one more case to add to our ever-growing file of reports. The Slittingmill connection was interesting, too. In one of my previous books, *Cosmic Crashes,* I had detailed the account of a family that had undergone a nightmarish encounter in the same area with a group of diminutive troll-like creatures who surrounded their broken-down car shortly after midnight in the latter part of October

1975. As we concluded our interview with Jackie Houghton and departed, we realized that our adventure was almost at an end. Almost, being the key word. There was one final thing that we had to do: attempt an invocation of the Man Monkey. If we couldn't find it, we would invoke it.

Richard's experience at Glastonbury had suggested to us that the action of invoking Cormon-like phenomena could prove highly successful. Similarly, our experience on the Yorkshire moors that had resulted in at least two sightings of big cats was eye-opening, to say the least. But the Man Monkey, the one beast more than any other that had set us off on our countrywide escapade, was the real prize. We thought back to what Mother Sarah had told us about how the beasts were most at home and at full strength within forests and woods. So with a curious sense of déjà vu coursing through our veins we attempted yet another monstrous invocation. By now, after six weeks of traveling, we believed fully in the Cormon phenomenon; it was complete and utter belief in the beasts that was the key to a successful invocation, the witch had told us. There was only one place that seemed fitting for our purpose: Castle Ring.

For the second time in a couple of days we found ourselves striding along the route to the ancient location. My mind flashed back to the late 1980s, when one Sunday morning, while walking my old Cairn terrier, Susie, I had entered one particularly dense part of the Cannock Chase that I had never been to before. A curious feeling overcame me and for a few minutes, as with Pauline Charlesworth, things didn't seem quite right and I vaguely remembered hearing strange noises among the trees and feeling disoriented. In a matter of minutes the feeling subsided and Susie and I continued on our walk. But it was strange, I thought, that I had totally forgotten about it until now.

By the time we reached Castle Ring, it was 10:00 P.M., and aside from the illumination provided by the flashlight, the whole area was enveloped in darkness and provided a spectacular view of the night sky. Whereas Richard's invocation at Loch Ness was conducted largely as a joke, the situation here and the attendant atmosphere were very different. Knowing what had happened to Pauline Charlesworth at Castle Ring, and with our complete belief in the existence of the Cormons, we were totally receptive to the presence of the beasts. The lighthearted banter that had been present throughout our quest had vanished. We headed to the center of Castle Ring and began a simple process of meditation. Twenty minutes later, we were relaxed and attuned to the world of the forest and all of its attendant mysteries and wonder.

This time we decided we would try something different. Instead of having Richard scream an invocation to some "mighty creature of old," as he seemed to particularly enjoy doing, we would envisage in our minds the image of the Man Monkey as it had been described to us by those with knowledge of the creature and try to imagine it standing at the edge of Castle Ring. For more than two hours we sat there in silence, with the man-beast's features firmly locked in our minds, and for more than two hours nothing happened. After 1:00 A.M., however, the atmosphere changed and changed radically. As we sat there, our minds still focused, I felt a sudden chill and opened my eyes. Richard was looking directly at me and then Jon opened his eyes, too.

"Do you feel that?" asked Jon quietly.

"Yeah," I whispered. Richard nodded. The temperature within Castle Ring had dropped alarmingly, despite the fact that there was no accompanying wind. I also felt the sensation that I had experienced more than a decade previously while walking on the Chase— the sensation of something being wrong, very wrong, indeed.

We felt like someone was watching us, so we turned our attention to the trees. We could see nothing but we knew that something was out there, watching us. Our eyes, by now accustomed to the darkness, darted left to right, sensing something bipedal stalking us and stealthily and carefully creeping outside of the Ring. And then, there it was.

I have debated whether or not to include the following information, because looking back on it today it just seems beyond belief. And yet, it happened; and so I feel that in an effort to portray the story as accurately as humanly possible, I am duty-bound to record the facts.

At a distance of perhaps forty feet, we could see two bright points of light flitting about the trees. There were two red glowing eyes—the veritable hallmark of a Cormon. The fact that they were approximately eight feet from the ground suggested to us that we had indeed successfully conjured up a man-beast. But it appeared to us that the creature was wary of showing itself and it continued to use the trees as cover. Nevertheless, we could make out its shadowy form as it moved slowly around us—perhaps inquisitive, perhaps stalking.

We were all holding our breath at this point, wondering what would happen next and still not quite believing what we were seeing. I looked at Richard and motioned that we should charge it; he nodded in agreement. Jon, seeing this, signaled us with his hand.

"We're gonna rush it, mate," I whispered.

"Are we really seeing this?" he said quietly.

"Yeah, we are," replied Richard, his lighthearted attitude that had accompanied much of the rest of the hunt now gone. Completely. The beast continued to circle us and we could see its eyes occasionally as it watched us, before it slinked back into the darkness only to reappear elsewhere on the outskirts of the Ring. The eyes were moving from left to right and closing in on a clearing when I motioned to Richard that we should make our move. As we did so, however, the glowing eyes suddenly came to a halt. There was a rustling in the trees and the animal turned and ran at full speed away from us.

Richard and I leapt to our feet, leaving Jon within the circle, and, unfortunately, with the flashlight. While this paralleled in some ways our experience at Glastonbury, in this case the beast seemed much more physical in nature and far less spectral. We could hear its feet padding on the forest floor and we could hear branches being flung aside as it crashed through them in its effort to escape. "The bastard's scared of us!" screamed Richard and, spurred on by having the upper hand, we increased our pace and were within perhaps thirty feet of it when we were met by a sudden and complete silence. We had run breathlessly for about five minutes and were unsure where we were, except to say that it was deep within the woods. The apelike figure had gone. Or so we thought.

"There it is," Richard said in hushed tones, pointing to the south. Sure enough, there were the wretched red eyes.

"No, wait, it's there now," I said, pointing north. "Look." And so it was. But it was still at the original location, too. And there was a third set to our right, no more than sixty or seventy feet away. Richard and I looked at each other, and although we were little more than silhouettes in the darkness, we both knew what the other was thinking. The creature hadn't been scared by our presence at all. It had cunningly lured us deep within the forest to where there were others of its kind. To this day, Richard and I differ on how many pairs of eyes we saw. He says six pairs; I say five. But that is hardly the point. Here we were in the middle of the night on Cannock Chase being stalked by creatures that we had summoned up from some nightmarish realm.

The eyes began to slowly walk around us and we could hear what was undoubtedly heavy breathing. I wish I could say that it was Jon making his wheezy way through the trees, but it wasn't. Richard and I stood back to back and turned slowly in every direction to ensure that we had our eyes on the creatures at all times.

"What do you want?" Richard shouted loudly. The figures stopped and for a moment I caught sight of the mighty form of one of the creatures as it reached a small clearing in the trees. Six to seven feet tall and totally black in color, it stared blankly in our direction. To our left we heard a low growl.

"Oh, shit," said Richard. "Oh, shit. Oh, shit." Suddenly there was a thump to the right somewhere, then to the left and then in front of us. It sounded like the animals were rhythmically banging on tree trunks. Suddenly, in my mind I saw the apocalyptic image of a giant atomic mushroom cloud. Washington, D.C., London, Paris, and Moscow were all gone, all destroyed in a radioactive holocaust. Richard cried that his mind was deluged with images of a huge flood. Whole cities and civilizations were buried under a torrent of water and fire rained down from the sky as Judgment Day arrived. Then I realized what was happening. We were not in any physical danger from the beasts and never had been; they didn't feed like lions, tigers, or bears. They were creating these images in our minds to ensure that they could feed upon and ingest the emotions that these horrific images provoked.

"Rich, it's not real," I cried. *"It's not real!"* We both crouched and tried to concentrate and think of other things, of *anything.* Slowly, as the minutes passed, the images faded, as did the glowing red eyes. And within five minutes, the calamity that had nearly befallen us was over. The forest, although still utterly black, seemed to return to normal and the evil presence in our midst was gone.

"Are you okay?" I asked.

"Yeah," Richard replied quietly. "Let's get back to Jon." We found Jon still sitting within Castle Ring and waving the flashlight in the general direction of where we had headed. We told him the remarkable tale and he sat there, eyes ever wider as the story unfolded. After six weeks, we had seen a Cormon for ourselves. Or at least Richard and I had. In fact, we had seen several of the things. There was no doubt in our minds that these things were diabolically evil and were both paradoxically physical and apparitional in nature. The old witch was right.

I now know that these things exist. *I know it.* I also know why no one has ever captured—or ever will capture—a lake monster, a Bigfoot, an alien big cat, or one of the phantom black dogs. Their reality is our nightmare and our reality is little more than a feeding ground for them that they make swift use of before vanishing again into the ethereal darkness from which they came.

17

ADIOS, AMIGOS

**Bad boys then, bad boys now,
good buddies, mau, mau, mau.**

"R.A.M.O.N.E.S.," THE RAMONES

It had been a remarkable six weeks—for all of us. In many ways the final hours of our excursion were sad ones. I would soon be flying out to the United States to begin a new life and I knew that it would probably be a long time before I would see my old and dear friends again, and Jon and Richard thought likewise. But it was also a joyous occasion and one to celebrate friendship, a new beginning for me and to reflect on the glad, sad, mad, and bad times that we had spent together since I had first met Jon back in the UFO-dominated year of 1997.

Indeed, the journey back to Jon's was filled with conversations that began, "Do you remember when," or "Who could forget when we," and so on. We took our time on the return journey and stopped twice at rest areas to fill our stomachs and to discuss old times. But the last leg of the journey was dominated by a discussion of what we had learned over the course of the past one and a half months.

To say that we found the collective events surreal was the understatement of the year. Before we set off from Jon's, none of us, I am sure, would have ever imagined—or *could* have imagined—that we would find ourselves running around secret passageways in the middle of the night, chasing a gargoyle and an ape-man in a wood, pursuing monstrous worms in Her Majesty's tunnels, wondering if there really were mutated cannibals hiding out in the wilds of the British countryside, and trying to summon up lake monsters from the depths of Loch Ness. After all, our initial plan had just been to try to resolve the mystery of the Man Monkey of Ranton! But the journey, however bizarre, had been a satisfying one.

But before we knew it we had reached the turning for Exeter and a short time later the driveway of Holne Court, where we had departed amid the sonic assault of the Sex Pistols six weeks previously. Richard and I carried the bags from the Mystery Machine to the front door, while Jon fumbled for his key.

"Do you want to come in for a drink?" asked Jon, with a sad tone and even a slight quiver in his voice.

"No, mate. Keep it for me until I visit next."

"You *are* going to visit again, aren't you?" he asked worriedly.

"Yeah, I'll be back. When, I don't know, but you'll see me again."

"You aren't going to start listening to all that country and western shit, are you, now that you're moving to Texas?" asked Richard, with genuine concern.

"Hell, no!" I cried. "Punk rock forever!"

I shook hands with Jon and Richard and then we did something that British men are curiously reluctant to do: We had a communal hug. I turned and headed down the steps from Jon's front door to the Mystery Machine and climbed into the cab. As I started the engine and began to maneuver the vehicle I waved to Jon and Richard for what would be the last time and they waved back, amid shouts of good luck and "bring me back some whiskey, you bastard!" I looked out of the vehicle's side window as I drove away and could see the door of 15 Holne Court slowly closing. We might be separated by the Atlantic Ocean, but we were, and always would be, as the Ramones so correctly put it, a happy family.

EPILOGUE

There's no stopping the cretins from hopping.

"CRETIN HOP," THE RAMONES

A lthough the events that you have just read occurred in the early summer of 2001, it was not until twelve months later that I began to work on this book. As I was writing, however, a number of curious things began to occur. The skeptic would say that what I am about to relate to you is simply the product of a mind that has immersed itself in its subject matter for too long. And perhaps it is. But then again, perhaps there is another explanation. One night in August 2002, after Dana and I had gone to bed, I had an extremely curious encounter.

It was around 4:00 A.M. and I was awake and yet not awake. And I couldn't move. I was suddenly aware that something was slowly heading down the corridor that links our bedroom to the living room. That something, even though I couldn't see it, I knew was a man-sized figure with the head of a wolf and dressed in a long black cape. It emitted strange and rapid growling noises that seemed to be a language, and the creature, whatever its origin was, seemed mightily ticked off about something. As it closed in on the room, I made a supreme effort to move my rigid form and finally succeeded, just as the man-beast entered the bedroom. In an instant it was gone and I was wide-awake.

Psychologists call this sleep paralysis and would say that the incident was purely a product of my subconscious. I hoped so, too, and largely forgot about the encounter until Dana and I traveled to her brother's house for the Labor Day weekend. As we headed home from dinner after a Saturday night out, I noticed out of the window what looked like the image of a large black dog in the road. I almost cried out to Dana but in an instant I could see that the image was made up of a series of complex shadows cast down from a nearby road sign. And then the next day, a close family member encountered a spectral cat.

I thought back to our experience with Colin Perks and the Glastonbury gargoyle. After meddling in things that didn't concern him, Perks told us that the gargoyle was forever plaguing his mind and that he would see it at all times, lurking in the shadows. Was something similar now happening to me, too? Had Jon, Richard, and I really uncovered the truth about the Cormons and the many other mysteries of our world? I was convinced that we had. And perhaps this was a warning. Or perhaps it was an attempt to emotionally feed on me and bleed me dry.

I elected to follow Jon's lead. He had once told me that the way to break a psychic backlash or to send the demons back to their dark abode was to use that most powerful of tools: humor. It was the one emotion that the beasts could not tolerate, he said, and was like garlic to a vampire "or like alcohol-free beer to me, you, and Richard." And it was with that in mind that I took steps to ensure that the book I was writing, the same one that you are now reading, was not quite as dark and as Gothic as it could have been. By injecting a little humor into its pages I found the images of the creatures fading from my mind to the point where they eventually vanished entirely.

Intriguingly, at the same time that I was having these bizarre encounters, Jon and Richard were experiencing an unparalleled interest in their monster-hunting activities on the other side of the globe. As I was busy typing in my office, they were once again heading north, this time in search of a giant and monstrous fish rumored to inhabit a Lancashire lake. Britain's media followed them on every step of their expedition and Jon even managed to write a new book on the events: *The Monster of the Mere.*[1] Then they found themselves immersed in an investigation of a bizarre and disturbing wallaby mutilation and were also offered the opportunity to hunt for sea serpents in the Gambia.[2] Was this all down to good luck after they had both toiled selflessly for years? Or were the Cormons manipulating Richard and Jon, too, and attempting to bolster belief in the existence of fantastic beasts by ensuring that the intrepid pair were in the right place at the right time to provide the added exposure and emotional feeding that the Cormons constantly required?

It could all have been a big coincidence, of course. But I had my doubts when Jon told me that he had taken on a new employee at the Center for Fortean Zoology. His name was John Fuller, which also happened to be the name of the man who had written *The Interrupted Journey,* perhaps the most famous book on so-called alien abductions. The manipulation game was continuing. Indeed, it showed no signs of stopping.

On October 19, 2002, Britain's *Western Mail* reported the sighting of what it termed a "rogue primate" on the loose in Pembrokeshire, West Wales. In this case, the creature was described as being the size of a dog—which might have meant that it was just an escaped, exotic pet, but the timing was interesting, to say the least.[3] But far stranger things followed.

Five days later fossil hunters in Yorkshire, England, discovered in a two-ton block of clay the fossilized remains of a plesiosaur, the long-necked and long-extinct sea beast that some have postulated survives within the waters of Loch Ness. While that is nothing to get too excited about, I was startled to learn that the site of the discovery was on the cliffs near Filey—the exact location where Richard had uncovered decades-old tales of sea monster sightings that he had regaled us with months before.[4] And the stories continued to flood in.

"Some Thing in the Woods" was the headline that appeared in the November 28, 2002, issue of the *Nottingham Evening Post.* It transpired that Chris Mullins, a well-respected British-based mystery-animal researcher, had been given details of an "eight foot, hairy man-beast with red glowing eyes" seen within the legendary Sherwood Forest of Robin Hood fame.[5]

And it was this newspaper article that would prompt an elderly man to contact Chris on December 4, 2002, with details of his own sighting of a seven- to eight-foot-tall apelike creature in the vicinity of Sherwood Forest late at night in 1982.[6]

Then, in mid-December 2002, the British *Express & Star* contacted me and asked me to write a feature for its readers about the accursed Man Monkey of Ranton—the beast that was responsible for Jon, Richard, and myself embarking on our quest in the first place. The article was published on December 21 and, lo and behold, it brought forth a report from a somewhat reluctant witness who nevertheless related that he and a friend had seen, only eight weeks previously, a huge apelike creature at the side of the road on Levedale Lane between Stafford and Penkridge, and in the direct vicinity of the sprawling Cannock Chase.[7]

"I saw something in the corner of my eye," said the witness. "It was coming toward the car, running very fast. It wasn't a dog or a deer. It was running like a human would run, but it was really hairy and dark. It came level and jumped at the car but just missed."

And as 2002 came to a close and a new year began, the madness continued unabated. An article published in the north of England *Evening Chronicle* of January 6, 2003, stated that, "A yeti with glowing eyes is living in a North East park, according to a fisherman's tale. A report on a website dedicated to hunters of the Yeti and his Big Foot buddy carries details of three encounters between the half-ape creature and three pals.

"They tell how they spend hours in Bolam Lake near Belsay, Northumberland, pike fishing late at night. But their tranquility was disturbed on one fishing trip by a catch they did not expect to make. The anonymous writer tells how he was between his friends Neil and Nathan walking on a wooden path back to the car park, just after midnight. 'About halfway along the path I turned around to talk to Nathan. He was further back along the path, picking his bag up off the track. Behind him, standing in the middle of the track, was a dark figure. The light was moonlight and shining through the trees.'

"The others did not see it at first until he pointed it out to them. He said it was 'a dark figure, looked about eight feet tall, heavy built, its eyes, or what seemed to be its eyes, glowed in the darkness. We ran, top speed, all the way back to the car.'"

Interestingly, the newspaper revealed that during the previous March, a similar creature had been seen on a hill close to the remains of an Iron Age settlement near the park's boundary. Here again was an example of a mysterious apelike beast seen in the vicinity of an archaeological structure not unlike that at Castle Ring on the Cannock Chase.[8]

Jon and Richard headed northward for Bolam Park in search of this latest British man-beast on January 15, 2003; once again they were armed with cameras and night-scopes. But this time, Jon had an ace up his sleeve: a paint-ball gun.

"It may not be a physical creature," Jon told me twenty-four hours before he and Richard set off on their quest, "but by God, I am going to do my utmost to mark the bastard with the paint gun." Needless to say, the image of Jon rampaging drunkenly around Bolam Park at midnight, armed with a paint-ball gun in pursuit of a Bigfoot, was a prize. Such is the nature of monster-hunting activities: Life is never dull. Jon also informed me that he and Richard intended to conduct what would probably be a yearlong investigation of the new sightings of man-beasts throughout the country.

In an interview for the *Evening Chronicle* on January 18, Richard stated: "I actually hate apes. They are filthy, vicious, dirty, horrible things. I prefer working with reptiles. If the Yeti were here, it would've been found centuries ago. But there's definitely something here—I think it's something paranormal." Richard's words would prove to be more than prophetic and echoed eerily our experience at Cannock Chase.

On the morning of January 19 I received a telephone call from Jon. "Nicky," he said quietly and with a degree of fear and trepidation in his voice, "I have seen the beast." It transpired that Jon and five members of a local research group, the Twilight Worlds Paranormal Research Group, were on watch at Bolam Park the previous evening as darkness began to fall. Suddenly "something" appeared that defied all explanation, said Jon. Jon and three of the group only caught a glimpse of it for the briefest of moments, he told me, but the fast-moving creature was around eight feet tall, three feet wide, and dark in color. Although lost in the failing light and the trees, Jon was able to determine that the "creature" seemed to be without real form and, incredibly, one-dimensional in appearance. "This has totally freaked me out," he told me, before being sidetracked by yet another call on his cell phone from Britain's frenzied media. And still things continued to escalate.

Only hours after speaking with John, I received another telephone call—this one from none other than Colin Perks. It seemed that Perks just couldn't forget about King Arthur and the accursed gargoyle and he informed me that he had spent the last three months trying to track down the mysterious Sarah Key, who had warned him to give up his research.

"I found her," he told me quietly.

"You did? Where?" I asked with genuine interest.

"She works for MI5," Perks replied, referring to the British equivalent of the FBI. "But Sarah Key isn't her real name." The strangest aspect of Perks's quest was still to come, however.

He told me how, only six days previously, he had traveled to London and had intended to confront Key at the futuristic-looking MI5 headquarters that overlooks the River Thames. Astonishingly, Perks said that as he walked toward the MI5 building across one of the many bridges that span the Thames, his attention was drawn to something moving in the deep water to his left. He looked closer, and, not quite believing his eyes, saw what appeared to be the head, neck, and back of an approximately six-foot-long, sea serpent–like creature staring directly at him. Perks told me that he quickly grabbed his camera and captured two images of the mysterious animal just before it vanished into the depths of the Thames.

Needless to say, Perks became seriously unhinged yet again and, interpreting this encounter as a warning similar to that of the gargoyle, decided against confronting Sarah Key, or whoever she really was. He quickly headed back to Glastonbury vowing, once again, to give up his research.

I have to confess that I was unsure what to make of this latest development in the saga of Colin Perks and the Glastonbury gargoyle, but true to his word, Perks mailed me a copy of one of the photographs, which does appear to show "something" in the River Thames. But the fact that the "animal" had appeared to a man who was already deeply immersed in the legends, monsters, and mythology of Britain was more evidence of the paranormal nature of these creatures—if, indeed, more evidence was needed.

🞔 🞔 🞔

Before Jon, Richard, and I set off on our adventure, I was a believer that alien beings from some far-flung corner of the galaxy were visiting the Earth and had been for millennia. I was also of the opinion that if Britain really *was* home to any unidentified species of animal, then matters probably began and ended with the big cats and possibly one or two mysterious creatures that existed in the country's lakes and lochs. But my views have now changed drastically.

No longer can I accept that UFOs and their black-eyed, bald-headed pilots are visiting us from Alpha Centauri or Zeta Reticuli. And neither can I accept that Britain is home to flesh-and-blood monsters of the type that we had been pursuing—or at least not flesh-and-blood in the way that we understand the term. No. I am now convinced that our aliens, our lake monsters, our phantom black dogs, our man-beasts, and all the rest of the assorted menagerie of unexplained creatures that inhabit our world, are much stranger than I had previously realized. Ironically, they are all alien in the literal sense of the word, but they come from a realm far closer to home than outer space, the depths of the oceans, or the snow-capped peaks of the Himalayas. Theirs is a shadowy, dreamlike world that is as close to ours as my fingers are to this keyboard as I sit typing these words, and yet that is as distant and as intangible as a forgotten dream. It is a realm where believing in something makes it so, whether fabulous, bizarre, or wretched, where the products of our nightmares can be brought to life, and from where, if one knows the ways of the ancients, our monsters and our aliens can be summoned up and given substance and the power and the will to exist in our domain.

The dark side of all this, however, is that I know that all of these creatures are little more than emotion-sucking parasites, manipulating us with bizarre games and charades that afford us brief glimpses of them while at the same time allowing them to emotionally milk us like cattle. The psychic backlash that Jon so often referred to, the images of Armageddon that the "aliens" show to so-called abductees, these are but cunning tools of the Cormons and their ever-growing offspring, designed to ensure that our minds operate in precisely the way they want them to, a way that continues to ensure their survival.

Perhaps most intriguing of all are the revelations that some people within the British government, at a restricted level at least, are also aware of the situation. And, if Colin Perks's account can be believed, elements of the government and the winged entity that Perks witnessed may be involved in a dark and unholy alliance designed to prevent the Cormons from having unlimited access to our world.

Conversely, it is very possible that the wild man that Alfred told us about could have been an entirely different breed of beast, one that is purely physical in nature. And if that is the case, then it adds even more to the wonderment of Britain's secret history and its catalog of monsters and mysterious creatures.

For me, the journey is now over, but I will never forget the six weeks I spent traveling Britain in pursuit of the unknown with Jon and Richard. At the start of our quest we were three men seeking monsters. Today, we are three men who can look back and say with a high degree of satisfaction and certainty that we found them.

ACKNOWLEDGMENTS

I would like to offer my sincere thanks to the following: Mark Fraser of the Scottish Big Cat Society; Geoff Lincoln of British Hominid Research; Chris Mullins of Beast-watch U.K.; Andy Roberts, for the use of material from *Cat Flaps!* and for generously allowing me to quote from his voluminous files on the Big Gray Man of Ben Macdhui; Jonathan Downes, Richard Freeman, Graham Inglis, and John Fuller of the Center for Fortean Zoology; and everyone at Paraview Publishing and Pocket Books, and particularly my editor, Patrick Huyghe, Louise Burke, Stephen Llano, Damian Fallon, and Joshua Martino. Thanks also to copyeditor Jean Lisa, and to Paul Slattery, for sharing his files on the Hexham Heads.

NOTES

CHAPTER 1
1. *The Owlman & Others*, Jonathan Downes, CFZ Communications, 2001.

CHAPTER 2
1. *Shropshire Folklore*, Charlotte S. Burne & Georgina F. Jackson, Trubner, 1883.
2. "Man Beasts and Beast Men," Jonathan Downes, *Encounters*, No. 3, 1996.
3. "Strangeness in Scotland," Mark Fraser, *Animals & Men*, No. 9, 1996.
4. *The A-Z of British Ghosts*, Peter Underwood, Chancellor, 1992.
5. *Legends of the Cairngorms*, Affleck Grey, Mainstream, 1987.
6. *Whitehaven News*, 5 March 1998.
7. *The Big Hairy Man Encounter*, Martin Jeffrey, www.mysterymag.com.

CHAPTER 3
1. *Bath Chronicle*, 9 September 2002.

CHAPTER 5
1. For more information, see: *The Black Dog of Bungay—A Brief History*, www.bungay-suffolk.co.uk.

CHAPTER 6
1. *The Cannibals of Clovelly: Fact or Fiction*, A. D. Hippisley-Coxe, Bideford, 1981. *A History of the Book in Devon*, www.devon.gov.uk.

CHAPTER 7
1. *Alien Animals*, Janet & Colin Bord, Granada, 1980.
2. For more information, see: *The Undying Monster*, Steven Elderedge, www.horror-wood.com.
3. "Going Underground—Rumors of London's Lost Cannibals," Michael Goss, *Fortean Times*, No. 105.

4. *Tunnel Vision,* Keith Lowe, Arrow, 2001. *Ghostly Tales of the Black Nun,* Jack Clark, www.thetube.com. *London Underground Ghosts,* www.bbc.co.uk.

5. "Wild Things," Paul Sieveking, *Fortean Times,* No. 161. *Of Wolves and Men,* Barry Lopez, Touchstone Books, 1982.

CHAPTER 8

1. *Werewolves,* Elliot O'Donnell, Brown Book Company, 1972.

2. *Cat Flaps!* Andy Roberts, CFZ Communications, 2001.

3. *Werewolf on the Prowl,* www.bbc.co.uk.

4. *The Beast of Exmoor,* Trevor Beer, Countryside Productions, 1985.

5. *Mystery Animals of Britain and Ireland,* Graham McEwan, Robert Hale Ltd., London, 1987. www.wolfcross.com. www.mysteriousbritain.co.uk. http://labete.7hunters.net. "The Skull of a Wulver?" Dr. Karl P.N. Shuker, *Fate,* November 2000.

6. Ibid. Additional information on the Hexham Heads supplied by Dr. Clare Sommers. *The Evening Chronicle,* 23 January 2003. *Nationwide,* BBC, 1976. *The Hexham Horror,* Paul Slattery, publication pending.

7. *The Owlman and Others,* Jonathan Downes, CFZ Communications, 2001.

CHAPTER 9

1. *The Rising of the Moon,* Jonathan Downes & Nigel Wright, Domra, 1999. *Magic and Mystery in Tibet,* Alexandra David-Neel, Dover Publications, Inc., 1971.

2. *The Rising of the Moon,* Jonathan Downes & Nigel Wright, Domra, 1999.

3. For more information on the Morrigan, see: www.tarot-decks.com.

4. *Mythago Wood,* Robert Holdstock, Grafton Books, 1986.

5. *The Rising of the Moon,* Jonathan Downes & Nigel Wright, Domra, 1999.

CHAPTER 10

1. For more information, see: www.glastonbury.co.uk and www.glastonbury-abbey.com.

2. *Psychic Self-Defense,* Dion Fortune, Aquarian Publishing Co., 1967.

CHAPTER 11

1. *A Covert Agenda,* Nick Redfern, Simon & Schuster, 1997.

2. Provost & Security Services brochure.

3. *Alien Liaison,* Timothy Good, Random Century Ltd., 1991.

4. Letters from Jonathan Turner dated 17 and 21 September 1994 and 10 May 1995.

5. Interview with Neil Rusling, 7 December 1996.
6. Letter to Martin Redmond, MP, from Nicholas Soames, Junior Minister for Defense, 28 October 1996.
7. *Strange Secrets*, Nick Redfern & Andy Roberts, Paraview Pocket Books, 2003.
8. For more information on Avebury and Stonehenge, see: www.stone-henge-avebury.net.
9. *Harmonic 33*, Bruce Cathie, A.H. & A.W. Reed Ltd., 1968. *Harmonic 695*, Bruce Cathie & P.N. Temm, A.H. & A.W. Reed Ltd., 1977.
10. *The Flight of Dragons*, Peter Dickinson, Pierrot, 1979. "The Dragons of Yorkshire," Richard Freeman, *Animals & Men*, issue 14.

CHAPTER 12
1. For more information on Woodbridge, see: www.woodbridgesuffolk.info.
2. For more information on Orford, see: www.orford.org.uk.
3. *To the Ends of the Earth*, Channel 4, 1998.
4. Nottingham County Library manuscript. "Black Dogs in Folklore," Bob Trubshaw, *Mercian Mysteries*, No. 20, August 1994.
5. *Historic Wells in and Around Bradford*, Val Shepherd, Heart of Albion Press, 1994.
6. *Phenomena: A Book of Wonders*, John Michell & Bob Rickard, Thames & Hudson, 1977.

CHAPTER 13
1. *Cat Flaps!* Andy Roberts, CFZ Communications, 2001.
2. Ibid.
3. *The Pennine UFO Mystery*, Jenny Randles, Granada, 1983.
4. *Cat Flaps!* Andy Roberts, CFZ Communications, 2001.

CHAPTER 14
1. For more information on Loch Ness, see: www.aboutscotland.com.
2. Ibid.
3. For more information on Aleister Crowley and Boleskine House, see: www.thelemicgoldendawn.org and www.mysteriousbritain.co.uk.
4. *The Dragon and the Disc*, F. W. Holliday, Sidgwick & Jackson, 1973. *Monster Hunter*, Jonathan Downes (publication pending).
5. *Glasgow Herald*, 13 December 1933. *Loch Ness Monster*, Rupert T. Gould, Geoffrey Bles, 1934.
6. For more information on Kelpies, see: www.mysteriousbritain.co.uk.
7. Ibid.

8. For more information on St. Columba and the Loch Ness Monster, see: www.lochnessguide.com.
9. *Inverness Courier,* 16 October 1833.
10. *Inverness Courier,* 1 July 1852.

CHAPTER 15

1. *Fortean Studies,* Vol. 5, John Brown Publishing, 1998; plus additional information supplied to the author by Andy Roberts.
2. For more information on Dundonald Castle, see: www.dundonald-castle.org. Further details of Mark Fraser's research into mystery animals can be found at www.beastwatch.co.uk and at www.scottishbigcats.org.

CHAPTER 16

1. *Strange Secrets,* Nick Redfern & Andy Roberts, Paraview Pocket Books, 2003.
2. For more information on Cannock Chase, see: www.cannock-chase.net.
3. Ibid.

EPILOGUE

1. *The Monster of the Mere,* Jonathan Downes, CFZ Publications, 2002.
2. For details of the wallaby killing, see: the CFZ website www.cfz.org.uk.
3. *Western Mail,* 19 October 2002.
4. *Yorkshire Today,* 24 October 2002.
5. *Nottingham Evening Post,* 28 November 2002.
6. Beastwatch UK. Contact the group's coordinator, Chris Mullins, at www.beastwatch.co.uk.
7. *Express & Star,* 21 December 2002.
8. *Evening Chronicle,* 6 January 2003. British Hominid Research. See the BHR website: http://homepage.ntlworld.com/lincolns. Or contact Geoff Lincoln and the BHR at: lincolns@ntlworld.com.

INDEX

Rudloe Manor. *See* Royal Air Force
Rusling, Neil, 147

Sacks, Mike, 197
St. Ledger Gordon, Ruth, 90
Sasquatch, 17
Sawney Beane, wild men of, 68, 79
sea-beasts, 161-62, 249, 252
sea serpent (Morgawr), 212–13
Sheila-Na-Gig, 119
Shiels, Tony "Doc", 99
Shug Monkey of Rendlesham Forest, 36,
    52, 165, 176, 177–79, 180, 182
Skegness
    Alien Big Cats of, 192–93
    cannibals at, 187, 188–91
Skunk-Apes, 17
Slemen, Tom, 91
Smitham Hill, man-beast of, 29
Snowdonia, man-beast of, 23
spider plague, in Leeds, 121–23
Stonehenge, Ancient Astronaut theory of,
    154–55
Story, Ronald, 154–55
Strange Secrets (Roberts and Redfern), 148,
    153
Strathmore, Lord, 20-21

Texas, wolf girl in, 84–85
To the Ends of the Earth, 177
Torphins, man-beast of, 19–20
troglodytes, in London Underground, 81–82
Tulku, 107
Tulp, Nicholas, 84
Tulpas, 104–07, 108, 121–22, 157
Tunnel Vision (Lowe), 83
Turner, Jonathan, 147

UFOs
    Ancient Astronaut scenario, 154–55
    conferences, 3–4, 11
    power grid theory of, 155
    RAF investigation of, 145, 146–48,
        149–50, 152
    RAF sightings of, 147

in Rendlesham Forest, 35-37, 174,
    175–76, 177
unexplained phenomena at sites of,
    32–37, 149–52, 197, 228–29
Underwood, Peter, 20, 20–21
Undying Monster, The, 80–81, 89

Von Koenigswald, Ralph, 16

Warren, Andrew, 95–96
Weird War Tales (Downes and Redfern), 11
Welsh, Hugh, 218
werewolves, 90–99
Widecombe-in-the-Moor, 47, 50–51, 71
    lightning strike at, 51, 180
wild men
    at Bottlebrush Down, 77–78
    cannibals, 67–69, 70, 72, 79, 90, 188–91
    capture of, 47–50, 52–54, 70, 79, 183–84
    at Crowlas, 71–72
    Daniel Defoe on, 68, 70, 79
    feral children, 83–85
    genetic defects as explanation for, 69
    in London Underground, 81–82
    at Lustleigh Cleave, 71, 77, 78
    in movies, 80–81, 82, 89
    relict colonies of, 69–71
Williams, Matthew, 3
wolf girl, 84–85
wormlike monsters
    dragons, 91, 157–60
    Handale Worm, 161
    Lambton worm, 162–65
    of Loschy Mill, 160–61
    at RAF Rudloe Manor, 151–53, 156,
        166–72
    sea-beasts, 161–62
    Stonehenge sightings of, 152, 156
    at UFO sites, 149–52
Wright, Jeremy, 148

Yeti, 16–17, 112, 250
Yowies, 17–18

zooforms, 5